LEARNING TO TEACH THROUGH DISCUSSION

SOPHIE HAROUTUNIAN-GORDON

Learning to Teach Through Discussion

THE ART OF TURNING THE SOUL

YALE UNIVERSITY PRESS   NEW HAVEN & LONDON

Published with assistance from the foundation established in memory of
William McKean Brown.

Set in FontShop Scala and Scala Sans by Duke & Company, Devon, Pennsylvania.
Printed in the United States of America by Sheridan Books, Ann Arbor, Michigan.

Library of Congress Cataloging-in-Publication Data

Haroutunian-Gordon, Sophie.
Learning to teach through discussion : the art of turning the soul / Sophie Haroutunian-
Gordon.
p. cm.
Includes bibliographical references and index.
ISBN 978-0-300-12000-4 (cloth : alk. paper)

1. Questioning. 2. Communication in education. I. Title.
LB1027.44.H38 2009
371.3'7—dc22

2009007111

A catalogue record for this book is available from the British Library.

This paper meets the requirements of ANSI/NISO Z39.48-1992 (Permanence of Paper).

10 9 8 7 6 5 4 3 2 1

In memory of my mother, Helen Augusta Halsey Haroutunian, 1914–2003

CONTENTS

Like every response, the sense of an interpretation is determined by
the question asked.
—Gadamer, *Truth and Method*

THE PHILOSOPHER Hans-Georg Gadamer locates questioning at the
heart of understanding: anything that is understood is understood as
the response to a question, for the question sets the context or perspective from which the answer is viewed. This book places questioning at
the center of teaching and learning, and it explores the way in which, in
a particular kind of teaching-and-learning situation, questions may be
cultivated.

As its centerpiece, the book presents a case study of two people who
are learning to teach. It shows both of these novice teachers and their
students as they engage in discussion, questioning, and thinking. We
follow them as their involvement in these activities becomes increasingly
impassioned and effective. Eventually, we see a learning community in
which the barriers of race and class seem to have been broken down.

Before I continue to describe the book, let me make clear what it is
not. First, it is not a method of cultivating questions or a step-by-step
procedure for doing so. Indeed, I argue that there can be no such method.

Second, the book is not a work of philosophy, although it draws on the philosophies of Plato, Gadamer, and Wittgenstein in order to develop its theoretical foundation. Third, it is not a work of literary theory, although it dwells on an approach to textual interpretation that falls within the tradition of reader-response literary theory. Fourth, it is not a psychological theory of learning, although it takes a "situated" approach to learning and belongs in the so-called constructivist tradition. It draws on Dewey's vision of a learning community and is consistent with modern learning science approaches. These contexts for the work are set out in Chapter 1, and they help locate its contribution. But because the book does not fall into any of these categories, many of the complex issues that abound in each are not addressed or are taken up briefly in the notes.

Instead, *Learning to Teach Through Discussion: The Art of Turning the Soul* is a work about pedagogy. As explained in Chapter 1, the title of the book is taken from book VII of *The Republic,* in which Plato defines the art of teaching as "the art of turning the soul." The present volume describes a pedagogical approach that I call "interpretive discussion," which emphasizes questioning and thinking as these occur when interpreting texts.[1] In an age when following a script has come to replace thoughtful, creative approaches to teaching[2] and students' attention has been turned from questioning and reflecting to scoring well on multiple standardized tests,[3] this book argues for a different focus. The claim is that life in school can be more engaging and productive for all—teachers included—if thinking, rooted in questioning, is placed at the center of at least some experiences. What better place than our educational institutions to develop habits of questioning and reflection?[4]

In chapter 1, I define the term "interpretive discussion" in detail and present some theoretical underpinnings. In Chapter 2 I introduce the case study: we meet the two teacher candidates and the two groups of fourth-grade students who participated in the project. I describe the way the two groups engage in their first interpretive discussions. Chapter 3 follows the progress of each group, and Chapter 4 presents excerpts from a discussion in which members of the two groups met together. That discussion is powerful in several respects, not the least of which is that differences of race and class seem to serve as resources for, rather than barriers between, the discussants. In Chapters 5 and 6 I focus on the development of the co-leaders so as to better understand the progress that was seen in the classroom conversations. Finally, in Chapter 7 I reflect on the implications of the study for educating teachers in the art of discussion-leading—the art of turning the soul.

I have come to imagine the reader of this book reflecting on his or her own teaching as the pages turn, for, although the teacher candidates discussed in the case study were preparing to teach in elementary school, my hope is that people who teach or care about teaching at any level—from elementary through graduate school—will find the book to be of interest.

Learning to Teach Through Discussion: The Art of Turning the Soul, more than ten years in the making, never would have been written but for my extraordinary good fortune on many counts. I came to Northwestern University to direct the Master of Science in Education Program in 1991. In so doing, I left "armchair" philosophy and began to live my philosophy of education in a way that I was only beginning to glimpse when I completed *Turning the Soul: Teaching Through Conversation in the High School* (University of Chicago Press, 1991). The Northwestern program is run under the auspices of the School of Education and Social Policy, and it prepares people with primarily liberal arts backgrounds to teach in elementary and secondary schools and to work as administrators in postsecondary settings. In my position as professor and director, I have used *Turning the Soul* to introduce teacher candidates to interpretive discussion, which I first encountered as a sixth-grade teacher in the summer of 1969, when I attended a workshop offered by the Great Books Foundation. The leader of that workshop, Edwin P. Moldof, vice president of the foundation, inspired not only my vision of teaching but also my later research and conception of teacher education. As indicated below, some important features of interpretive discussion as I present it were identified by the Great Books Foundation and are exemplified in their Shared Inquiry discussion format, publications, and professional development.[5]

In the fall of 1996, when two women who were preparing to teach at the elementary level approached me about doing a research project with two fourth grade classes that involved interpretive discussion, I jumped at the chance. Marsha and Paula, as I call them, were both wonderful to behold in their development as discussion leaders and were immensely cooperative and helpful to me. Not only did they pursue the project with great energy, but they worked carefully to assist me in every way possible so that we were able to collect multiple kinds of data. In addition, they read drafts of chapters, presented the research with me on numerous occasions, and advised me about many matters. Without their many contributions the book never could have come to be, and I am deeply indebted to each of them.

I have enjoyed the generous support of both the Spencer Foundation and Northwestern University for the research and the writing of the book.[6] I am indeed grateful to the dean, Penelope Peterson, who, with the Spencer Foundation, made possible a leave of absence in 1999–2000, when much of a first draft of the manuscript was completed. The chapters have undergone multiple revisions since that time, and again, Northwestern has supported me with assistance of various sorts.

Several individuals have made significant contributions to the work, some laboring for several years. Bradley Wadle, a former teacher candidate at Northwestern and now a high school teacher of German, assisted me with many aspects of the project, including data analysis, particularly the statistics (with Jeff Pasch), library and Internet research, and all phases of manuscript preparation. His generous help has been invaluable. Jeanne Olson, a former teacher candidate, created DVDs of the discussions held during the project and otherwise assisted in data preparation and analysis. Donna Rabin and Gabrielle Lensch, former teacher candidates and current teachers of high school English, worked with me on manuscript revision and research. Leslie Bjornkrantz, a now-retired Northwestern University librarian, assisted with library research. Sara Savini, former teacher candidate who is currently teaching high school social studies, assisted with permissions.

In addition, many colleagues have given generously of their time and expertise in reading drafts of chapters and related pieces over the years, in some cases multiple chapters and multiple versions. In particular, I thank Kal Alston, Rene Arcilla, Nicholas Burbules, Walter Feinberg, Daniel B. Frank, James W. Garrison, David T. Hansen, Alison Hilsabeck, Julie W. Johnson, Carol D. Lee, Elizabeth Meadows, Sharon Feiman Nemser, Barry O'Connell, Penelope Peterson, Denis Phillips, Suzanne Rice, Rosalie Romano, Alan Schoenfeld, Kathryn Schultz, Joseph Senese, Miriam Gameran Sherin, Richard A. Shweder, Harvey Siegel, Susan Stodolsky, Richard Strier, Leonard J. Waks, Stanton Wortham, and Karen Zumwalt. These people have offered invaluable support and criticism. Indeed, Barry O'Connell, on a leave of absence from Amherst College, assisted me directly in carrying out the project.

I have been enormously fortunate in having highly competent and dedicated colleagues in the Master of Science in Education Program, many of whom have labored overtime for years in the effort to help me bring the book to completion. In particular, I mention Ellen Esrick, Mary Gajewski, Mary Goosby, Peg Kritzler, Andre Nickow, Dave Renz, Patricia Rodriguez, Lois Trautvetter, and Theresa Watson. In addition, many teacher candidates and teaching assistants have enabled me to refine my understanding of interpretive discussion and my pedagogical approach to it. They have taught me to grasp its power and introduce that power to others in ways that, without their help, I simply would not have done.

I must add, too, that my wonderful piano teacher, Deborah Sobol, has helped me sustain my musical life through this long project. To her I owe the fact that I have become a somewhat better player and perhaps that I have finished the book.

When it came time to find a publisher for the book, luck was again with me when I met Keith Condon, associate editor at Yale University Press, who immediately became excited about the project. He has understood it from the start and has worked to find excellent readers whose commentaries have been enormously helpful. That the book is better for his and their efforts I have no doubt.

Finally, my husband, Robert P. Gordon, has weathered the long overdue birth of this book with steadfast patience and support. He has read and commented on chapters for years. In many ways he enables our home to be a place of peace and comfort where creative work, including questioning, is happily pursued.

The following publishers have given permission to quote from texts that were discussed in the research project:

1. "Jean Labadie's Big Black Dog," by Natalie Savage Carlson, in *The Talking Cat and Other Stories of French Canada*, by N. S. Carlson. Copyright © by Natalie Savage Carlson, 1952. Reprinted by permission of Harper-Collins Publishers.
2. *The Giving Tree*, by Shel Silverstein. Copyright © by Evil Eye Music, Inc., 1964. Reprinted by permission of HarperCollins Publishers.
3. "Kaddo's Wall," from *The Cow Tail Switch and Other West African Stories* by Harold Courlander and George Herzog. © 1947, 1974 by Harold Courlander. Reprinted by permission of Henry Holt and Company, LLC.
4. "Allah Will Provide" from *The Sultan's Fool and Other North African Tales* by Robert Gilstrap and Irene Estabrook. Copyright 1958 by Robert

Gilstrap and Irene Estabrook. Reprinted by permission of Henry Holt and Company, LLC.

5. "About What Happened to a Young Man Who Married a Very Wild, Unruly Wife," by Don Juan Manuel, from *Spanish Stories/Cuentos Españoles—A Dual Language Book*, translated by Angel Flores © 1987. Courtesy of Dover Publications, Inc., New York.

"Jean Labadie's Big Black Dog," "Kaddo's Wall," and "Allah Will Provide" were brought to the co-leaders' attention because the stories appear in the Great Books Foundation's Junior Great Books reading anthologies.[7]

CHAPTER ONE

Introduction to Interpretive Discussion

We must, in Empson's wonderful phrase, "taste each text with as clean a palate as we can. . . ." To do what Empson recommends mean[s] trying to appreciate each text's distinctive qualities, however strange or familiar.

—*Richard Strier*

INTERPRETIVE DISCUSSION is discussion about the meaning of texts. It aims to understand a text, to appreciate its features and meanings, whether one eventually judges them to be right or wrong. It grows from genuine questions that discussants have when they study the text, questions provoked by the desire to understand it. The "clean palate" that Strier, Empson, and others call for is what one might refer to as an open mind: a mind seeking to know the text on its own terms.

To have an open mind does not mean that one's understanding is unbiased or that the time, place, and sociocultural context of discussants can be set aside in interpreting the text. Indeed, in what follows, I argue to the contrary. Nevertheless, I begin by underscoring the central motive driving interpretive discussion. That motive is to understand the text as the expression of some idea or ideas that may or may not agree with the discussants' beliefs.

The chapter begins with a brief definition of interpretive discussion that is then elaborated. Next, I consider its three phases: preparation, leading the discussion, and reflection. In the course of describing the three phases, I relate interpretive discussion to traditions in philosophy, interpretive theory, literary theory and criticism, and learning. I thereby place in context the pedagogical approach as a whole, as well as a particular aspect of it, namely, forming or cultivating questions. I also begin to defend interpretive discussion as a way to go about teaching and learning. In conclusion, I outline the scope of the book and briefly introduce the case study of two teacher candidates who led a series of interpretive discussions in fourth-grade classrooms.

DEFINITION OF INTERPRETIVE DISCUSSION

Interpretive discussion is conversation between people who together seek to understand the meaning of a text. Now, what is meant by "seek" and by "understand the meaning of a text"? Because there are long traditions of literature behind these terms, let me begin by clarifying the meanings that I intend.

Seeking

Interpretive discussion is carried on by a group of "seekers," that is, a group of people who do not know something, who recognize that they do not know it, and who want to find out what they do not know. Generally speaking, the group numbers twelve to fifteen people, and there is a leader or pair of co-leaders who help the group proceed with the investigation. The conversation may take place in elementary, secondary, or college classroom settings or outside the classroom. Leaders as well as discussants believe themselves to be ignorant of the answer to the query that confronts the group. So leaders, as well as participants, are seekers.

I take Socrates and at least some of his interlocutors as paradigms of seekers. So, for example, in Plato's *Meno*, Socrates and Meno try to discover whether virtue can be taught. Socrates begins by declaring that he cannot answer the question because he does not know what virtue is.[1] In the course of trying to learn from Meno the definition of virtue, both men find themselves in a state of aporia, or perplexity—a moment of recognizing that they do not know what virtue is and wish to find out.[2] In each case, the character admits his ignorance, thereby acknowledging that he believes, at least at that moment, that there is something about which he is in doubt.

Yet seekers do not merely acknowledge their ignorance. In addition, they must want to find out the answer and work to do so. In the dialogues of Plato the characters often work by questioning what they or others think they know in order to resolve the uncertainty. In trying to discover what virtue is, Socrates repeatedly asks Meno what he thinks it is, and the responses are then examined.[3] Some responses are found to be sound, and others are not. Once some claims are accepted, the answer to the query is constructed or created on the basis of what is said to be known.[4] Seeking involves discovery of both what is not in doubt and what is. And it is motivated by the desire to distinguish the two in order to resolve a point of uncertainty.

Seeking has been of interest to many since the time of Plato, and his vision of it has proved robust. For example, the philosopher Martin Heidegger speaks of "gathering," by which he means not merely amassing but garnering in relation what is needed, for example, what is needed to answer the question.[5] Turning to modern theories of education, we find Beck,[6] Bruer,[7] Lampert and Ball,[8] Palinscar and Brown,[9] Palinscar and Ladewski,[10] Pea,[11] Edelson and Reiser,[12] Resnick,[13] Rogoff and Lave,[14] and Schoenfeld,[15] to name but a few who call for emphasis on seeking to discover what one does not know.

Understanding the Meaning of a Text

The seekers in an interpretive discussion are searching to understand the meaning of some text. A text may be an oral statement or set of statements such as those offered by Meno. It may also be a set of data, a picture, an artifact of some sort, or a film, for example. How does one go about seeking an understanding of a text?

The pedagogical orientation of interpretive discussion falls within the tradition of the reader-response theory of interpretation.[16] Many in that tradition would say, with Gadamer, that understanding the meaning of a text involves making an interpretation of it[17] and that an interpretation is a "translation."[18] Interpreters, as translators, do not reproduce the original text but instead present it as they understand it to themselves and others. That is, they try to say, in their own words, what the text says.[19] The interpretation will depend not only on what is given in the text but also on the terms and concepts that an interpreter uses in trying to say what it says.[20]

Making an interpretation of a text is like playing a game, says Gadamer.[21] The games that people play generally follow rules. In games such as chess players follow the rules for moving particular pieces. Following the rules involves repeating the actions dictated by the rules, and this keeps the game going.[22] In an interpretive discussion this involves following rules by which an interpretation of the text is created. I will have more to say about the nature of the rules in what follows. Let me point out, however, that in following the rules, one is not following a method or step-by-step procedure that renders an interpretation, for there are several activities involved in text interpretation, some of which are not amenable to strict procedure. For example, in order to make an interpretation, one sometimes needs to identify assumptions that are present in the text. How do the interpreters discover those assumptions and beliefs? Gadamer answers that the discovery begins when something in the text "addresses us," or draws our attention.[23] When that happens, a question arises. Gadamer writes: "The recognition that an object is different and not as we first thought obviously involves the question of whether it is this or that. . . . This is the famous Socratic [ignorance] which opens the way . . . to the true superiority of questioning."[24]

In the passage quoted above, Gadamer aligns himself with Plato in maintaining that questioning is the route to understanding. Questioning begins with the recognition that something is not what we first thought, and we ask: Is it a case of X or of Y (or neither)? The seeker does not know and tries to determine the answer. Addressing the question takes the seeker back into the text to locate an answer, into further interpreting (or translating) the text. What part of the text receives further scrutiny? That depends on the question. What assumptions in the text are identified? That depends on the question. Heidegger makes a similar point.[25] With Gadamer and Heidegger, I argue that the questions arise from the particular circumstances of the interpreters. Hence, there can be no method or step-by-step procedure for detecting assumptions in the text, for there can be no method for generating questions.

THE THREE PHASES OF INTERPRETIVE DISCUSSION

An interpretive discussion is a conversation about the meaning of a text that takes place among participants and their leaders or co-leaders, all of whom have access to the text. I turn now to the three phases of the discussion. The first phase involves preparing for the discussion. Leaders as well as participants prepare for the discussion. If there is one leader, that person engages in preparation alone.[26] If there are co-leaders, they prepare for the discussion together. The goal of this phase is to develop questions about the meaning of the text. In Chapter 5 I give examples of questions prepared prior to discussion and describe the general orientation that the leaders adopt in developing them, as well as criteria used to evaluate them. Here I introduce the concepts of a "discussable text" and a "cluster of questions." In so doing, I show that questioning is the focus of interpretive discussion even in the preparation phase.

In the second phase, leading, participants and leaders work together to understand the meaning of a text. It may be described as a game that involves following the rules of textual interpretation and additional rules. The goals of the discussion include identifying a question that the members of the group wish to resolve (that is, a shared question), addressing it, and evaluating arguments for proposed resolutions. In what follows, I describe these goals. I also identify the goals and some of the practices of the discussion leaders.

The reflection phase involves assessing the accomplishments of the group conversation. Two categories of accomplishments are identified: those related to building a learning community via participation in the discussion and those related to identifying the content of the discussion, including the shared questions that were (or were not) formed and the answers that the conversation revealed. In the second category I take up a few issues related to interpretation, including the topic of correctness and the development of the ability to engage in interpretive discussion.

Preparation

Finding a Discussable Text

The leaders must first identify a discussable text. Although many kinds of objects could be texts, a suitable text is one about which leaders can raise questions. In trying to do so, leaders test whether those with whom the text will be discussed may also be able to question its meaning. Jauss,[27] Iser,[28] and Grondin[29] side with Gadamer and Heidegger in recognizing the centrality of the reader's questions in textual interpretation.

In order to raise questions about the meaning of a text, leaders try to put the text in their own words. In so doing, they discover questions that they have about what it says. The questions are functions not only of what is in the text but also of the reader's translation of it.

The questions that arise may fall into three categories, which, with the Great Books Foundation, I call "factual" questions, "interpretive" questions, and "evaluative" questions.[30] The questions of fact may be answered by pointing to a particular place in the text and resolving it definitively (or recognizing that the question cannot be addressed by anything in the text). An interpretive question may be addressed by looking at places in the text, but the resolution seems to be in doubt. An evaluative question does not concern the meaning of the text but instead calls for judgment about whether what it says is right or wrong, good or bad, that is, whether the text or something therein meets the reader's criteria for evaluation. Here are some examples: Is the little girl who falls down the rabbit hole in *Alice in Wonderland* named Alice? (factual question); Is *Alice in Wonderland* anyone's view of a mad world or a child's view of the adult world? (interpretive question); Is *Alice in Wonderland* a good story? (evaluative question). All three types of questions are good and useful in some situations, and all may be asked at some point during interpretive discussions.

In preparing for discussion, leaders write down questions that come to mind while reading without regard to type. When the first reading is complete, however, they read through their questions and put to one side those that are factual or evaluative. In perusing the questions that are left—those that are interpretive—they try to discover the question about the meaning of the text that they most wish to resolve. I call that question the deepest point of doubt (DPD).

Why should leaders focus on interpretive rather than evaluative or factual questions in preparing to lead discussion? Donoghue,[31] another reader-response theorist, writes, "Interpretation is not the whole story but only the first part of it, a necessary labor of explication. Without such labor, we could hardly think ourselves engaged with the [text] at all."[32]

Interpretation, or saying in one's own words what the text says, is necessary in order to relate to the text. The interpretive questions that leaders write while reading arise because of beliefs, concepts, and terms that are employed in the course of trying to interpret the text. And they are the questions that, if addressed, will take a leader back into the text in order to discover more meaning in it. Answering factual questions, though it can help one find new facts in the text, opens new possibilities for understanding meaning only if the answers are viewed in the context of some interpretive question, that is, some question about meaning. And answering evaluative questions, which ask for judgment about the position offered by the text or some aspect of it, takes readers away from exploring further meaning to focus instead on whether their criteria for evaluation have been met. Therefore, in preparing for discussion, leaders focus on their interpretive questions in order to identify what they wish most to resolve with further study of the work.

Preparing a Cluster of Questions

Interpretive questions may or may not concern what the creators of the work intended.[33] They may or may not concern what the text, exclusive of the creator's intentions, intends to say.[34] Interpretive questions may be about any aspect of the text that leaders find puzzling. And what they find puzzling will depend not only on the content of the text but also on the beliefs, prejudices, concepts, and terms with which they try to understand it.[35]

Wolfgang Iser, a reader-response theorist whose views parallel Gadamer's at many points, describes how questions arise as one reads.[36] In so doing, he helps explain how the reader's terms and concepts determine the questions that are raised by the text. Iser says that textual interpretation is a dialectic process: it moves back and forth between what one remembers, what one expects to see, and particular places in the text where memory and expectation are related to one another.[37] The goal of this movement is to build a consistent understanding of what is read.[38] And that goal creates questions when what is remembered or expected appears to be inconsistent with what is encountered as the reading proceeds. At such moments, the reader asks: Is my memory of X incorrect? Is my memory of X correct but my expectation of Y inaccurately inferred? Such are the questions that arise when inconsistency is detected.[39] And the nature of the inconsistency will depend on the terms and concepts into which the text has been translated.

The presence of inconsistency may drive the reader to seek the cause and in so doing to discover a point of ambiguity in the text. Empson defines an ambiguity as "any verbal nuance, however slight, which gives room for alternative reactions to the same piece of language."[40] He identifies seven types of ambiguity,[41] any of which may arise as one reads and may provoke questioning. The situation in which two conflicting meanings are possible, given the context (Empson's Type 7), is particularly provocative. One may understand either one of two things, and the two cannot both be the case. Until such ambiguity is resolved, it prevents the reader from making a consistent interpretation.

In preparing to lead an interpretive discussion, leaders develop a set of questions that identifies the deepest point of doubt about the meaning of a text.[42] That question is likely to rest on a point of ambiguity.[43] The question set also includes at least eight interpretive questions that, if addressed in at least one way, imply some resolution of the DPD. The set is called the Basic Question (BQ) set. Generally speaking, those eight questions focus on eight different places in the text.

Why is it important to write eight follow-up questions? Though the number eight is arbitrarily chosen, there are good reasons to adopt it, for by definition, a follow-up question concerns some particular place in the text whose interpretation suggests ideas about the resolution of the BQ. If the deepest point of doubt about *Alice in Wonderland* is: Is *Alice in Wonderland* a child's view of the adult world or anyone's view of a mad world? then one might also ask: If the story is anyone's view of a mad world, does the Queen of Hearts insist, "Sentence first, verdict later," because normal cause-and-effect relations are reversed in the story? If one answers that question in the affirmative, the Queen's declaration may be taken as evidence for the "mad world" view. So, if leaders can write eight follow-up questions, then it is clear that the BQ can be addressed by studying at least eight places in the text. It is likewise clear that the DPD can sustain discussion of the text for forty-five minutes and probably more, if it is so desired. In Chapter 5 I consider examples of clusters of questions made up of BQs with eight follow-up questions. I also present criteria that clusters of questions need to meet before the leaders are ready to begin the discussion with a group of participants.

Leading the Discussion

The Language Game of Interpretive Discussion

An interpretive discussion is what the philosopher Ludwig Wittgenstein would call a "language game."[44] That is, it is language and actions woven together, and playing the game involves following rules, or practices, that are defined by the particular game. Gadamer concurs that textual interpretation is a kind of language game.[45] Wittgenstein and Gadamer agree that one who "knows" the game is one who knows how to follow the rules and play, who knows how to go on acting in the context of the game.[46]

The language game of interpretive discussion is played by engaging in rule-governed behaviors that bring about three outcomes. First, the players, or discussants, having read or otherwise gained access to a discussable text, try to find a point of doubt about its meaning that is of interest to many if not all of them. That question may or may not be the point of doubt identified by the leader(s) in preparing for the discussion. Addressing the question will open the text to further interpretation. By following certain rules,[47] participants in a discussion come to a question about the meaning of the text that they care to resolve. This is the first outcome.

Second, again by following rules, discussants seek evidence in the text to build an argument about its meaning and thereby answer the question.[48] They seek to resolve their shared point of doubt by looking for evidence in the text and building arguments using the evidence. The construction of arguments to resolve the shared point of doubt is the second outcome of the leading phase.

Third, the participants evaluate the strength of the arguments about textual evidence that are put forth, again by following rules. For example, they look at evidence in the text that supports their arguments and counter-arguments; they weigh the value of various pieces of evidence because not all are of equal value; they modify their arguments in light of the evidence and counterevidence. In so doing, they interpret and judge the value of the textual evidence that they find with respect to a proposed interpretation. Argument evaluation and modification make up the third outcome of the leading phase.

Two points are in order. To begin with, the rules that participants follow in working toward these three outcomes are complex and numerous and come in several forms. Some are practices that are followed routinely, as when a competent English speaker decodes the word "rule" in a written sentence. Some are practices that are followed intentionally by executing routines, as when one turns to a page that contains endnotes and looks for the desired note. And some are intentional practices that are not routine, such as searching for confirming evidence.

Second, the language game of interpretive discussion, though it is a pedagogical orientation or approach, cannot be described as a pedagogical method. This is true in part because interpretation is not pursued by following a fixed step-by-step procedure, as argued above. In addition, the activities of the group—identifying a shared point of doubt, building arguments to resolve the question, and evaluating those arguments—

cannot themselves be turned into such procedures. The evidence for the latter claim becomes clearer as we identify some of the practices followed in leading the discussion.

The Practices of Leaders

Leaders of an interpretive discussion function as does the teacher described by Socrates in Book 7 of Plato's *Republic:*

> Education is not what the professions of certain men assert it to be. They presumably assert that they put into the soul knowledge that isn't in it, as though they were putting sight into blind eyes . . . but the present argument . . . indicates that this power is in the soul of each, and that the instrument with which each learns . . . must be turned around. . . . There [is] an art to this turning around, concerned with the way in which this power can most easily and efficiently be turned around. . . . This art takes as given that sight is there, but not rightly turned nor looking at what it ought to look at, and accomplishes this object.[49]

Socrates indicates that the goal of the educator is not to put knowledge into a soul but to "turn" the student's gaze to the proper place, for by looking there, the student draws out or comes to realize what he or she knows and does not know. Hence, teaching is an art—the art of turning the student's attention to the proper point. There is no fixed procedure—no method—for doing so.

The first goal of interpretive discussion leaders, according to Socrates, is to direct the attention of the students and thereby help them identify what they think they do not know and want to find out. Accordingly, leaders question the participants in order to help them form and clarify their questions and identify the deepest point of doubt, their ideas, and their arguments for or against resolution of the point of doubt and other queries.

There is no method for such questioning because what is asked depends on what participants say. Thus it is that Socrates speaks of the "art" of turning the soul. Likewise, learning to lead interpretive discussion is, indeed, learning the art of turning the soul. What each person says is unique, so the dialogue that transpires in an interpretive discussion is also unique.

Socrates was skilled in helping others draw out their beliefs and questions, and of necessity, he proceeded differently in each case. For example, when he holds a discourse with a young mathematician named Theaetetus[50] he asks Theaetetus to answer the questions as best he can and then examines whether the beliefs Theaetetus offers seem to be true. In the dialogue, Socrates uses the interests, assumptions, and, indeed, the personal history of Theaetetus to pursue resolution of the query that they choose to address.[51] What he says to Theaetetus depends on what Theaetetus says and hence on listening carefully to his remarks.

Because the first aim of discussion leaders is to help the group identify a question it wishes to resolve, they query the participants about the meaning of what they say. Hence, they try to unearth vagueness and inconsistency, as well as connections and implications, in the discussants' thinking. They also question discussants about the terms they use to interpret the text. Are those terms justified, given textual evidence? Is the term "mad world" suitable in reference to *Alice in Wonderland*? Is "child's view of the adult world" a better phrase? Through the questioning, leaders hope to arouse perplexity about what the text says. Again, there can be no method to follow. Rather, the leader must listen to individuals and query them so as to understand their meaning.

If the shared point of doubt that the group identifies and works to resolve is a genuine question, it will be addressed by the text, for it is the text that the group is trying to understand. Furthermore, it will be a question that can be explored by looking at different places in the text. Because leaders prepare a cluster of questions consisting of a BQ and follow-up questions, all of which are interpretive questions, they know that there is at least one question (the BQ) that can be addressed by sustained study of the text. There may be others that the participants identify and pursue.

In addition to assisting in the formation of the question, leaders also try to help the participants resolve it. This requires relating different perspectives to one another, or achieving a "fus[ing] of horizons," in Gadamer's words. A "horizon" includes everything that can be seen from a particular vantage point.[52] The "fusion" must occur between what can be seen by the interpreters and what can be seen by the text. How is the perspective of the text identified? The discussion creates a set of terms that mean the same to the interpreters and the text. In other words, they are terms that "fit" the text and are understood by the discussants. A group that is discussing *Alice in Wonderland* might, for example, try to determine whether the phrase "mad world" fits that text. Gadamer writes:

> Texts are "permanently fixed expressions of life" which have to be understood, and that means one partner in the . . . conversation, the text, is expressed only through the other partner, the interpreter. Only through him are the written marks changed back into meaning. . . . By being changed back into intelligible terms, the object of which the text speaks itself finds expression. . . . It is the common object that unifies the two partners, the text and the interpreter. . . . [They] find a common language [which] coincides with the very act of understanding.[53]

The common "object" is an idea that the text and the interpreters come to share via the activity of textual interpretation and interpretive discussion. That idea—the "object"—which the text conveys must be translated into terms that the discussants use to interpret it. When they question the meaning of the text and try to express that meaning in their own words, they are working to create a set of terms that, they agree, expresses its meaning: a "common language." If the discussants fail to identify a suitable set of terms for understanding the text, they will not be able to grasp its meaning. Hence, the object of the text will be undisclosed to that group of discussants. In Chapter 6 I look carefully at some patterns of discussion leading that can help groups find terms that express the ideas found in texts.

Reflection

The third phase of interpretive discussion, reflection, takes place after the group discussion has ended. It may occur with or without the discussants. The goal of the reflection phase is to assess the accomplishments of the discussion. The reader will find references to this phase throughout the chapters because reflection occurred during the case study and after it was completed.

Let me now identify more specifically the accomplishments with which the reflection phase may be concerned. They fall into two categories: the accomplishments of the discussion with respect to building a community of learners and the accomplishments of the discussion with respect to the content of the discussion.

Building a Community of Learners

As indicated in the preface, one of the most exciting moments in the project occurred when, after several interpretive discussions, students from the urban and the suburban groups came together to talk about the meaning of a text. In Chapter 4 in which we read excerpts from one of these mixed discussions, we see a community of learners take form in a most remarkable way. What is meant by "community of learners"?

Interpretive discussion can be described as an example of what Jean Lave calls "situated social practice."[54] According to Lave, "learning," "thinking," and "knowing" do not refer to mental events that take place in the minds of individuals, as Piaget,[55] Fodor,[56] and others have maintained. Rather, they are words that refer to relations. As argued above, interpretive discussion engages leaders and participants in sets of practices that weave language and activities together in particular situations, according to rules. The rules are agreed on in the sense that they are conventions.[57] The conventions are defined by particular social and cultural traditions. Thus our "knowledge" is related to—indeed, depends on—the social and cultural traditions in which the text was written and in which the discussion occurs.[58]

As we will observe, those who participated in the case study come to follow the rules of interpretive discussion by engaging in discussions: over time, with the help of the co-leaders, they become more competent in following its practices. Likewise, the co-leaders come to follow more effective practices of discussion leading as they work with me to clarify their preparations and engage the students in textual analysis. Lave and Wenger would say that discussants and leaders learn by "legitimate peripheral access," that is, by participating in the practices to a greater extent and with greater expertise over time.[59] The vision of learning as engaging in rule-governed practices with more experienced players may be likened to Lev Vygotsky's idea of the zone of proximal development, particularly as understood by Lave and Wenger: participant practices as well as the rules of the game undergo transformation as the game of interpretive discussion is played.[60] One might say, with Lave, that interpretive discussion is situated in "historical development of on-going activity."[61]

Hence reflection on an interpretive discussion can help leaders identify growth in their and the discussants' ability to play the game, that is, engage in its rule-governed practices. An interpreter, like a historian or a social scientist, understands that his or her interpretation is a function of the situation, including the moment in time when it occurs—a point with which Gadamer would agree.[62] Reflection on discussion enables participants to identify changes in the way people participate in discussion because they can compare new patterns with those seen on previous occasions. They can also try to view the changes in terms of the conditions under which they occurred.

Now, one of the greatest sources of power in an interpretive discussion is its potential for building a community, that is, for helping people work together to achieve a common goal. John Dewey, perhaps the most influential educational thinker of the twentieth century, helps us understand what a community is and why it is important: "The extension in space of the number of individuals who participate in an interest so that each has to refer his own action to that of others, and to consider the action of others to give point and direction to his own, is equivalent to the breaking down of . . . barriers of class, race, and national territory."[63]

When Dewey writes of "individuals who participate in an interest," he refers to those working together to achieve goals that the group has agreed to pursue. The group members use the actions of one another to define their next steps, if not their long-term courses of action. Where members relate their actions to those of others in this way, they are not separated by geographical, racial, or social class differences because their actions are regulated with respect to the common goal. Hence, their differences are broken down.

In reflecting on an interpretive discussion that has taken place, one might ask: Did the discussants have a shared point of doubt that they wished to resolve? Did they use the comments of others to determine their own so that they worked together to resolve the shared point of doubt? Did the differences between people serve as resources for addressing the question of concern or did they divide the participants?

We know that working cooperatively to achieve shared goals as Dewey describes is not easy in our complex society.[64] Austin Sarat puts it well:

> To be an American is to live with an ambivalent relationship to
> difference: it is to be a neighbor to difference and at the same
> time harbor suspicions that difference may be our national un-
> doing, that differences can never be bridged, and that without

assimilation disorder lurks just below the surface of our national life. Yet . . . difference is an integral part of American
culture; America is a hybrid nation. Difference . . . has been
a part of the cultural life of Americans since the nation's
founding.[65]

I take Sarat to mean that Americans are surrounded by yet fearful of
those who come from different racial, ethnic, and cultural groups: Americans fear that the interests of groups other than their own will diminish
their power to get what they want. Hence, unless the other groups become
assimilated, that is, their goals become consistent with the national goals,
they may undermine others, and disorder may follow.

In interpretive discussion, people work together to identify both a
question about the meaning of a text and its resolution. In doing so, they
develop something that is needed in order to navigate the tension between
the desire to pursue one's own interests and the fear that others doing
likewise will limit one's success, namely, what Shweder, speaking about
immigration, calls "tolerance": "Tolerance means setting aside readily
aroused and powerfully negative feelings about the practices of immi-
grant minority groups long enough to get the facts straight and engage
the 'other' in a serious moral dialogue."[66]

Here, Shweder is saying that tolerance involves reserving judgment
about the ideas or practices of others that strike one as negative long
enough to find points people agree on, or the "facts." It may involve coming to understand the point of view of the other so that ideas and practices
are seen in that context rather than from one's own vantage point—a difficult goal to achieve, at times. When one begins to grasp the perspective
of another, one is able to think about ideas or practices in a different way
than is possible if that perspective remains unknown. One may ask: Are
the ideas or practices fair? Are they legitimate? Should they be modified?
Are they ones to which the other might contribute, given his or her talents,
skills, and resources? Such questioning permits a moral dialogue, that
is, a dialogue about what those concerned believe to be good and bad,
desirable and undesirable.

So in reflecting on an interpretive discussion, the leaders and participants might ask: Were group members tolerant of one another? Did
they listen so as to clarify facts or points of agreement about the meaning

of a text? Did they listen so as to understand the perspectives of one another, even where these differed from their own? Such tolerance is useful not only for understanding others but for studying the value of one's own ideas. And it is critical in a community of learners. Without tolerance, horizons cannot be fused; perspectives cannot be related to one another.

The Accomplishments of the Discussion with Respect to Content

In reflecting on the discussion, one may pose several questions about its content and about the ability of the group to engage in conversation concerning the meaning of the text. The leaders and participants may ask: What was the shared concern for the group, the question it wished most to resolve? At what idea did the group arrive in answer to the question? Was that idea what Gadamer calls the "object" of the conversation? If so, the discussion reaches a "truth":

> Understanding . . . is a genuine experience, i.e., an encounter with something that asserts itself as truth. . . . What we mean by truth here can [be understood] in terms of our concept of play. . . . Language games are where we, as learners—and when do we cease to be that?—rise to the understanding of the world. . . . [In playing language games], the play of language itself, which addresses us, proposes and withdraws, asks and fulfills itself in the answer.[67]

In an interpretive discussion, the experience of understanding occurs in the context of a question, for the question presents terms in which the answer may be given. The relations exist between the interpreters and the text, and the nature of the relations will be defined by the social and cultural traditions to which the text and interpreters belong, as well as the point in time when the discussion occurs. The question "Is *Alice in Wonderland* a child's view of the adult world or anyone's view of a mad world?" may arise because of things that one reads in the story (for example, people drinking potions and changing size or a queen insisting, "sentence first, verdict later"). But it is also not likely to be asked by very young children, who would lack the necessary perspective, or by adults unaccustomed to thinking in terms of cause-and-effect relations.[68] Hence the truth that emerges from an interpretive discussion is a necessary truth—necessary given the terms of the question and the evidence in the text as it is understood by the interpreters at that time.[69]

One might also ask another question in reflecting on an interpretive discussion: How is the group progressing in terms of its ability to question the meaning of a text? Indeed, this very question is addressed in the chapters that follow with respect to the two groups of students who participated in a series of interpretive discussions.

OVERVIEW OF *THE ART OF TURNING THE SOUL*

As indicated in the preface, the centerpiece of the book is a case study of two teacher candidates who were learning to lead interpretive discussion with two groups of fourth-grade students. We will see how these groups and their discussion leaders developed the capacity to engage in textual interpretation. I show that at first both groups had difficulty. Participants did not clearly distinguish between trying to grasp what the text was saying and judging it using particular criteria. Instead, they veered back and forth between these two poles, mixing evaluation with interpretation while seemingly unaware that they were doing so. Their co-leaders, who were completing the Master of Science in Education program at Northwestern University and preparing to teach in elementary school, did likewise at first. As the project progressed, all became more focused on textual interpretation, that is, on forming questions they wished to resolve about the meaning of the text, interpreting it using the evidence therein so as to address the questions, and evaluating the strength of their arguments and interpretations. Over time, they began to work together to identify and address questions, study the texts, and develop their positions.

Chapters 2, 3, and 4 present excerpts from interpretive discussions that took place in two schools, one urban and one suburban. In Chapter 2, I introduce the case study in detail and present excerpts from the first discussions that were held in the two classrooms. I also look closely at several of the participants who responded in interesting ways to the opportunity for discussion.

Chapter 3 offers excerpts from some additional discussions that took place. We see that the groups of students begin to understand how to question the text, to locate convincing evidence therein, and to build arguments for their views. We continue focused study of a few of the discussants.

In Chapter 4 we explore excerpts from the last discussion that was held in the project, one in which students from both classes came together to talk about a story that was new to all of them. That discussion was in some ways the highlight of the project, for students worked together to develop understanding of the story. Furthermore, the differences between them served as resources for the conversation rather than barriers to it. Once again, I examine changes in the discussion participation patterns of a few students.

In Chapters 5 and 6 I focus on development of the novice teachers as discussion leaders in order to understand why the group discussions changed as they did over time. Chapter 5 presents the clusters of questions that the co-leaders developed before leading the discussions about each text. I argue that progress in the classroom conversations is related to the progress in the development of the clusters of questions.

Chapter 6 explores the patterns of discussion leading that the co-leaders gradually developed over the course of the project. I argue that the patterns are related both to changes in the preparations and to events that occurred in the classroom conversations. I show that less productive patterns were replaced with ones that facilitated the development of questions among the students and the pursuit of resolution.

Finally, in Chapter 7 I examine implications of the case study for the preparation of leaders of interpretive discussion. I argue that they need opportunities to lead, to select discussable texts, to prepare clusters of questions, and to participate in interpretive discussions themselves. I provide ways in which these goals may be realized in practice by offering insights gleaned from work on interpretive discussion with teacher candidates at Northwestern University.

Thus, in the chapters that follow, we watch as the two groups of students and their co-leaders learn to develop interpretations of texts. and so build arguments together in order to learn.[70] Eventually, we will see the partners in the conversation "come under the influence of the truth of the object and [be] thus bound to one another in a new community."[71]

CHAPTER TWO

Finding a Shared Concern

THE PROJECT BEGINS

INTRODUCTION OF THE CASE STUDY

One day in late November 1996, Paula Baron and Marsha Mason, two graduate education students who aspired to teach in elementary school, entered my office.[1] They shared the following frustrating situation:

> We were sitting in the hallway [of a suburban school] discussing Langston Hughes's poem "Mother to Son" with a group of fourth graders. It was a poem we both loved about an African American woman who gives her son advice about how to handle the struggles in life. As the conversation advanced, we began to exchange disturbed glances as we listened to what our students were saying about the mother: "She has very bad grammar." "She needs to go to the Reading Lab." "She sounds like she didn't learn English very good." "She had a bad life, maybe she did drugs or something." Just a week earlier, we had led a similar discussion with a group of inner-city fourth graders. Their comments about the mother had been strikingly different: "She didn't depend on anyone, and she worked for herself." "She didn't have people doing things for her." "She's been through rough days and good days, too."[2]

Paula and Marsha were struck by the contrast between the responses of the students in the two schools. It seemed to them that the fourth graders in the urban school tried to understand the speaker of the poem. Their statements seemed consistent with the words of the poem. By contrast, those in the suburban school judged the mother instead of trying to understand her situation. One student in the suburban group drew inferences that seemed to go beyond the literary work: "Maybe she did drugs or something." Marsha and Paula wondered why the two groups had responded so differently to the poem.

I was intrigued by the question and by these two people. Marsha, a business and finance major, had been working for more than two years in financial consulting. Paula had majored in journalism as an undergraduate and had been working in public relations for eight years. Like most students in the Master of Science in Education program at Northwestern University, these young women struck me as bright, articulate, and serious about issues related to teaching and learning. And, like many, they told me that they had come to the teaching profession looking for fulfillment in their work.

But there was something else about these two: Marsha and Paula appeared to be unusually reflective people. In the fall of 1996, they were participating in a program initiative called the Urban/Suburban Northwestern Consortium Project, which involved twelve teacher education candidates who observed and taught in both urban and suburban settings.[3] Participation in the project was voluntary, and it led Paula and Marsha into the two fourth-grade classrooms where they had the discrepant experiences with the poetry of Langston Hughes.

The three of us continued to reflect on the two schools, imagining that both might be isolated from the experiences of people belonging to cultures outside their own. The suburban school, which I call Sheridan, is an elementary school that includes pre-K to grade four, with about twenty students per class. The urban school, which I call Central, is located west of the Dan Ryan Expressway in Chicago near a housing project. Central, part of the Chicago public school system, houses grades K–8, with about twenty-one students in each class. The teachers with whom Marsha and Paula worked at each school were very supportive of reading and provided their students with many opportunities to read in the classroom. Nevertheless, IGAP reading scores at Central were well below the 1996 Illinois state mean of 238 (of 500), whereas the scores on the same test at Sheridan were significantly higher than the state mean (see table 2.1).[4]

Table 2.1. Profile of Central and Sheridan Schools, 1996

	CENTRAL	SHERIDAN
School population	733	444
African American (%)	99.3	0.0
Caucasian (%)	0.3	98.4
Low-income (%)	72.7	0.0
Average third-grade IGAP reading score	186 (of 500)	303 (of 500)

During our initial conversations, Marsha and Paula conjectured that the Central students worked to understand the mother's perspective because they shared her cultural background and so could imagine her experience. As we talked further, they began to ask: If fourth-grade students from these two schools had the opportunity to read and discuss stories that depicted life in cultures beyond their own, would they become more tolerant? That is, would they try to understand the perspective of cultural groups other than their own before or instead of judging it right or wrong, good or bad? Would they work to "get the facts straight," as Shweder puts it? (See Chapter 1.)

I began to realize that Paula and Marsha had set before me an opportunity that I had long been seeking. Since coming to Northwestern, I had been preparing aspiring novice teachers to lead discussion. This, then, might be a chance to learn more about how to make my teaching more effective. If I coached these two closely in discussion preparation and leading, what effect would the coaching have? Would their approach to preparation change over time? Would their leading styles evolve as they led the discussions, and if so, in what ways? Could I help them learn to lead discussions that would help students break down the barriers of class and race?

Our next step was to develop a methodology for conducting both investigations—theirs and mine—and for recording the experiences of the fourth-grade students, the co-leaders, and me, their professor. The method we followed is consistent with "grounded theory" approaches as these are defined by Glaser, Strauss, Miles, Huberman, and Corbin.[5] Hence the goal was to make discoveries on the basis of data that were gathered systematically. Consistent with Cochran-Smith and Lytle, we proceeded on the assumption that inquiry into our own teaching could provide "a distinctive and important way of knowing about teaching."[6]

We agreed that Marsha and Paula would work as co-leaders with a group of students at each of the two schools. They would lead discussions of five texts. Each group would consist of ten fourth-grade students selected at random who would participate for the duration of the five discussions. The conversations would be held during the internship quarter, when the co-leaders would be at either Central or Sheridan all day long for ten weeks. We planned that one week, they would take the group from Central into a quiet spot, read the text aloud, and lead discussion about its meaning for forty-five minutes to an hour. The next week, they would meet with Sheridan group, read the same text aloud, and lead discussion for approximately the same period of time. By reading to the students, the co-leaders hoped to focus attention upon interpreting the meaning of a work rather than decoding the words.

Please note that neither group in the study was a control group because both received the experimental treatment. The aim was to "sample theoretically," a process that, as Harris states, is "designed to discover categories and their properties" in the service of developing theory[7]—in the case of Marsha and Paula, theory about helping students become tolerant of others, and in my case, theory about how to prepare effective discussion leaders.

We agreed that the co-leaders would choose the texts for the discussions, given criteria that they and I accepted. They would also develop a cluster of questions before leading discussion of each text. Recall that a cluster of questions is a set of interpretive questions consisting of a basic question (BQ), or a point of ambiguity that one hopes to resolve about the meaning of the text, and eight additional interpretive questions, which focus on different passages that seem to have implication for resolving the BQ. By studying their clusters of questions over the course of the project, I hoped to learn whether the clarity of the preparations would affect the character of the subsequent discussion. I also hoped to discover how to help Marsha and Paula develop clear clusters of questions. Hence, we agreed that before the discussion of each text with the students, they would prepare and I would review the cluster, and they would revise the questions so as to eliminate points of confusion and vagueness. Our procedure is summarized in table 2.2.

Table 2.2. Preparing a cluster of questions

1. MM and PB select a text.
2. SHG reviews the text to determine whether it satisfies criteria for use in interpretive discussion.
3. MM and PB develop the Basic Question (BQ).
4. MM and PB develop eight follow-up questions that refer to places in the text that may help to resolve BQ.
5. SHG reviews the cluster. Is the BQ clear? Is there a genuine concern? Do the follow-up questions, if resolved in at least one way, have implications for resolving the BQ?
6. MM and PB revise the cluster.
7. Repeat steps 5–6 as necessary.

Eventually, we collected a lot of data. First, there were data related to the preparation phase of the discussions. As it turned out, several drafts of each cluster were needed in order to clarify the question that Marsha and Paula wanted to address. I preserved each draft of each cluster, together with my comments on the questions. Furthermore, we decided to meet after the three of us had read and written questions but before Marsha and Paula began to prepare the cluster so as to explore possible points of doubt. We recorded our conversations on audiotape and these were later transcribed.

From the leading phase of the project, we collected data in the following ways. First, we hired a professional videographer to tape all ten classroom discussions. These tapes were transcribed and retranscribed, and the transcriptions were checked for accuracy. Second, after each classroom discussion, Marsha, Paula, and I met to review the events that had taken place. We also met at least one more time between the first and second discussion of each text. We made audiotapes of all these conversations, and the audiotapes were transcribed. Third, the co-leaders wrote reflective journal entries after each classroom conversation. They emailed the entries to me so that I had more information about their experiences of preparing for and leading the discussions. Fourth, I, too, kept a journal in which I reflected on our preparation sessions and on my observations of their leading.

The pages that follow tell the story of Paula and Marsha's project and their evolution as co-leaders. I present excerpts from the discussion transcripts so that the reader may see actual exchanges. The excerpted comments are numbered for ease of reference. In presenting these excerpts, I offer my interpretations of them as well, together with analysis. The analyses address particular questions that are raised about the investigation as it proceeds. Because these questions need to be addressed by data about what was said rather than how it was said, and because I hope the reader will find the excerpts easy to follow, I present them without indication of intonation or description of gestures, except in a few instances.[8]

THE GIVING TREE

The co-leaders selected a picture book by the American author Shel Silverstein titled *The Giving Tree* as the first text to be read and discussed with the fourth-grade students. Now, one may wonder why this work was chosen, given the question they wished to resolve. Indeed, the book seems to shed little light on values and practices that one finds in cultures outside of the Caucasian middle class in the United States. That, however, was its seeming virtue. Marsha and Paula worried that teachers, administrators, or parents at Sheridan might think that the two novice teachers were introducing literature with the intent of persuading discussants to accept values and practices of other cultures. Because *The Giving Tree* did not present such an issue, it seemed a safe way to begin, and so it became the first text used in the study.

A Synopsis of The Giving Tree

The story concerns a tree whose feelings are personified: "And she loved a little boy."[9] The boy she loves would gather the tree's leaves, climb up her trunk, and swing from her branches. "And the boy loved the tree very much and the tree was happy," the story says.[10] As the boy grows older, he stops visiting the tree until one day he comes and asks the tree for money, to which the tree responds by offering him her apples to sell for money. The boy takes the apples, "And the tree was happy," the story says.[11] The boy again is away for a long time, and when he returns, he is pictured as a man. He asks the tree if she can give him a house, to which she responds by telling him to cut off her branches and use the wood to build the house. He cuts off the branches, and again, the story tells us that the tree is happy. After a long time, the "boy" returns and asks the tree for a boat "that will take me far away from here."[12] The tree tells him to cut down her trunk and make a boat, and he does so. "And the tree was happy . . . but not really,"[13] says the story. Again, after a long time, the "boy" returns to the tree, and this time she says, "I am sorry, Boy, . . . but I have nothing left to give you." " 'I don't need very much now,' says the boy, 'just a quiet place to sit and rest. I am very tired.' 'Well,' says the tree . . . , 'an old stump is good for sitting and resting. Come, Boy, sit down. Sit down and rest.' "[14]

The Giving Tree, *Central School—Discussion 1*
The first discussion took place in Central School. The area where the discussions were held was not separated from the rest of the classroom by physical barriers, but the desks in the room, where other students sat working quietly, were at a distance from our group. Of the ten students who had been selected to participate in the project, three were absent. The other seven sat in the discussion area behind name tags that read Cynthia, Ethan, Grace, Joseph, Tanis, Tracy, and Troy. They were seated on chairs facing one another, and Marsha and Paula sat with them in the circle.

After introducing themselves and handing each child a pencil, the co-leaders passed out copies of the text with the lines numbered. They explained that once the story had been read aloud, the discussants would have the opportunity to write down questions about its meaning on their personal copies and in discussing the story, could refer to places of interest by line number. Marsha then read *The Giving Tree* to the group. She looked at the discussants as she read and turned the pages. They seemed to be watching the pages as she held the book so as to display its contents. When the reading ended, the students were given time to jot down notes and questions. Then the discussion began—most remarkably:

[GT1]   TRACY: I want to know why the tree kept on calling him, "Come, boy," and he was grown.[15]

[GT2]   MARSHA (MM): Who else wondered that? I wondered that same thing, Tracy. Because, you know, in that picture, when it's talking about the old man, and he's all hunched over, and the tree is still calling him "Boy," isn't she?

[GT3]   TRACY: I think she must still think he's young in some kind of way.

[GT4]   MM: She still thinks he's young in some kind of way? What do you think, Ethan? Do you think the tree sees the boy as being young?

[GT5]   ETHAN: No.

[GT6]   TRACY: I think because she said, "Come and swing on my branches."

[GT7]   ETHAN: He's too strong.

[GT8]   PAULA (PB): Tracy, can you show us? Can you refer to the line where she says, "Come and swing on my branches?"

[GT9]   TRACY: On line twenty-four. "Boy, climb up my trunk and swing from my branches and be happy."

[GT10]   MM: And what did the boy tell the tree?

[GT11]   TRACY: "I'm too big to climb trees," said the boy. "I want a house to keep me warm," he said. "I want a wife and I want children and so I need a house. Can you give me a house?" That was line twenty-five and twenty-six.

Some of the student behaviors that we see here are characteristic of experienced rather than novice discussants. To begin with, the very first question is an interpretive one—a question about the meaning of the text. So when Tracy asks why the tree addresses the boy as "Boy" even when he was grown up [GT1], she poses a question whose resolution requires interpretation of the story; it cannot be answered definitively by pointing to one passage. Because the majority of questions posed by teachers in the United States call not for interpretation but rather the recitation of fact,[16] it is somewhat surprising that this fourth-grade student, who has lived in classrooms for at least five years, opens the first discussion with an interpretive question.

In the second place, when Ethan and Tracy disagree about the resolution of the question, each provides a reason for his or her position, and Tracy spontaneously supports hers with textual evidence, albeit without a specific line reference. Tracy says that the tree's invitation, "Come and swing from my branches," supports her idea that the tree may find the boy "young in some kind of way" [GT3]. We see discussants beginning to find ambiguity in the text and supporting their questions and claims with textual evidence, both hallmark practices of interpretive discussion and behaviors characteristic of experienced participants.

One goal of discussion is to arrive at a clear question that those in the group wish to answer—what I have called a shared point of doubt, or shared concern. Why is it important to reach a shared concern? To begin with, if a point of doubt is shared by several people, then they may work together to try to resolve it, especially if the question is clear. They may listen with care to the comments of one another so that they can both get and give ideas that work toward resolution. Consequently, the discussion has coherence that all can feel, for everyone is speaking to the same question. Given the running start, will the group at Central move toward the formation and resolution of a shared concern? The following exchange took place somewhat later in the discussion:

[GT12]   TANIS: I think that the boy wasn't happy even when he had all the stuff the tree was giving him.

[GT13]   MM: What makes you think the boy wasn't happy, Tanis? What line?

[GT14]   TANIS: Because he . . . it's not in a line . . . because he kept on coming back and coming back for more things.

[GT15]   PB: So was he not happy with what he got from the tree? Because he always wanted more stuff from the tree? Can you show us one of the places where he wanted more stuff?

[GT16]   TANIS: Line twenty-six. "I want a wife and I want children and so I need a house. Can you give me a house?"

[GT17]   MM: Tanis, when he's saying these things, when he says, "I want a wife and I want children" and he keeps coming back like you said, when the boy says those things, is he being selfish because he keeps taking things from the tree?

[GT18]   TANIS: Kind of.

[GT19]   MM: Kind of? Tracy?

[GT20]   TRACY: In the book, I never heard him say "Thank you" after the tree gave him stuff.

[GT21]   MM: Never heard him say "Thank you"?

Marsha poses a question about whether the boy is selfish [GT17]. Unlike Tracy's initial question, resolution of Marsha's does not require textual interpretation. Indeed, she has worded it as an evaluative question—a question that may be answered with reference to the respondents' criteria, not criteria that are offered by the text. In order to answer the question of whether the boy is selfish, the respondents may evaluate his actions and character using their own criteria for judging someone selfish. Indeed, Tracy does just that when she suggests that the boy is selfish because she "never heard him say 'Thank you'" [GT20].

What are the consequences of posing an evaluative rather than an interpretive question? I continue to explore the answer to this question in the remainder of the chapter. First of all, the evaluative question asks students to express their beliefs about an issue on the basis of personal experience.[17] Sometimes a leader may want them to do just that.[18] But at the moment when evaluation occurs, the search for meaning in the text comes to a halt, at least temporarily. So the focus of the discussion shifts. And in order to return to a focus on the text, the discussion must shift yet again, as we see in the next exchange, which immediately followed the one reprinted above in the discussion:

[GT22]   CYNTHIA: I think that the tree wanted to give him stuff, because they used to play together and stuff. It was like they were best friends.

[GT23]   MM: Find a place, Cynthia, where you think that the tree wants to give things to the boy. Why, Cynthia, when the boy keeps coming back and the tree gives him apples: what is it about giving the boy apples that the tree likes?

[GT24]   CYNTHIA: What I think is that she knows that she's going to grow some more. Because you have to pick them. It's like farmers pick apples from trees to give to grocery stores so they can sell them and get money, so I think that's [what] she's doing here.

[GT25]   PB: So do you think she minds giving up these things?

[GT26]   CYNTHIA: Yes.

[GT27]   TRACY: No.

Marsha had posed an evaluative question when she had asked whether the boy was selfish in taking things from the tree [GT17]. That question seems to interest Tracy and perhaps Cynthia, for Tracy argues that the boy was selfish—"I never heard him say 'Thank you'" [GT20]—and Cynthia argues that the tree wanted to give things to the boy "because they were best friends" [GT22], suggesting, perhaps, that the boy was not selfish in taking things from the tree. Paula then shifts away from Marsha's evaluative question when she asks whether the tree minds giving the things to the boy [GT25]. That question is interpretive, and, indeed, Cynthia and Tracy answer it in two different ways. In posing the interpretive question, Paula may have wished to return the discussion to a focus on the text. Her next query suggests as much.

[GT28]   PB: No? Then why doesn't she mind giving them up?

[GT29]   TRACY: Because she wanted to be nice to him. She wouldn't want to be selfish because she wouldn't want anybody to kick the tree or [do] something like that to her. Like if someone would kick the tree or throw pebbles or rocks at it.

[GT30]   PB: So even though the boy doesn't say "Thank you" every time he comes back for something, you think she doesn't mind?

When Paula asks Tracy why the tree doesn't mind giving things to the boy [GT28], she begins to explore the student's reasoning about the answer to the interpretive question that she posed [GT25]. Paula could have asked Cynthia why she says yes [GT26] in answer to the question, but she does not do so. Perhaps she queries Tracy because Cynthia's reply seems to contradict the line of reasoning she has offered: if the tree and the boy are "best friends" [GT22], and she knows that the apples will grow back if she gives them to the boy [GT24], then why would she mind doing so? Paula may ask Tracy to explain why she answered no in the belief that, having heard Cynthia's argument, Tracy will defend the answer that is consistent with it—and with the evidence in the text.[19]

Once again, like Marsha [GT17], Paula does not make it clear that she is posing an interpretive question [GT28]. She does not ask, According to the text, does the tree mind giving things to the boy? Therefore the fact that Tracy responds by evaluating the text [GT29] is understandable.

When she says that the tree does not mind giving the boy apples because the boy might harm her if she were selfish, Tracy offers reasoning based on her own experience, not textual evidence. Indeed, there is no evidence that the tree has concern for her own safety or well-being—quite the contrary. Marsha then says:

[GT31]   MM: Tracy, when the tree gives the boy things, look at lines twenty-nine and thirty, and it says, "And so the boy cut off her branches." This time he's taking her branches, not just her apples, "and he carried them away to build his house." And line thirty says, "And the tree was happy." So, Tracy, do you think when the tree gives the boy things, is that what makes the tree happy?

Marsha draws attention to lines where there is evidence that is relevant to the question of whether the tree minds giving things to the boy. In doing so, she treats Paula's question as one about the meaning of the text although Paula did not explicitly pose it as such. Because there is evidence elsewhere in the story that the tree does mind giving some things to the boy, the answer to Marsha's question calls for careful interpretation: the evidence must be scrutinized in order to decide which answer it best supports. And the consequence of posing a question that is clearly interpretive is that the question points the way for continuing the discussion: it shows how the discussion should go on, as Wittgenstein would say.[20] Unlike the evaluative question, the interpretive question directs the discussants back into the text in order to resolve a point of ambiguity about its meaning.

Now let us step back for a moment and ask: Has the group at Central arrived at a shared point of doubt? The exchange that follows the one reprinted above is telling.

[GT32]   MM: Joseph, what do you think?

[GT33]   JOSEPH: I think the boy is taking too many things from the tree because after all those things he was taking, she might not be anything. She might be gone . . .

[GT34]   MM: What line are you looking at, Joseph? Line twenty-three?

[GT35]   JOSEPH: Yeah, because it says, "And one day the boy came back and the tree shook with joy and said, 'Come boy, climb my trunk,' and he said, 'I'm too big to climb trees,' and she . . ."

[GT36]   MM: Okay, so then, Joseph, in line twenty-three, that you just read . . . do you think when it says, "the tree shook with joy" that the tree is happy because the boy came back and because she missed him, or do you think the tree is shaking with joy there because of something else?

[GT37]   JOSEPH: I think the tree is shaking with joy because he came back.

[GT38]   MM: Because he came back.

[GT39]   PB: Tanis, what do you think?

[GT40]   TANIS: I think in line one, it says, "Once there was a tree, and she loved a little boy." She probably wanted to give him stuff because she loved him.

[GT41]   MM: Oh, Tanis just said that the tree probably loved the boy.

[GT42]   TANIS: That's why she wanted to give him stuff.

At this point, there seem to be three issues that discussants are trying to resolve. The first, pursued by Joseph, is the evaluative question of whether the boy is selfish, and Joseph argues that he is. At [GT33], Joseph offers his own criterion of selfishness: whereas Tracy had argued that the boy was selfish because he never said "Thank you" to the tree, Joseph maintains that the boy is selfish because he destroys the tree in the process of taking things from her to meet his own needs.

The second issue arises when Marsha asks why the tree is happy [GT36]. This is an interpretive question, for it can be addressed, though not resolved definitively, by interpreting lines from the story. Thus Marsha introduces a totally new interpretive question.

Finally, Tanis seems to shift back to a question raised previously by Paula, namely, whether the tree minds giving things to the boy [GT40]. Tanis quotes and interprets line one of the story. She may mean that the tree does not mind giving things to the boy because the story says that she loved the boy.

In short, there seem to be three issues on the floor: Is the boy selfish? Why is the tree happy, as stated in line twenty-three? Did the tree mind giving things to the boy? We have seen how each of these questions seemed to arise as another was being discussed. But they are separate questions, and the presence of all three at once may distract the discussants from working together to explore all passages that might help resolve any one of them. In fact, the group at Central never did focus on any one question and work to resolve it during that first discussion.

As we explore the conversations that took place during the project, we will look closely at two students from each group. We will watch as their participation patterns shift over time. In subsequent chapters I try to show why the changes occur.

A Closer Look at Tracy

The first of these students is Tracy, an African American female with a soft, gentle face and hair in pigtails who attended Central School. Tracy participated actively from the first discussion to the last. In the conversation about *The Giving Tree*, she spoke a total of twenty times. In the excerpts printed above, she did several things that are worth noting. I have already remarked on her opening the discussion with an interpretive question. In addition, after one request by Paula to give a line number in order to locate her reference to the story [GT8], Tracy complied [GT9] and then spontaneously offered a line-numbered reference in answer to the next question, which was asked by Marsha [GT11]. In fact, Tracy spontaneously referred to the text nine times over the course of the conversation.[21] She seemed to have grasped a practice that is essential to interpretive discussion—that of addressing questions with reference to specific places in the text.

At the same time, her devotion to the practice is not consistent. For example, when Marsha asks her whether the boy is acting selfishly when he takes things from the tree [GT17], Tracy says, "I never heard him say 'Thank you' after the tree gave him stuff" [GT20]. As explained above, Tracy evaluates rather than interprets the text; that is, she invokes a criterion for judging the boy that is her own rather than appealing to criteria that are offered by the text. She may be making use of personal experience that inclines her to associate selfishness with impoliteness. It is not surprising that she fails to give a line number in making her comment at [GT20], for there is none to give.

Nor does she give a line number when answering Paula's question about whether the tree minds giving things to the boy [GT28]. Again, Tracy responds by evaluating rather than interpreting the text when she says that the tree did not mind giving the boy things "[b]ecause she wanted to be nice to him. She wouldn't want to be selfish because she wouldn't want anybody to kick the tree [or] . . . throw pebbles or rocks at it" [GT29]. When Tracy responds as she does, she creates a fantasy about what the tree is thinking and judges the tree's feelings on the basis of that fantasy.

At this point in the project, Tracy may not discriminate between evaluating and interpreting the text. In theory, however, and often though not always in practice, there is a clear distinction between these alternatives, and the consequences of evaluating and interpreting can be very different.[22] In what follows we continue to ponder those differences. The other Central student at whom I take a closer look is introduced in Discussion 3.

The Giving Tree, *Sheridan School—Discussion 2*
The second discussion took place at Sheridan School, which is located on a quiet street in a suburb north of Chicago. The space available allowed the co-leaders to take the discussion group out of the classroom to a quieter spot. On the day of the first discussion there, I arrived to find the discussants and the co-leaders seated in a small room outside the regular fourth-grade classroom. Apparently restless, the students had begun to make paper airplanes of the line-numbered pages of *The Giving Tree*.

Seated in this group were nine of the ten students participating in the project at Sheridan: Arnie, Beth, Brian, Daphne, Jeremy, Katie, Maggie, Parker, and Walter. Marsha introduced the discussion activity much as she had done at Central and then proceeded to read the story. The students started to watch as the pictures flashed by. They seemed to grow more attentive as the story proceeded, and conversation began as soon as the reading ended.

[GT43]   JEREMY: I have a question. Why was the tree happy? . . .
           He cut off its branches, and like, sort of killed it.

Jeremy, like Tracy at Central School, has started right off with an interpretive question, for he seems to be asking: Why is the tree happy if the boy cut off its branches and "sort of killed it?" The question is interpretive because there is textual evidence to address it, but at no point is it resolved definitively. Arnie responds, followed by Beth:

[GT44]   ARNIE: Well, the tree was happy to give something to the
           boy. . . .

[GT45]   BETH: Well, he was happy because he was making another
           person happy. . . .

[GT46]   MM: Where? So you're saying the tree was happy because
           she's making the boy happy?

[GT47]   BETH: Mm hmm [Yes].

[GT48]   MM: Okay, let's look at line thirty. It says, "And the tree
           was happy." And you said you think the tree's happy
           because she's making the boy happy, right? How is she
           making the boy happy?

[GT49]   BETH: By giving him things to survive.

[GT50]   MM: Okay, Jeremy?

[GT51]   JEREMY: But it's like sort of saying, you can have my hair,
           just scalp it off and you can like donate it to science or
           something. . . . Sort of like cutting off your ear [someone
           says "Ow!"] and . . . here [gestures giving it away]. Cause
           you're cutting off your branches.

[GT52]   MM: But you know, it's kind of strange, Jeremy, though,
           because each time she cuts something off, it says she's
           happy.

At this point the discussion seems to clarify an issue that Jeremy first
posed. He began by asking why the tree was happy [GT43], to which Arnie responded that the tree was made happy by giving to the boy [GT44].
Beth said that the tree was happy because she was making the boy happy
[GT45]. When Marsha points to textual evidence and asks how the tree
was making the boy happy [GT48], Beth's answer [GT49] seems to prompt
Jeremy to reiterate his dilemma, this time embellished with examples to
show that giving the boy things as the tree did should cause her pain, not
happiness [GT51]. Marsha then underscores Jeremy's dilemma [GT52]. So
it seems that the interpretive question, Why does the story say that the
tree is happy? is on the floor. Maggie continues:

[GT53]   MAGGIE: On number one, it says, "And she loved a little
           boy," and if she loves the boy, then if she gives him things
           that he likes and that he needs, she'll be helping him and
           so . . .

[GT54]   M M : And so that's why she's happy?

[GT55]   MAGGIE: Yeah.

[GT56]   BETH: [She's] grateful and happy because she thinks she's
           doing the right thing.

[GT57]   PB: She's doing the right thing. Is she doing the right
           thing? Or is she happy [to give him things]? You know how
           there are two different things? I'm giving you something
           because I'm happy to do it, or I'm giving you something
           because I think it's the right thing to do.

[GT58]   ARNIE: It's the right thing to do.

[GT59]   BETH: Well, I mean, you never have . . .

[GT60]   ARNIE: [Interrupting.] Because it's better to give than to
           receive.

[GT61]   BETH: You never have to give somebody something, but it
           makes you feel good that you can do that and the other
           person will be very grateful.

[GT62]   KATIE: It's not exactly the right thing to do, it's just that,
           like, it is the right thing to do but it also makes you happy.
           That you would actually do something. In her case I think
           it makes her happy because she's doing something for a
           boy who doesn't have anything. Like he doesn't have a
           house or a boat, enough money . . .

In the excerpt above, the discussants remain focused on the question of why the story says that the tree is happy. Furthermore, they seem
to grasp the difference between the two options that Paula poses [GT57],
and they move to determine the value of each. Arnie opts for "It's the
right thing to do," by which he seems to mean that doing the right thing
makes the tree happy. Beth may be adding justification for Arnie's claim
at [GT61]. Beth seems to mean that one gets pleasure from doing the
right thing, even if it is not necessary to do it, and that the gratitude of
the receiver increases the giver's pleasure. At [GT62] Katie may disagree
with Arnie and Beth. Her point seems to be that it may be right to give
things to the boy, but it is the giving that produces the pleasure that the
tree feels, and that feeling of pleasure is equivalent to happiness.

So is the tree happy because she does the right thing in giving things to
the boy or because she gets pleasure from giving? The debate continues:

[GT63]   WALTER: I don't feel like it would be the right thing to do because it's killing itself to make somebody have a house and a boat and it's, like, killing itself just for them.

[GT64]   PB: Walter, I'm sorry. You're saying that she is doing it because it is the right thing to do?

[GT65]   WALTER: She's not.

[GT66]   PB: She's not doing it for that reason.

[GT67]   WALTER: Yeah, I don't think she is. She's doing it to make him happy.

[GT68]   PB: To make him happy? And show us again somewhere in the poem—that's not so hard for us to find, is it?—Can you help us find somewhere in the poem where it says she's doing it because she's happy? Is it because she's happy, though?

[GT69]   WALTER: No, because she wants the boy to be happy.

[GT70]   PB: Ohhh.

[GT71]   MM: Because she wants the boy to be happy, Walter?

Again, evaluation finds its way into the interpretive discussion. When Paula asks Walter why the tree acts as she does [GT64], he responds by rejecting one of the possibilities on the floor [GT65]—that the tree acts from a desire to do the right thing when she gives the boy her apples and branches. Indeed, Walter declares that the tree is motivated by the desire to bring the boy happiness, not the desire to do what is right [GT67]. In response, Paula asks Walter to give evidence from the text for his position [GT68]. Yet the student may not believe that Paula has grasped his meaning, for he repeats his position [GT69]: the tree gives things to the boy because she wants him to be happy, not because she wants to do the right thing.

Notice the different forms that appeal to personal experience as a basis for evaluation can take. In the first instance that we saw, when Tracy argued that the boy was selfish because he didn't say "Thank you" to the tree [GT20], she judged the boy's character with respect to her own criterion. As suggested previously, perhaps in her experience selfish people are also ungrateful people, and hence her criterion.

In the second instance, in which Tracy argues that the boy does not mind giving things to the tree [GT29], she attributes reasoning to it that seems to be based on her fantasy about the tree's thinking—fantasy grounded in personal experience, although the nature of that experience is unclear. Again, there is no evidence in the text that the tree had concern for her own safety and well-being.

In the third place, when Walter argues that the tree is happy not because she does "the right thing" but, rather, because she gives things to the boy, he neither appeals directly to his own experience nor imagines a scenario in which he uses his experience as a basis for his argument. Instead, he opts for one resolution—the tree acts as she does to make the boy happy [GT69]—because he rejects the other possibility, namely, his own statement at [GT63] that what the tree does is not right. Evaluating the appropriateness of one of the options for resolution on the basis of his own idea of right and wrong brings Walter to reject it and, as a consequence, choose the other option.

All three instances of evaluation are similar in that the speakers judge the text (or characters therein) on the basis of criteria they bring to bear on it from without. The criteria arise in some way from the personal experience of the speaker. As we have seen, the personal experience could express itself in the form of reference to the speaker's personal history, an imagined scenario or course of reasoning, or an expression of the speaker's personal values. And the criteria can come from other sources, as we shall soon see.

But first, let us ask: What has happened to the discussion? Jeremy began by asking why the story says that the tree was happy because it is losing its branches and trunk—"killing itself." The reasons that the group members have offered thus far include the following: (1) it is giving (Arnie, [GT44]); (2) it is making another happy (Beth, [GT45]); (3) it is helping the boy survive (Beth, [GT49]); (4) the tree loves the boy, and giving to him helps him, so helping him makes the tree happy (Maggie, [GT53]); (5) it is doing the right thing (Beth, [GT56]).

When Walter argues that the fifth possibility—doing the right thing makes the tree happy—is unacceptable because the tree isn't doing the right thing (since it is killing itself), he evaluates the tree's actions on the basis of his personal values. When he does so, he interrupts the movement of the group toward the formation of a question about the meaning of the text that the members share. As the next excerpt shows, the group again moved on to address a new question:

[GT72]   ARNIE: The tree was sad because . . . the tree was giving the boy her branches and her apples, but the boy wasn't giving anything in return and then it says, "The boy stayed away for a long time and the tree was sad" [reading from the text].

[GT73]   PB: So you think she's sad because she gives him all this stuff and then he [the boy] goes away and isn't giving her anything back?

[GT74]   ARNIE: Yeah, he comes back and takes some more stuff.

[GT75]   PB: So every time he comes back he's just taking? OK. Jeremy?

[GT76]   JEREMY: I think that she's sad because she's, like, giving him things, like she's giving him money, giving him a house, giving him a boat, but each time he just goes away and she thinks that—she's sad because she doesn't get to have more time with him. She just stays there and waits until he comes back, and then they see each other for, like, five seconds and then he leaves again.

[GT77]   PB: So it sounds like what Jeremy's saying is that [the tree] is sad because [the boy] goes away and they don't have their friendship, as opposed to she's sad because when he's gone she can't be giving him stuff. Right? You think it has more to do with friendship?

[GT78]   JEREMY: Yeah. Because she doesn't even get to . . . she gives him a house and then he goes away. He doesn't even stay with her for, like, five minutes.

In the exchange above, the students are discussing the question of why the story says that the tree is sad—another new question. In so doing, they are looking at a line that Arnie reads [GT72]. Arnie argues that the tree is unhappy because she does all the giving and the boy never offers to give her anything in return. Jeremy, at [GT76], suggests another idea: the sadness is caused by the boy's too-swift departure. Marsha seems to take up Arnie's suggestion that the tree might be sad because the boy takes from her without giving in return, and she poses a question to Jeremy that explores the idea:

[GT79]   MM: So Jeremy, when [the boy] keeps taking these things, is he, like, on line twenty-nine when it says, "He cut off her branches and carried them away to go build a house," is he being selfish when he takes these branches from her?

[GT80]   JEREMY: I think he is, because he's just taking, he's taking it and then he's not even giving things to the tree.

[GT81]   ARNIE: The boy doesn't even say "Thank you."

At [GT79] Marsha introduces the question of whether the boy is selfish, just as she did in the discussion at Central School. Perhaps the question is still of interest to her, and perhaps she takes it up because Arnie [GT74] has suggested a new idea—the boy's failure to give the tree things in return. Here we see that criteria for evaluating the text can come from other discussants. That is, they may introduce criteria that their peers find acceptable for some reason. If there is an evaluative question on the floor, they may use the suggested criteria to judge the text in some way.

Regardless of the source of the external criteria, the presence of an evaluation question shifts the focus of the discussion. Once Marsha invites Jeremy to evaluate the boy [GT79], Jeremy does not hesitate to respond. At [GT80] he says that the boy is selfish because he takes without giving in return—much the point that Arnie made at [GT72]. Both discussants seem to evaluate the boy on the basis of their own values. Arnie, for his part, continues evaluating when he says, "The boy doesn't even say 'Thank you'" [GT81]. As in the Central School discussion, we again see a participant suggest the failure to give thanks as a criterion of selfishness, perhaps on the basis of his own experience with selfish people.

In asking whether the boy is selfish, Marsha moves away from Jeremy's claim that the tree is sad because she can't see the boy [GT76, GT78]. She shifts the focus away from the interpretive question "Why does the story say that the tree is sad?" to the evaluative question of whether the boy is selfish. And what is the consequence? As was true in the Central School discussion of *The Giving Tree*, the conversation comes to a halt when the evaluative question is posed. It is not clear how to go on. The discussants could question one another about the suitability of the external criteria that have been brought to bear. Or they could question each other about whether, given those criteria, a suitable judgment has been rendered. Such questioning may not go very far, for now the evidence in the text may be irrelevant to the dispute. For example, if the external criteria are based on one person's personal history, discussion may break down altogether if the experiences of others differ such that they do not find the criteria acceptable. If the criteria are based on personal values, the discussion may break down if people hold conflicting values and cannot persuade one another to modify any of them. In short, once the evaluative question is posed, there is no clear sense of how to address it and how to resolve disputes.

As a consequence, in many instances where an evaluation question is introduced, the participants are forced to shift to another question in order to resume discussion. As we have seen, the movement is often to an interpretive question. Why? If the group is engaged in trying to figure out the meaning of the text, as opposed to judging its truth or merit, then it is clear how to proceed: examine the textual evidence to determine the meaning and hence resolve the question.[23]

Not only is the direction clear, but each member of the group has access to the material that is used as the basis for resolving the question, that is, the text. In evaluative discussions, the basis for resolving the issue often is not shared by all. For example, if the basis is personal history, then each discussant may have different grounds for making the judgment. One person may tell the group about his or her particular history, but the others may not have direct access to the events described and may not be in a position to judge their usefulness or relevance to the situation at hand. If others are not persuaded of the relevance of the speaker's experience, the discussion will come to a halt with perhaps no indication of how to proceed further.

In short, the presence of evaluative questions in an interpretive discussion has three consequences: It shifts the focus of the discussion away from trying to understand the meaning of the text, at least temporarily; it interrupts the movement toward the formation of a question that the members of the group share about the meaning of the text; and it does not indicate how the discussion is to proceed, especially where there is controversy about the criteria for judgment or their application.

I am not suggesting that leaders should never ask evaluative questions or that evaluative discussions are always unproductive. On the contrary, there are times when leaving exploration of the text aside so as to learn about participants' experiences, values, or personal reasoning (which is based on experience, values, or fantasy) is very suitable. Such may be the case, for example, when the text has been thoroughly explored as to its meaning, and a group wishes to consider its truth or worth.

On the other hand, the move to evaluate the text before it has been analyzed with respect to points of ambiguity—before it has been well interpreted—may be costly because the participants may forgo opportunities for insight that careful study of its meaning can yield. Furthermore, if the group moves from one question to another without fully resolving any of them, it is hard to feel that the discussion has made progress, whether in understanding the text or articulating and evaluating personal beliefs.

The question before us now is: How does a group move from evaluating to interpreting a text or to mixing the two approaches to the text appropriately in an interpretive discussion? It is to that question that I turn in Chapter 3, which presents excerpts from conversations that took place later in the project.

A Closer Look at Jeremy

Jeremy was an active participant from the first discussion to the last. He spoke often—thirty-eight times in the discussion of *The Giving Tree*—and moved frequently in his chair. Like Tracy, he was the first to speak in the discussion, and he opened it with an interpretive question [GT43]. At [GT51], Jeremy reiterates his question, and one has the sense that he is interested in resolving it.

Also like Tracy, Jeremy sometimes appeals to textual evidence in articulating questions and arguing conclusions. In the questions that he poses at both [GT43] and [GT51], he refers to facts that the story gives, for instance, that the boy cuts off the tree's branches. At [GT76] he says that the tree gives the boy "money, a house, and a boat."

Unlike Tracy, however, Jeremy does not cite line numbers in defending his claims about what happens in the story—not even once. He is not alone in failing to do so. But his failure suggests that at this point in the project he is not interested in defending his claims in a precise way. Furthermore, he slips in claims for which there is no textual evidence, as when he says that the tree gave the boy "money, a house and a boat." The story explicitly states that the tree gave the boy apples, not money.[24]

Finally, Jeremy, like Tracy, does not hesitate to evaluate the text. Jeremy made ten evaluative comments over the course of the conversation about *The Giving Tree.* In comment [GT76] he claims that when the boy returns to the tree after having been gone for a long time, "they see each other for . . . five seconds and then he leaves again." At [GT78] he says that the tree "gives [the boy] a house and then he goes away. He doesn't even stay for . . . five minutes." There is no indication in the story of how much time elapses when the boy is with the tree—or when he is away from her, for that matter. We know only that the boy progresses from youth to old age over the course of the tale. At [GT76] and [GT78] Jeremy evaluates the text by imagining a scenario and makes judgments about the feelings of the tree on the basis of his fantasies. At [GT80] he refers to the boy's actions in a vague way—"he's just taking, he's taking it and then he's not even giving things to the tree"—and defends his claim that the boy is selfish on the basis of that generalization.

In sum, then, while Jeremy is inclined to speak frequently, he is also inclined to evaluate the text with frequency, to mix evaluative with interpretive commentary indiscriminately, and when appealing to the text, to do so in vague, imprecise ways. Finally, we have seen him attribute certain statements to the text, seemingly unaware of and unconcerned about the lack of textual evidence to support his claims.

As the analysis continues in Chapter 3, we will watch as the participation patterns of Tracy and Jeremy change. We will also see how the two groups of discussants move from an evaluative to an interpretive focus on the text and the consequences that arise from doing so.

CHAPTER THREE

Finding a Shared Concern

THE PROJECT CONTINUES

IN WEEK 3 of the project, after they had led the discussions of *The Giving Tree* in both schools, Marsha and Paula returned to Central to help the group there reflect on a story from Africa called "Kaddo's Wall." Week 4 took them back to Sheridan with "Kaddo's Wall," and in Weeks 5 and 6 they visited Central and Sheridan, respectively, to explore a story from Africa titled "Allah Will Provide." In Weeks 7 and 8 the co-leaders turned to a tale from the French Canadian tradition titled "Jean Labadie's Big Black Dog."

For reasons of space, clarity, and ease of focus, I explore excerpts from three of these six discussions: "Kaddo's Wall" at Sheridan, "Allah Will Provide" at Central, and "Jean Labadie's Big Black Dog" at Sheridan. In each case I present the excerpts with a particular question in mind. In analyzing the discussion of "Kaddo's Wall," I return to the question posed at the end of Chapter 2: How did the groups move from evaluating the text to interpreting it? When considering the discussion of "Allah Will Provide," the question is: How do students become committed to resolving a shared question about meaning by using textual evidence? And in perusing excerpts from the Sheridan discussion of "Jean Labadie's Big Black Dog," I ask: How do the students become committed to evaluating the strength of possible text-based resolutions of the shared question? As the analysis proceeds, we take a closer look at the performances of Tracy, Jeremy, and two other students—Grace and Kurt.

"KADDO'S WALL"

Synopsis
This traditional folktale from Africa focuses on a rich man named Kaddo who uses his excess corn to build a wall around his house.[1] Indeed, he does so while ignoring the cries of protest from the townspeople, who object that many around him have nothing to eat. One year, when drought robs Kaddo of his crops, he consumes his wall, for he himself is starving. He then seeks aid from Sogole, king of a neighboring territory called Ganna. Sogole responds by loading Kaddo down with enough corn to begin new crops, and Kaddo starts to return to his home. But on the way, the once-rich man becomes hungry, begins to devour the gift, and before reaching his home, kills himself by overeating.

"Kaddo's Wall," Sheridan School—Discussion 4
How did the groups move from evaluating the text to interpreting it? In reviewing the excerpts from the discussion of "Kaddo's Wall" at Sheridan, we see the shift taking place—a shift that occurred in both groups, as it turned out. Consider, for example, an issue that arose in the discussions, namely, Why did Kaddo behave as he did? Was he selfish? Greedy? Although students in both schools raised and reflected on these possibilities, Jeremy, with Marsha's help, introduced another possible motive:

[KW1]   JEREMY: Well, I don't see why [Kaddo] made so much corn in the first place. He should've just made how much he needed. Then he wouldn't have a problem. Then he wouldn't have to make a wall out of it. And then when he made the wall, that's how he screwed up.

[KW2]   MM: In the beginning, Jeremy, look at what it says on lines five and six; it says that "[h]is grain bulged in his granary, because each season he harvested far more than he could use." So did he harvest more grain than he could use because—what Beth brought up—that he's greedy?

[KW3]   JEREMY: I don't know.

[KW4]   MM: Or did he harvest more grain because maybe he just thought . . . that he didn't know what else to do with it, and he's just kinda maybe an ignorant man . . . [he] doesn't realize that there are other things to do with the corn?

[KW5] JEREMY: No, um, he had so much harvest that he didn't know what to do with it but I think since he had all of it, he should've just saved it because, like, what happened at the very end . . . he died because his stomach didn't know what to do with food, but he lost the food first . . . but if he just made as much as he needed every, like, time then he could do better.

[KW6] MM: So why, Jeremy, did he do that? Why did [Kaddo] harvest far more corn than he could ever eat?

[KW7] JEREMY: I think because maybe he didn't . . . he wasn't a good gardener. I don't know.

Jeremy and Marsha consider the possibility that Kaddo is ignorant, rather than selfish or greedy, as others had maintained. Now, of what is Kaddo ignorant? Jeremy may have more than one idea about the answer to the question. For at [KW1] he suggests that Kaddo was ignorant about what to do with all the excess corn and therefore would have been better off without it. At [KW5], however, he seems to mean that Kaddo was ignorant about how to raise just enough corn to meet his needs.

Perhaps, in listening to Jeremy, Marsha hears several possible topics about which Kaddo may be ignorant, for she asks him to think further about his position [KW6]. At [KW7] Jeremy admits that he is in a state of perplexity.

The importance of perplexity in learning was underscored by Socrates when, in questioning a young slave about the answer to a geometry problem, he says to Meno, the onlooker: "Observe, Meno, the stage he has reached. . . . At the beginning he did not know . . . nor indeed does he know . . . now, but then he thought he knew it and answered boldly[;] . . . he felt no perplexity. Now however he does feel perplexed. Not only does he not know the answer; he doesn't even think he knows."[2] Socrates indicates that becoming perplexed is important because perplexity motivates further seeking. When one does not know, and recognizes as much, one will continue to look for the answer. Does Jeremy's perplexity move him to reflect further on the nature of Kaddo's ignorance? Has he become a seeker, as described in Chapter 1?

[KW8]   PB: Well, Walter, I have a question for you. You said if you
             were Kaddo . . . that you would have given some of your
             corn away? Would you have given some of your corn away
             because you're a generous person and you just would want
             to share with others, or would you have given your corn
             away because you realize that someday you might need
             their help in return?

[KW9]   JEREMY [Interrupting]: Yeah! Except I don't . . . and that
             would be the good thing to do at the same time.

[KW10]   WALTER: Yeah, well, because . . . if I were Kaddo, I'd have
             millions of pieces of corn, but I'd just give it up . . . give
             them away.

Paula [KW8] asks Walter whether he would have given to people
because of generosity or because of the recognition that he might be de-
pendent on others at some point in the future. Walter's response [KW10]
to Paula's question is unclear, and she queries him further:

[KW11]   PB: So, hold on one second, Jeremy . . . [Walter], so would
             you, simply because you were wealthy, say, "Well, I'm just
             a generous person. I have so much that giving some away,
             I won't feel it?" Or might you be thinking, "Wow, what
             if I don't have all this forever and I might need their help
             some day?"

[KW12]   WALTER: Yeah!

[KW13]   PB: Is [it] one or the other?

[KW14]   WALTER: Well, because if you give it away then you might
             need their help because . . . let's say you don't give it away
             and you run out of corn, then they . . . and they don't like
             you so they don't want to help you.

[KW15]   PB: And [the story] said that Kaddo knew he couldn't go to
             those people, right?

When Paula asks Walter to imagine how he might reason if he were a
rich person confronted with hungry people [KW11], she tries to help him
understand the dilemma she is posing by articulating each component
of it as a thought.[3] At [KW14] Walter affirms one of the possibilities that
Paula has offered (people will not help you if you have not been helpful to

them), but he does not indicate whether such might be Kaddo's reasoning. Jeremy, however, seems to hear Walter's idea, and he continues:

[KW16]   JEREMY: Because [Kaddo] didn't help them so they aren't going to help him, but . . . he could have been . . . generous by giving them stuff. And, well, if you're smart enough, you'll know. Like, since you helped somebody else, they will probably help you in return if you need help.

[KW17]   MM: So, Jeremy, is he just not being smart? Is he being kind of ignorant that, not helping people, he doesn't realize that later on down the road no one is going to help him?

[KW18]   JEREMY: He doesn't know what's going to happen. He thinks forever he'll be . . . he is not planning ahead because he thinks, "Oh, I'm always going to be rich for the rest of my life."

Jeremy comes to two new ideas about the nature of Kaddo's ignorance. At [KW16] he appears to repeat Walter's assertion: an intelligent person will realize that if he or she gives help to another, the recipient will return the assistance at some point in the future, if it is needed. At [KW18], however, Jeremy seems to say that Kaddo is ignorant not so much about human relations as about the importance of "planning ahead," meaning, perhaps, imagining that life might be different in the future and making provision for that possibility.

In total, Jeremy has mentioned four points about which Kaddo may be ignorant: (1) he may not know that one can do a variety of things with excess corn besides try to store it [KW1]; (2) he may not know how to garden and hence how to raise only as much corn as he can use or manage [KW7]; (3) he may not understand human relations very well and fails to recognize that if he does not help others, they will not help him [KW16]; (4) he may not be able to imagine and plan ahead for a future in which he is not so well off [KW18]. Here we see evidence that the state of perplexity has moved Jeremy to keep pondering the nature of Kaddo's ignorance.

Let us now return to the question raised above: How did the groups move from evaluating the text to interpreting it? In order to begin to answer the question, let us first notice that unlike the discussions of *The Giving Tree*, in this discussion the question on the floor does not change in the excerpts reprinted above. So the first thing to say about the shift that occurs in the discussion of "Kaddo's Wall" is that students tended to focus on one interpretive question for a longer period of time—in some instances, more than twenty minutes. The group wondered: Why did Kaddo behave as he did? Jeremy explores the possibility that ignorance was the reason. Indeed, Jeremy seems to ponder possible topics of Kaddo's ignorance even as Paula questions Walter about how he would reason if he were a rich man at [KW8] and [KW11].

The second thing to notice is that Jeremy's state of perplexity is sufficiently strong to send him into the text repeatedly to look for the answer. For example, Walter does not reference textual evidence to defend his claim [KW14], and Paula offers him some [KW15]—that Kaddo knew he could not turn to the townspeople for help—although she does not mention a line number. At [KW16] Jeremy uses that evidence to argue that because Kaddo didn't comply when people asked for help, he may have been ignorant about the problematic relations he was engendering. It seems that Jeremy's state of perplexity moved him to continue to reflect, to hear in Walter's statement [KW14] a useful idea about the resolution, and to appeal to the evidence that Paula offered [KW15] to defend his new idea about the answer.

So, interpreting rather than evaluating a text seems to occur when students focus on a question about its meaning for a period of time long enough to find evidence in the text to address the question. If perplexity about the answer is sufficient, the discussant will return to the text repeatedly—perhaps to examine new evidence, perhaps to look at evidence from a different perspective.

Notice, however, that at [KW18] Jeremy begins to speculate about Kaddo's thinking without reference to the text, suggesting that his commitment to defending claims on the basis of textual evidence is inconsistent. Furthermore, he seems to be unaware that he has, in fact, considered four possible sources of Kaddo's ignorance. He makes no attempt to evaluate the possibilities against the text to try to determine whether some are better justified than others. Perhaps his perplexity is not great, meaning that while he admits to not knowing the basis of Kaddo's ignorance [KW7], he may not care very much about resolving the issue.

I take a closer look at Jeremy at the conclusion of the chapter. For now, let us turn to excerpts from a discussion of the third story that the co-leaders presented to the two groups of students. Again we see increased emphasis on textual interpretation. In addition, we find the group members moving toward the formation of questions about the text that they seem eager to resolve.

"ALLAH WILL PROVIDE"

Synopsis
The protagonist of "Allah Will Provide" is Bou Azza, "an honest woodcutter" who cuts down trees and sells them in the market each day, earning "barely enough" money to feed and clothe his wife and himself.[4] Growing old, he worries that he will no longer be able to chop wood and will therefore starve. One day, he watches a snake hypnotize a bird until it falls from its perch in a stupor. Then the snake gobbles its prey.

> As Bou Azza walked home in the twilight . . . , he said to himself, "I am a fool! The serpent finds much food without really working for it, thanks to Allah, whereas I, a man, must work very hard in the hottest part of the day to earn just a mouthful of food. Allah alone is good, and with his help I will be like the serpent. No longer will I work so hard to get food when the serpent gets it for nothing. So shall it be."[5]

The following day, Bou Azza says that he will not stir from his mat "even if [he] die[s] of hunger." He holds to his word when his wife entreats him to help her carry a pot of gold that she has unearthed in the forest while looking for mushrooms to sell at the market. His wife's brothers agree to help in return for a share of the riches, and Bou Azza and his wife live in luxury thereafter.

"Allah Will Provide," Central School—Discussion 5
In both groups the emphasis on interpreting the text developed over the course of the project, and that development continued as the students at Central School conversed with one another. Now, how do students become committed to resolving a shared question about meaning by using textual evidence? The Central School group is assembled in its usual spot. Once the reading of the story is complete and the co-leaders tell the group that "Allah is like God," Paula begins:

[AP1]   PB: If no one has an immediate question right now, I want
             to ask whether the snake was working hard when he was
             hypnotizing the bird. Do you think that his hypnosis . . .
             of the bird is something that took work? Or it didn't take
             work? What do people think about that? Let's hear some
             answers. Okay, Grace and then Cynthia and Tracy [these
             students raise their hands, thereby requesting to speak]
             and let's see where we are after that and see if we can add
             anything new to it. Do you think he was working?

[AP2]   GRACE: Yes, I think he [the snake] was working trying to
             get the bird to fall down out of the tree, but Bou Azza
             didn't know that. He thought [the snake] wasn't working.
             He thought that Allah provided that for [the snake].

[AP3]   PB: And could you show us where that is, 'cause I'm think-
             ing the same thing and I think it's somewhere . . . at about
             line fifty-five or so. Can you read what Bou Azza thought
             about that?

[AP4]   GRACE [reading at line fifty-five]: "As Bou Azza walked
             home in the twilight, he thought more and more about his
             idea. After a time, he said to himself, 'I am a fool! The ser-
             pent finds much food without even working for it, thanks
             to Allah, whereas I, a man, must work very hard in the hot-
             test part of the day, to earn just a mouthful of food.'"

[AP5]   PB: So you think that, even though the snake is working,
             Bou Azza sees that and says, "He's not working very hard.
             Allah is providing it?"

[AP6]   GRACE: I think he [Bou Azza] was mad because he had to
             work, but he thought the snake wasn't working to get his
             food.

At [AP1] above, Paula seems to be asking an evaluative question meaning: Do you call what the snake was doing when it hypnotized the bird
"work"? Grace responds [AP2] that she believes that the snake was working when it hypnotized the bird. But on what grounds does Grace render
her judgment? Is she using her own criteria of what working involves,
or is she measuring the behavior of the snake against criteria that the
text offers?

Paula asks Grace for textual evidence in support of her claim and mentions a line number [AP3]. She then asks Grace to read a passage that describes Bou Azza's view of whether the snake was working, perhaps thinking that Bou Azza's view might shed light on the text's criteria for working hard. It seems, then, that Paula's initial question may have meant: According to the text, is the snake working hard when it hypnotizes the bird? Given her wording, however, the question could have been taken as either evaluative or interpretive. The issue of whether the snake works persists, and the criteria for judgment seem to come from personal experience:

[AP7]   PB: Okay, Cynthia, what do you think?

[AP8]   CYNTHIA: I think Bou Azza was just looking at the snake
             to . . . I think he was just thinking that the snake was just
             being a snake. Like, you know how it moves and slithers? I
             think that Bou Azza didn't think that the snake wanted the
             bird to come out of the tree.

[AP9]   MM: So, Cynthia, are you thinking along the same lines as
             Grace is when Grace says that Bou Azza kind of . . . Grace,
             and correct me if I'm wrong . . . that [Bou Azza] made a
             mistake when he said, "Boy, that snake doesn't seem to be
             working very hard," or do you think the snake was working
             hard?

[AP10]   CYNTHIA: Mmm, I don't think he was working hard.

[AP11]   MM: Okay, you don't think he was working hard? So Grace,
             we talked about that you thought the snake probably was
             working hard, and Cynthia is saying that the snake wasn't
             working hard. Is that right?

[AP12]   GRACE: No, I said the snake wasn't working hard.

[AP13]   PB: Was not. Right. Cynthia, what did you say?

[AP14]   CYNTHIA: I don't think he was working hard either.

[AP15]   PB: And one last person who was going to comment on
             that was Tracy.

[AP16]   TRACY: I think the snake wasn't working hard either be-
             cause I agree with Cynthia and Grace, the snake was just
             moving his body, that's all. And I think he wanted the bird
             to fall out of the tree. But he wasn't working hard.

Although Grace at first says that the snake is working hard [AP2], she later denies that claim [AP12], signaling a change of mind about the correct interpretation. At [AP12], however, Grace states her position as though it has not changed.[6] Cynthia and Tracy, at [AP14] and [AP16], respectively, agree that the snake did not work hard. At [AP8] Cynthia supports her claim on the basis of knowledge garnered from sources outside the text—including the speculation that the snake did not want the bird to fall out of the tree, which, as we shall see, seems contrary to textual evidence. At [AP16] Tracy may also be evaluating the text when she says that the snake's movements cannot be called "work" because a snake does not expend much effort in moving its body. Her comments seem to be based on knowledge of snakes that she brings to bear on the text. Damian, however, treats the issue of whether the snake is working differently:

[AP17]   DAMIAN: I have a question. I wanted to ask . . . I don't think. . . . I think the snake was working real hard.

[AP18]   MM: Wait, you do or don't?

[AP19]   DAMIAN: I do.

[AP20]   PB: So we have a new opinion here . . . that the snake is working hard. Tell us about that.

[AP21]   DAMIAN: I think the snake is working hard because he tried to hypnotize . . . if . . . he wasn't trying to hypnotize him, why did the bird fall out . . . of the tree? If he wasn't working, if it was just being, like, a snake, why did the bird fall out of the tree?

Damian's judgment, unlike the judgments rendered by Grace, Cynthia, and Tracy, seems to be based on evidence given by the text [AP21]. He asks: If the bird fell out of the tree after the snake stared at him, doesn't this mean that the snake had to stare long enough for the bird to fall into a stupor, and isn't the text therefore showing that the snake did have to work to achieve its end? Damian, then, seems to take the discussion back to the story "Allah Will Provide" in treating as interpretive the question of whether the snake was working when it hypnotized the bird. His doing so seems to affect others' views:

[AP22]   SYLVIA: First of all, I think he was working. I know that, in the other part he didn't do it, but I know that the snake was working because everybody has to work for their food.

[AP23]   TANIS: I agree with Sylvia and Damian because . . . I saw on TV how people hypnotize people. They work. And sometimes if you want to get food to, like, carry home. Like, if you want to carry groceries home. That's work because sometimes groceries [can] be heavy.

Sylvia and Tanis agree with Damian's conclusion that the snake was working. Damian, however, interprets the text in order to make his case, and Sylvia and Tanis make their arguments by using criteria drawn from sources outside the story. Sylvia [AP22] appeals to her beliefs about the human condition—people work to get their food—and Tanis [AP23] appeals to things she has seen on television. Furthermore, she seems to draw on another source of personal experience when she adds that carrying groceries home—one way human beings get food—is work because the groceries may be heavy [AP23].

[AP24]   PB: Sounds to me like we're starting to have a split between what people think. Some of us are thinking that the snake was working hard and it was a part of his nature to hypnotize animals to get food. Other people were saying, "I don't know if he was working hard, he was just swaying his body." Is there anyone who hasn't spoken yet who wants to say whether they think the snake was working hard or not? Joseph?

[AP25]   JOSEPH: I think, I think the snake was working hard because can't nobody just hypnotize something like quick, it takes time.

[AP26]   CYNTHIA: I've changed my mind. I agree with Joseph. Because it does take time to hypnotize somebody because sometimes people look like, "What are you doing?" [puts an incredulous look on her face] and they start gettin' like [sways head back and forth] and then they start falling asleep, but it does take time.

[AP27]   PB: Okay, Tracy, how 'bout you?

[AP28]   TRACY: I agree with Joseph, too. [laughter]

[AP29]   MM: Everyone's agreeing with you, Joseph!

[AP30]   TRACY: Because sometimes people be like, "You can't hypnotize me," but then when they get ready they just start going with the flow. And I want to go back . . . when Joseph
was saying about the hypnotizing and stuff? I want to add
something on to it about the hypnotizing. He was right
when the snake had to work hard for his food because
sometimes the bird was ready to fly but he couldn't move!
And then he was thinking he could get away. But then he
started going with the flow with the snake, so that's why I
think the bird got ate.

[AP31]   DAMIAN: Those three still didn't answer my question.
Why did they think, if the bird was . . . if y'all [looking at
the discussants directly] said the snake was just being a
snake by moving around, why did the bird get hypnotized
and fall and he [the snake] ate him?

Cynthia, at [AP26], unlike Grace at [AP12], declares that she has
changed her mind. Tracy seems to shift her position as well [AP28], although she does not acknowledge doing so. The evidence that Cynthia
gives in support of her claim is based on personal experience rather than
further evidence found in the text. Tracy begins to appeal to the text at
[AP30], however, when she recounts, in her own words, lines from the
story that read, "As Bou Azza looked . . . the viper held the bird in its
merciless stare, swaying from side to side . . . while the helpless victim
became more and more paralyzed."[7] These lines lend credence to the idea
that the bird wanted to fly away but was mesmerized, so the snake must
have wanted the bird to be in that state and worked to attain it.

When Damian reiterates the question he asked of Cynthia, Grace, and
Tracy at [AP31], he does two things that we have not seen before in these
discussions. First, he insists that his question be answered—that those
who argue that the snake was not working explain why the bird eventually
fell out of the tree, which, as Tracy might now agree, is evidence that the
snake was working. Second, because Cynthia and Tracy do change their
positions and agree that the snake was working (at [AP26] and [AP28], respectively), Damian reiterates his question, possibly because he feels some
commitment to resolving the issue he has raised and thereby explaining

why the bird fell out of the tree. In short, Damian may be insisting that the discussion be interpretative rather than evaluative. Interestingly enough, Tracy may be coming to a similar conclusion.

So let us return to the question of how students become committed to resolving a shared question about meaning by using textual evidence. What has happened to Damian and perhaps to Tracy is nicely described by Gadamer in the following passage from *Truth and Method:* "The movement of understanding is constantly from the whole to the part and back to the whole. Our task is to extend in concentric circles the unity of the understood meaning. The harmony of all the details with the whole is the criterion of correct understanding."[8] Gadamer seems to be saying that making a correct interpretation requires looking at the details in the text together with the work as a whole. As details are interpreted and related to overall meanings, consistency—or "harmony"—between the two must be established in order for one's understanding to be correct. His point is similar to one made by Iser and discussed in Chapter 1—that reading is a dialectic process.[9] A group becomes committed to resolving a question about the meaning of a text when consistency of interpretation is called into question. When this happens, the goal of being right about one's interpretation is set up. At that moment, the desire to resolve the question becomes intense, and the will to examine the textual evidence is no longer lacking.

So when Damian focuses on the textual detail that the bird fell out of the tree, or, as the story puts it, the snake held the bird in its "merciless stare" until it fell to the ground in a stupor, he recognizes the power of that detail. The answer to the question of whether, according to the text, the snake was working when it hypnotized the bird must be consistent with that detail. As students come to see that correct interpretation requires consistency between the factual details and overall meanings, they focus on those details—the textual evidence—with greater energy and perseverance. The question they are trying to resolve becomes more pressing as the relevant evidence is identified and scrutinized. We see the scrutiny of evidence build desire to resolve the question as we watch the group at Sheridan discuss the fourth text used in the project.

"JEAN LABADIE'S BIG BLACK DOG"

Synopsis

This story comes from the French Canadian tradition.[10] The plot is as follows: Jean Labadie is a farmer and storyteller who can terrify all with his dramatic portrayals of the *loup-garou,* a demon "who takes the shape of a terrible animal."[11] Jean suspects his neighbor André of stealing his chickens ("pullets"), and in order to scare André away from the henhouse, Jean invents a big black watchdog whose red tongue hangs out as he runs. Jean says that he got the dog from the Indians, and he describes the dog to André, saying, "He is a very fierce dog, bigger than a wolf and twice as wild. . . . Surely you must see him. He runs along so so fast. He lifts one paw this way and another paw that way."[12] André says that he sees the dog and describes it to others in the town as well. The chickens no longer disappear.

In time, the townspeople, as well as André, complain that the dog runs wild and growls at them. When Jean says he has chained the dog, a neighbor reports that the dog has broken loose. After Jean pretends to drive off with the dog to return him to the Indians, André reports the dog's return. Jean calls André a liar, and he responds, "Wait until the others see your big black dog running around again."[13] Many report that they have seen the creature, and one day André, his hand bleeding, charges that the big black dog has bitten him. At the end of his wits, Jean agrees to compensate André with two plump pullets and then, in the presence of witnesses, "shoots" at what he believes to be nothing but air, and the townspeople all agree the big black dog is dead.

"Jean Labadie's Big Black Dog," Sheridan School—Discussion 8

How do the students become committed to evaluating the strength of possible text-based resolutions of the shared question? This is the third question raised at the start of the chapter, and it is to this question that we now turn as we peruse excerpts from the discussion of "Jean Labadie's Big Black Dog" that took place at Sheridan School. Here, as in the discussion of the story that took place at Central School, students came to a question about the meaning of the text that they focused on at length. In both cases, the groups wondered whether there was an actual big black dog running around the town. We pick up the conversation at Sheridan:

[JL1]   MM: So Parker just threw out another option. . . . Maybe there's just a big black dog running free and [it] just happens to be coming along whenever they're talking about it. And so people think that's the big black dog. Kurt, I've got you next on my list.

[JL2]   KURT: Uh, I think the dog isn't real . . . Jean Labadie's dog . . . but I think there might be a loose black dog, like Parker said.

[JL3]   PARKER [delighted]: Yeah?

[JL4]   PB: Well, if that's so, if there is this big, black dog that was loose, how come at the very end of the story Jean gathers all the townspeople and he shoots this big black dog? And you see the picture—there's no big black dog there—and he shoots it. And it says, "And everyone agreed that the dog was gone for good." So maybe this is a question for Kurt and Parker.

[JL5]   KURT: Well, on page 177, lines 311 and 312, it says, "Jean Labadie lifted his gun to his shoulder, pointed it at nothing, and pulled the trigger." So he didn't shoot anything.

[JL6]   MM: But, Kurt, it says everyone agreed that the dog was gone.

[JL7]   KURT: That's what I don't get.

[JL8]   MM: And earlier it says, if you guys are following along, I'm on line, like [lines] 309 and 310 [on page 177]. And it says, "See how he runs with his big red tongue hanging out. And everyone saw the big black dog."

[JL9]   KURT: Yeah, I don't get it.

The students are confronting a point of doubt about the meaning of the story. On one hand, the reader is told that the big black dog is a character that Jean fabricates in order to frighten André so that he will stop stealing chickens. On the other, the reader is also told that the townspeople see the dog running around the town and complain about its behavior. If the big black dog is fictional, why do the people see it? Kurt [JL2] and Parker [JL3] put forth the hypothesis that there is an actual dog running around, although the story mentions no such character. Paula [JL4] then confronts them with textual evidence when she reminds them that the story shows Jean "shooting" the dog, although no dog is pictured, and that after the "shooting," everyone agrees that the dog is gone for good. If there is a real dog that people see, why do they agree that the dog is gone after Jean pulls the trigger while aiming at nothing?

At [JL7] Kurt expresses perplexity about the answer to that question. At [JL9] he expresses further doubt about the evidence in lines 309 and 310, which say that the people saw the dog. How could people see a fictional dog? The loose-dog hypothesis explains how people could see a dog, but because the text does not show a dog being shot, the hypothesis seems to contradict the evidence. Parker presses on:

[JL10]   PARKER: Well maybe, like, the dog . . . was right next to where he was shooting.

[JL11]   PB: Okay, so you still think that there is a dog.

[JL12]   PARKER: Like, next to . . . like behind the barn. . . . Jean Labadie didn't know that, like, a dog was behind the barn.

[JL13]   JEREMY: Wait! Wait! I . . .

[JL14]   MM: Hold on a second, Jeremy, I see hands, remember, but I don't hear, like, "Oh! Oh! Oh!" Kurt, what do you think? Do you agree with Parker or—you pointed out that there was nothing there but everyone saw it?

[JL15]   KURT: Well, I think there's a loose dog, but I don't think he was there when [Jean] shot because it says "he pointed at nothing."

[JL16]   PB: But it also says that everyone saw the dog.

At [JL12] Parker seems to mean that the loose dog ran behind the barn when the gun was fired, which would explain why no dog is pictured when Jean "shoots" the dog and why the story says that people saw a dog. At [JL14] Marsha appears unconvinced of the loose-dog hypothesis when she asks Kurt whether he agrees with Parker. Marsha seems to say: If the dog ran behind the barn when Jean fired the gun, why does the story say that everyone saw the dog and agreed that the dog was gone for good? Kurt responds that the dog might have been behind the barn [JL15], much as Parker had maintained, because the story says that Jean pointed "at nothing" when he fired the gun. At [JL16] Paula, like Marsha, seems unconvinced when she points to textual evidence and asks: If the dog was behind the barn, why does it say that everyone saw the dog?

How do the students become committed to evaluating the strength of possible resolutions of the shared question based on textual evidence? I suggest the following. First, the students recognize a point of ambiguity in the text, namely, that Jean shot at nothing, but the story says that everyone saw the dog and agreed it was dead. It is not simply that the teacher (or anyone else) has posed a question. Rather, these participants recognize the dilemma as such—they feel it.

Second, members of the group have proposed an idea about the answer that seems to resolve the dilemma: if there is a loose dog running around the town, that could explain why the story says that the people saw the dog even if they also saw Jean shoot at nothing. Having an idea about the resolution to the dilemma allows the discussants to move on to test its worth. And because they care about answering the question, they become seekers like the slave who converses with Socrates and recognizes that he does not know an answer that he thought he knew. In both cases, the problem is clear and is of concern, and so a solution is desired.

Third, the dilemma before the students concerns the meaning of the text, and they see how to test the merit of the proposed resolution: look at it in relation to textual evidence. In other words, they know what to do in order to determine whether the loose-dog hypothesis is sound. Hence, we see them become more focused on details in the story—to try to get them exactly right—so as to use them to determine whether the proposed resolution should be accepted or rejected. Marsha [JL14] asks Kurt whether he agrees with Parker, given the lines Kurt read at [JL5]. Kurt [JL15] agrees with Parker that there was a loose dog—he seems to like the hypothesis—but recognizes that only if the hypothesis is consistent with textual evidence can it be accepted. Consequently, at [JL15] Kurt adds that the loose dog was not there when Jean pointed the gun because the story says that Jean "pointed at nothing." At [JL13] Jeremy needs to be restrained by Marsha [JL14], so great is his excitement. Here is more:

[JL17]   PARKER: But he could be shooting right next to a barn.
[JL18]   MM: [To Jeremy] What do you think about Parker's option, then?
[JL19]   JEREMY: But then how . . . would [Jean] see the big black dog if [the story] says he shot at nothing? He shot at nothing and everybody else saw the big black dog?

Maybe there was a wild one. But he [Jean] said he saw nothing.

[JL20]   KURT: It didn't say he saw nothing.

[JL21]   MM: He pointed at . . . he pointed at nothing.

[JL22]   KURT: It said he shot at nothing.

[JL23]   JEREMY: Well, then that's the same thing. He pointed at nothing. He shot at nothing.

[JL24]   KURT: But he could've, like, seen a dog that was, like, over here, and the people saw it, and he shot, and it looked like he pointed at the dog, but [he didn't].

[JL25]   JEREMY: It said that he pointed at nothing and he shot.

[JL26]   KURT: But you could be a dog now and I could go like this [aims his finger at Parker] and make it look like I'm pointing at you but I'm not.

[JL27]   JEREMY: You see me! But it said that he pointed at nothing!

[JL28]   KURT: Yeah, but that doesn't mean that we don't see you.

[JL29]   PARKER: The dog could be behind the barn . . .

[JL30]   JEREMY [sarcastic]: Oh, so he pointed at nothing but he saw the dog?!

At [JL30] Jeremy seems to reject the loose-dog hypothesis as incredible. He has reasoned that because the story says that Jean "shot at nothing," he saw no dog running loose [JL19]—that if there was a loose dog, Jean did not see it. Kurt objects at [JL20], arguing that the story does not say that Jean "saw nothing." Marsha then rereads the line in question from the text—"he pointed at nothing" [JL21]. Kurt takes the line to mean that Jean "shot at nothing" [JL22]. Jeremy [JL23] says that "pointed at nothing" and "shot at nothing" are equivalent in meaning. At this point, Kurt introduces the possibility that Jean pointed at nothing, shot at nothing, but nonetheless saw the dog, as did all the people [JL24]. It is that option—that Jean saw a dog yet shot at nothing—that Jeremy rejects at [JL30]. He again points to textual evidence when he continues.

[JL31]   JEREMY: But he [Jean] just made the big black dog up!

[JL32]   MM: He made that big black dog up!

[JL33]   KURT: Yeah, I know what they're saying. It could've been a loose one.

[JL34]   JEREMY: OK, there's a loose one. Yeah, but it says that
           he pointed at nothing. He pointed at nothing.
[JL35]   KURT: Yeah, you're right.

Once again, Jeremy argues against the loose-dog hypothesis at [JL31] by using textual evidence: the story tells us that Jean made up the big black dog. In saying this Jeremy points to different evidence than that which Kurt cites at [JL5]. Furthermore, even if there is a loose dog, maintains Jeremy, it means nothing in terms of what happens in the story, for we are told that Jean pointed at nothing and shot at nothing [JL34]. At this point Jeremy returns to the lines that Kurt cited at [JL5] to argue against the loose-dog hypothesis. Has Kurt been persuaded by Jeremy at [JL35]? The conversation continues:

[JL36]   JEREMY: [Jean] could have seen it but he didn't.
[JL37]   KURT: [Jean] could've seen it but pretended like he didn't.
[JL38]   JEREMY: Aw, [Jean may have thought:] "I see a dog but I
           don't want to kill it." He said he wanted to kill it.
[JL39]   KURT: No he didn't.
[JL40]   JEREMY: Yeah, he said, "I'm going to end this," so he shot
           at nothing.
[JL41]   MM: You know what, hold on, Jeremy. I want to ask you a
           question, then. What do you think? What are you saying?
[JL42]   JEREMY: I'm saying there's no black dog. Maybe there
           would've been, but not at that part. Maybe those people
           are complete idiots.
[JL43]   MM: Well, then, Jeremy . . . why do people see the big
           black dog?
[JL44]   JEREMY: I know: because [the story] said he shot at nothing.
[JL45]   MM: So why do people see [the dog]? Is it because, like
           Brian said [earlier in the discussion], because [Jean is] a
           powerful storyteller who could hypnotize people?
[JL46]   JEREMY: [makes no response, chin in his hands, staring
           at the floor]

At [JL36] Jeremy continues his reasoning: even if there was a loose dog running around and Jean could have seen it, in fact he did not see it, because the story said he pointed at nothing when he "shot" the dog.

Kurt [JL37] counters that Jean could have seen the loose dog but pretended he did not see it, which could explain why the story says he pointed at nothing when he shot the dog. Jeremy rejects Kurt's suggestion at [JL38], again on the basis of textual evidence: Jean said he wanted to kill the dog, so why would he pretend he didn't see it, point the gun, and fire at nothing? Jeremy cites no line number when he offers his evidence, and Kurt rejects Jeremy's evidence [JL39].

Next, Jeremy appears to read a line from the text supporting his claim that Jean wanted to kill the dog [JL40]. The line in the story is not exactly what Jeremy gives, but it is close. Jean says: "I am going to shoot my big black dog. I want everyone to see this happen."[14] Perhaps because the meaning of the written words is close to what Jeremy indicates, neither Kurt nor the co-leaders challenge him further. Instead, Marsha asks for clarification [JL41]. In response, Jeremy reasserts his position: there is no big black dog running around, at least not at the moment when Jean shoots the dog [JL42].

At the end of [JL42], Jeremy adds that the people, who see Jean point and shoot at nothing and yet agree that the dog is gone, not to return, are deluded. In so saying, he gives further evidence that he understands what is required in an interpretive discussion for resolution of a dilemma about the meaning of the text. He seems to recognize that in order to explain why the people agree that the dog is gone for good after Jean pulls the trigger at nothing, it is insufficient to reject the loose-dog hypothesis. Instead, he still needs to provide a resolution that is justified by the textual evidence and that answers the question. At [JL44] and again at [JL46], Jeremy indicates that he is still in a state of perplexity about the proper resolution. Even his suggestion that the people "were complete idiots" seems not to satisfy him, for he does not try to mount an argument that is based on textual evidence in support of the claim.

In the passages reprinted above, we see examples of students' pointing to different pieces of textual evidence, working to interpret them, and then using the interpretation to evaluate the strength of the hypothesis about the overall meaning of the text. In order to judge the truth of the loose-dog hypothesis, they look at lines 311–312 (mentioned first at [JL5]), the fact that story tells us that the dog is made up (mentioned, without line number, at [JL31]), Jean's statement that he wanted to kill the dog (mentioned at [JL38]–[JL40]), and the fact that the people see the dog (mentioned at [JL16] and [JL45]). Participants argue about what these facts permit and preclude in terms of accepting or rejecting the loose-dog hypothesis. In sum, we see that the discussants become committed to testing possible resolutions against textual evidence when there is a dilemma about the meaning of the text that they care to resolve, when there is an idea about its resolution on the floor (for example, the loose-dog hypothesis), and when they understand that the idea about resolution can be evaluated—judged correct or incorrect—using textual evidence. That is, the members have something to resolve and they know how to carry on with the discussion that will address it.[15]

A CLOSER LOOK AT TRACY, GRACE, KURT, AND JEREMY

The excerpts from the discussions above reveal changes in the ways in which four students participated in the conversations. Let us begin with Tracy, who, in the discussion of *The Giving Tree,* spoke twenty times and referred to the text spontaneously nine times. She also made five evaluative comments. In the discussion of "Allah Will Provide," she spoke a total of seventeen times, made four evaluative comments, and appealed to the text spontaneously seven times. On the surface, the patterns of her participation in the two discussions appear similar.

Although in the discussion of "Allah Will Provide" she may be making an evaluative statement at [AP16], at [AP30], she makes a clear move toward answering the question of whether the snake is working when it hypnotizes the bird on the basis of textual evidence. She says that she wants to add something to Joseph's argument and proceeds to give facts from the text that support Joseph's claim that the snake was working: "The bird was ready to fly but he couldn't move. And then he was thinking that he could get away." Tracy does not read from the text and mention a line number, but she mentions a fact that is easily referenced. She seems to believe that textual evidence should be offered in order to defend Joseph's claim and moves toward doing so.

Grace, another student at Central, was present for the discussion of *The Giving Tree,* although she spoke only four times. Of those four contributions, two were evaluative comments, and she offered no spontaneous references to the text. In the discussion of "Allah Will Provide," Grace spoke seven times and again made two evaluative comments. This time, she twice referred to the text spontaneously. When Paula asked her to read a passage that supported her view [AP3], Grace found and read appropriate lines [AP4].

At [AP12] Grace seems to change her position regarding the issue of whether the snake was working hard when it hypnotized the bird. She does not acknowledge doing so and may not realize that she has done so. Perhaps she is persuaded by Cynthia's reasoning at [AP8]. Although Grace fails to acknowledge that she has changed her position, the fact that she seems to have done so suggests that she is listening to others and can be persuaded.

Kurt, another discussant whom we meet for the first time in the present chapter, participated in the Sheridan discussion of "Jean Labadie's Big Black Dog." He was absent for the discussion of *The Giving Tree*. He spoke only four times in the discussion of "Kaddo's Wall" (we observed none of his contributions), and at that time, he made no spontaneous references to the text. In the discussion of "Jean Labadie's Big Black Dog," however, he spoke thirty times, and his comments included four spontaneous textual references (seen at [JL5], [JL15], [JL20], and [JL22]). His argument concluded at [JL24].

Now, it is interesting that all four of these references are to the same passage—the one cited in [JL5], lines 311 and 312: "he pointed at nothing and pulled the trigger." At [JL5] Kurt uses the lines to argue that Jean did not shoot at anything. At [JL15], he uses the lines to argue that the loose dog was not present when Jean shot the gun because it says he "pointed at nothing." At [JL20] he uses them to argue that Jean might have "seen" the dog, because the text says only that he "pointed at nothing." And at [JL22] he uses the lines to argue that Jean "shot at nothing" but that it does not mean that he saw nothing. His final argument is further elaborated at [JL24].

Here then, is an example of a discussant's returning to the text repeatedly—in this case, the same passage in the text—to argue for the plausibility of a suggested interpretation. Kurt seems to grasp the point stressed by Gadamer in the quotation given above: the truth of an interpretation depends on whether it is consistent with facts in the text.

Finally, we look once again at Jeremy. In the discussion of "Kaddo's Wall," Jeremy spoke twenty-eight times, as compared with the thirty-eight times he spoke in the conversation about *The Giving Tree*. He made fourteen evaluative comments while dealing with "Kaddo's Wall" and appealed spontaneously to the text seven times. In the discussion of "Jean Labadie's Big Black Dog," Jeremy spoke thirty-two times, made two evaluative comments, and referred spontaneously to the text a total of fifteen times. Therefore, he made the most dramatic progress toward focusing on textual interpretation, as opposed to evaluating the text.

In addition, whereas Kurt returned to the same passage repeatedly, Jeremy wrestles with that and with several other facts found in the story, as indicated above. He objects to Kurt's suggestions repeatedly and always begins with textual evidence, although he does not always cite line numbers: At [JL19] he questions the possibility that Jean saw a loose dog running around because the text says that he shot at nothing; at [JL25], [JL27], and [JL30], Jeremy continues to resist the suggestion; at [JL31] he asserts that the dog is fictional and hence there is no loose dog. At [JL34] he argues that even if one grants the validity of the loose-dog hypothesis, it does not explain Jean's behavior because he "pointed at nothing" and therefore did not see a dog. At [JL38] he rejects Kurt's suggestion that Jean may have seen the dog but pretended that he didn't by saying that, according to the text, he said he wanted to kill it. Jeremy's reasoning seems to be that if Jean said he wanted to kill the dog, he would not pretend not to see it and shoot at nothing.

Yet Jeremy cannot account for all the facts in the text satisfactorily in his interpretation, for, as he acknowledges at [JL42] and [JL44], he cannot explain why the story says that the people see the dog. So although he has argued convincingly against the loose-dog hypothesis, he has not explained why people see the dog and agree it is gone when Jean pulls the trigger.[16] Indeed, he seems unable to consider the plausible suggestion that Marsha offers him at [JL45].

As we will see in Chapter 4, the co-leaders mixed the groups of students from the two schools for discussions of the fifth text in the sequence. They took some students from Sheridan to Central and some from Central to Sheridan. One might wonder: Did the mixed groups work to define and pursue resolution of genuine questions about the meaning of the story, just as the groups had begun to do when working separately? Or did the changes in setting and the composition of the groups disrupt the patterns of discussion that were beginning to take form? In fact, the conversations provide some dramatic evidence about the extent and power of the discussion practices that these students appeared to be acquiring.

CHAPTER FOUR

Mixing the Groups

FROM THE beginning of the project, the co-leaders had considered mixing the two groups for conversations about the fifth and final text. They wanted to give all participants an opportunity to converse with students from the other group. Yet they had been hesitant, fearing that the discussions might not go well.

One question that had been present from the start moved the co-leaders to take the plunge and mix the two groups: Would experience in the discussions help participants draw out ideas and gain insight from each other despite differences in race, socioeconomic class, and school or home culture? Furthermore, would they show tolerance and perhaps appreciation for the others and their views—others who might appear unlike themselves in some ways?

As indicated at the end of Chapter 3, I wondered about the discussion patterns that the groups had begun to form. Would the mixed groups define and pursue resolution of queries that they shared about the meaning of the text? If so, would they use textual evidence to address their questions? And would they work to evaluate the strength of proposed resolutions using textual evidence?

Let me be more precise. The transition from evaluating to interpreting texts had been made gradually by both of the groups. The first step in the transition was to focus on a question about the meaning of the text for a sustained period of time—at least long enough to identify possible resolutions. In the discussion of "Kaddo's Wall," for instance, we saw Jeremy identify four topics about which Kaddo may have been ignorant. The second step was to recognize that in an interpretive discussion, the most effective defense of a resolution involves textual evidence—a realization at which Damian and perhaps Tracy arrived in the discussion of "Allah Will Provide." The third step was to defend resolutions using textual evidence because in doing so, the question becomes clearer, the relative strength of the resolutions is revealed, and the desire to find the best resolution intensifies. In the discussion of "Jean Labadie's Big Black Dog," participants discovered that it is necessary not only to explain facts in the text well but also to note when relevant facts are unexplained by a particular interpretation. Would the newly mixed groups invoke and further develop these practices or would they revert to evaluating the text before, or instead of, trying to interpret it?

"ABOUT WHAT HAPPENED TO A YOUNG MAN WHO MARRIED A VERY WILD AND UNRULY WIFE"

The final text that was chosen for the project had been given to me by a second-grade teacher who taught in a public school attended by many Latino and Latina students. It is a dramatic tale written by Don Juan Manuel, who lived in thirteenth-century Moorish Spain.[1] Over the years, I had led discussions about the text with people of various ages, and all seemed to enjoy it. So when the co-leaders asked me for a recommendation concerning the fifth text, this story came to mind. They read it, liked it, and decided to bring it to the fourth-grade mixed groups.[2]

Synopsis

Once there was a Moor with a good son and very little money and a rich Moor with a wicked daughter.[3] The young man chose to marry the wicked daughter in order to be poor no longer. His father tried to stop him, but to no avail. The girl's father consented to the marriage, saying, "But if your son wants her I shall give her to him or to anyone who would get her out of this house for me."[4] Following their wedding, the newlyweds were left alone in their home, causing the townspeople to worry that the young man would be dead by the time they returned in the morning.

Before the wife had a chance to speak, however, the husband demanded that his dog fetch water for him to wash his hands. When the dog failed to do so, the husband drew his sword and slew it. He next demanded that his cat and his only horse fetch water for him. When the animals did not comply, he butchered them as well, making a big bloody show of the killings. He declared that any living thing that disobeyed his orders would meet a similar fate. Then he turned to his wife and demanded that she bring him water to wash his hands. Terrified, she quickly obeyed. He next demanded that she make him a meal while he slept. Then he retired.

The following morning the townspeople returned to the home. To their amazement, the wife greeted them with a hushed voice, urging them to be quieter lest they awaken her husband. And so, the story says, the couple lived happily ever after, and the young man was held high in esteem for having tamed his unruly wife.

The discussions of the story that took place at Sheridan and at Central were both fascinating. Again, for reasons of space, clarity, and ease of focus, I explore what happened in only one of them—that which occurred at Central School. The case allows us to see how the students interacted with one another in discussing the story and so to address the questions raised by the co-leaders and by me. It serves as an illustration of the criteria that good discussions meet.

"The Unruly Wife," Central School—Discussion 10
The visitors from Sheridan School to Central School included *Arnie, Jeremy, Katie, Maggie,* and *Parker.*[5] They would be talking with Grace, Sylvia, Tanis, Tracy, and Troy. The introductions were made in the fourth-grade classroom, and then the group, consisting of ten students, two co-leaders, and the fourth-grade teacher from Sheridan, made their way toward a room where they would have lunch together. After lunch, the group returned to the classroom, and Paula read the story. The conversation began as follows:

[UW1]   MM: You guys have written stuff down. Raise your hands if you have a comment or question, like always. Then we'll ... as we do, we'll write down names and we'll just go in that order. I'll write down Tracy, Tanis, Grace, anyone else? Want to start with those three? Okay, Tracy.

[UW2]   TRACY: I thought that the wife was the crazy one, but he's

the crazy one. 'Cause . . . I think he did that when his
father told him that, that she was crazy, and . . . and
then, that girl, after then . . .

[UW3]   MM: Wait. What was that last thing you said now?

[UW4]   TRACY: I thought that after he did all that, after he killed
the dog and stuff, after that the girl hadn't said anything to
him. She just did what he told her to 'cause she didn't want
her head chopped off.

[UW5]   PB: So do I have this right? At first you thought that she
was crazy 'cause the story told us that. But then as the
story went on, you started to think that he was the one who
was crazy?

[UW6]   TRACY: I know that he was crazy 'cause when they say in
the beginning, they say she was rude and stuff and then
and at the end he started killing the horse, the cat, and the
dog.

[UW7]   PB: Okay.

Tracy opens the discussion, just as she had done in the conversation
about *The Giving Tree*. At [UW2], she does not pose a question but instead
admits perplexity about exactly which character was crazy. In doing so,
she begins to interpret the facts that are given in the story and asserts
that the husband was crazy [UW6] because he butchered the animals.
Grace, however, sees the story differently.

[UW8]   GRACE: I think he was doing that to teach his wife a
lesson.

[UW9]   MM: Doing what?

[UW10]   GRACE: To, like, chop off the cat's head and dog and the
horse's head. I think he wanted to do that because, like,
he wanted to teach his wife a lesson. And I think he had
planned to do that all along.

[UW11]   PB: So, Grace, Tracy said she thought he was crazy. Do you
think he was crazy, like Tracy thinks, or do you think he's
pretending to be crazy?

[UW12]   GRACE: I think he's not crazy. I think he was smart if he
did that.

When Grace disagrees with Tracy's assertion that the husband is crazy, she presents another perspective on the story: the husband planned to kill the animals in order to teach his wife something [UW10]. By interpreting the husband's actions differently, Tracy and Grace have begun to raise a question about the husband's character. The conversation continues:

[UW13]   MM: Okay, okay. Troy, do you have something else?

[UW14]   TROY: When he told all them animals to fetch him some water to wash his hands, he shoulda got up and done it his own self.

[UW15]   PB: Troy, is there any reason you think that he didn't fetch [it] for himself? Why do you think. . . . Why would he tell the animals to fetch it instead of fetching it himself?

[UW16]   TROY: Because he was lazy.

[UW17]   MM: Okay. So Tracy started off with, "He's crazy for doing all those things." Grace is saying, "No, you guys, he's smart. He's a smart guy because all along he had this plan in his head to get his wife to do what he wanted." So she thinks he's smart. And Troy, you think he's being a lazy guy by not getting the water himself. Okay, what about you, *Parker?* You're next on my list.

Students have given three suggestions about the husband's character —he is irrational, he has a plan, and he is lazy. Will there be further suggestions? Or will the discussants begin the process of evaluating the strength of the possible resolutions, given the textual evidence?

[UW18]   PARKER: Well, I think that he's a bit lazy because umm . . . and smart . . . 'cause he knows that the animals can't get water for him, so he probably just set up the entire thing before the wife got to his house . . . and he killed his animals because, it didn't say what he did, but just to set him up so she would do everything for him.

[UW19]   MM: So *Parker,* you started off by saying he's lazy, too, but it sounds like you're talking about setting up this whole thing. And I mean, fetching water or chopping a horse's head off—I mean, fetching water . . . which do you think sounds like the easier thing to do? You know what I mean?

[UW20]   *PARKER*: Get it yourself.

Although *Parker* begins by asserting that the husband was lazy [UW18], the argument that he mounts supports Grace's suggestion that the husband was strategic, or acted so as to accomplish a plan: because the husband knows the animals will not bring the water to him, says *Parker*, he demands that they do so and kills them when they do not obey in order to teach his wife to obey him. At [UW20], he seems to concede that killing the animals did not constitute taking the easy way out. This suggests that he is no longer persuaded that the husband was lazy. Evaluation of the proposed resolutions continues:

[UW21]   TRACY: Then I got a question for Grace and *Parker*. . . . If it was all a plan, why would he cut off his only horse's head? His only horse, and cut off his head?

[UW22]   MM: That's a great question because both Grace and *Parker* were kind of touching at this; sounds like a plan that he has in his head for a while. He set it all up, right? You guys were similar in your thinking, right? So that's a good question for them. Tracy, say that one more time.

[UW23]   TRACY: Why do you think he cut off his only horse's head?

[UW24]   MM: *Parker*, you want to start? Then we'll go to Grace.

[UW25]   *PARKER*: Yeah. Maybe just to scare his wife so . . . enough so . . . to get the water 'cause maybe the dog and horse was [sic] something but I mean, like, even his only horse? Then she might get pretty scared.

[UW26]   MM: What do you think about what *Parker* just said, Grace? Did you have the same reason in your mind?

[UW27]   GRACE: No.

[UW28]   MM: What do you think?

[UW29]   GRACE: Well, I think that . . . I have another thing to show it must have been a plan. Because everyone knows that cats can't get water and dogs can't get water, and horses can't get water. So I think he set that up again right there. Everyone knows that cats and dogs and horses cannot get water.

When Tracy poses a question to Grace and *Parker* at [UW21], she seems to ask: If the husband planned the killing of the animals, why would he make a plan that included chopping off the head of his only horse? Like Damian in the discussion of "Allah Will Provide," Tracy seems to be testing a theory—in this case, the theory that the husband acted as he did because he planned to do so—against a fact found in the text (he killed his only horse). In other words, Tracy is testing the possible resolution that Grace and *Parker* have offered against textual evidence.

At [UW25] *Parker* seems to argue that the husband made the drastic plan to kill his only horse in order to frighten his wife into obeying his commands. In advancing this idea, he seems to address Tracy's question. Grace at [UW29], however, appears to ignore the issue that Tracy has raised. Instead, she continues to argue that the husband must have planned to kill the animals when he asked them to fetch water because he and everyone knows that they would not obey. Grace seems unwilling to acknowledge the importance of explaining why the husband killed his only horse. Rather, she prefers to focus on evidence that supports her position. The conversation continues.

[UW30]   MM: How about we take *Katie* and *Maggie* and *Jeremy* in that order? Oh, I'm sorry, *Katie*, can we have *Jeremy* go first because he's been . . . ?

[UW31]   KATIE: Yeah.

[UW32]   MM: Go ahead, *Jeremy*.

[UW33]   JEREMY: I don't see why he got up and started running after it. It said he got up and started running after his dog. And he kind of, like, passed the sink. He could've just, like, stopped and got the water.

[UW34]   MM: Ah-ha, I see what you're saying, *Jeremy*. If he, like *Parker* and . . . who else said he was lazy? Like *Parker* and Troy . . .

[UW35]   JEREMY: And also that the horse was outside. Why would he go outside while getting up and opening the door and going outside, then coming back in. And also, going all the way . . . it would have been shorter just to have just gotten the water yourself.

[UW36]   M M : So it sounds like he put a little more effort into it than he needed to. So does that sound like a lazy man?

[UW37]   J E R E M Y : No, I think that he was just setting it up.

Jeremy, like *Parker*, may feel perplexed, and he works to evaluate the power of a suggested resolution. When he points out that the husband could have gotten the water himself more easily than chasing down the dog [UW33] and the horse [UW35], he provides justification for rejecting the hypothesis that the husband was lazy. Hence, he proceeds to conclude that the husband was acting according to a plan [UW37]. Notice that *Jeremy*'s reasoning appeals to two "facts" found in the story: that the husband got up and chased the dog [UW33] and that the horse was outside [UW35]. The first fact is indeed given by the story, but the second is not:[6] nowhere does it mention that the man went in and out of doors to slay the horse. Instead, *Jeremy* imagines the horse's location and offers a liberal mixing of fact with fantasy. When it is her turn to speak, *Maggie* returns to the question that Tracy raised:

[UW38]   M M : We'll go to *Maggie*.

[UW39]   M A G G I E : Well, since what *Parker* and Troy said, about why he would cut off his only horse's head, well, maybe he would scare his wife so much so she might get him another horse.

[UW40]   M M : So *Maggie*, do you think that it was part of his plan, like . . .

[UW41]   M A G G I E : No, I think he was crazy.

[UW42]   M M : You think he was crazy like Tracy said in the beginning? So you don't think, like Grace said—he's been setting this up all along. You think the guy's just nuts.

[UW43]   M A G G I E : Umm-hmm [nodding affirmatively].

When Tracy asks *Parker* and Grace about why the husband would create a plan that involved killing his only horse [UW21], she may do so because the act seems to her "crazy" or irrational. At [UW39], *Maggie* returns to Tracy's question and suggests that such a drastic action might be needed to terrify the wife into replacing the lost creature. Although *Maggie* can imagine a motive for killing the horse, she does not conclude that the husband was acting so as to realize a plan. Instead, she agrees with Tracy's claim that the husband is irrational [UW41], and she may have returned to Tracy's question in order to press those who disagree to think further about it. Grace responds:

[UW44]   GRACE: I still think it was all a plan.

[UW45]   MM: Tell us why.

[UW46]   GRACE: Because when [the husband says to the wife] on line 99, "How I thank God you have done as you were told or I would have done to you what I've done to the others," I don't believe that.

[UW47]   PB: If you were [the wife]?

[UW48]   MM: You wouldn't have believed what?

[UW49]   GRACE: I wouldn't have believed when he said on line 99. I wouldn't have believed that because . . . Why would he chop off the neck of his only horse? So I still think it was all a plan, because if it wasn't a plan, then he wouldn't have chopped off the head of his horse and his cat and his dog. Because they can't carry water and they . . . it's silly for you to think they can carry water. So I think his wife shouldn't have believed that.

[UW50]   MM: His wife shouldn't believe what? That he would have killed her?

[UW51]   GRACE: Mm-hmm [nods].

Grace offers new evidence from the text to argue that the husband killed the animals because he was executing a plan, not because he was crazy. For the first time in the discussion, we see someone citing and reading a line from the text. She says the evidence at line 99 indicates that the husband was prevaricating when he threatened the wife [UW46]. At [UW49], Grace turns to Tracy's question, arguing that the husband would not have killed the animals unless he had a plan because everyone knows they will not bring the water when ordered to do so. Hence, the wife should have suspected that the husband was trying to frighten her when he butchered his dog, cat, and horse and that he did not really intend to kill her ([UW49] and [UW51]).

As the conversation continues, we see that Grace's interpretation of the story raises another question.

[UW52]   MM: She should not have believed him? Okay, so you think that it was all planned and that he. . . . Why do you think he was doing this plan, though, Grace? You think it's all a plan, but why?

[UW53]   GRACE: Because he probably didn't want to get killed.

[UW54]   MM: He didn't want to get killed? So was he scared of the wife, or did he want to turn the wife into something else?

[UW55]   GRACE: I think that he was scared of her at first but then I think he wanted to make *her* scared of *him*.[7]

[UW56]   MM: Why would he want her scared of him?

[UW57]   GRACE: So that he wouldn't get killed by her bad temper.

In the foregoing exchange, Marsha, at [UW52], confronts Grace with the issue that her position raises: If the husband killed the animals because he was executing a plan, what did he aim to accomplish? At [UW55] and [UW57], Grace asserts that the intention was to terrify the wife so that she would not terrorize him.[8] In offering a justification for the plan, Grace adds further reasoning for her claim that the husband acted from intention rather than craziness. Other ideas about the motivation behind the plan continue to emerge.

[UW58]   MM: I have *Maggie* and then *Parker* and then *Katie.*

[UW59]   MAGGIE: Well, I just kinda thought that maybe he did plan it. 'Cause like I said earlier he might have just killed his animals to make her really scared and he might get some new ones from her 'cause she's scared so much.

[UW60]   MM: So, *Maggie,* it sounds like you're changing your mind because, in the beginning, you were talking about how you felt you agreed with Tracy when she said, "He's crazy." But now are you changing your mind to what Grace . . . is talking about? And *Parker,* too, he talked about this, too. About how it was planned?

[UW61]   MAGGIE: Yes.

At [UW59], *Maggie* declares that she has shifted her position and is now agreeing with Grace that the husband planned to kill the animals. Why has she changed her mind? Perhaps she had decided that if he killed the animals in order to frighten his wife into purchasing replacements, the reasonable inference is that he was strategic rather than crazy. Hence, she may be persuaded by her own reasoning rather than, or in addition to, Grace's.[9] Marsha then puts the same question to *Maggie* that she had put to Grace:

[UW62]   MM: Okay, then I'm going to ask you the same question: Why did he plan this?

[UW63]   MAGGIE: Maybe because it said she was the devil and he wanted someone to work for him and so he acted like he was a nut case.

[UW64]   MM: So, like, was he scared of his wife?

[UW65]   MAGGIE: No.

[UW66]   MM: Like [Grace] said? Or did he want to turn his wife into something else? [The story said] she was a devil. Did he want to make her a different kind of person?

[UW67]   MAGGIE: Yeah, someone who'd be really scared and would do anything that he'd say.

[UW68]   MM: What kind of person did he want to turn her into?

[UW69]   MAGGIE: Maybe to, like, someone [who] if he said, "Go get me some water," maybe she would do that.

Marsha seems to recognize that although Grace and *Maggie* are arguing the same claim about the husband—that he was executing a plan; he was not crazy—they have different ideas about the aim of the plan. Grace had maintained that the husband was afraid of the wife and wanted to make her afraid of him [UW55], but *Maggie* disagreed [UW65], arguing that the husband wanted the wife to be obedient [UW67, UW69]. For which idea is there more textual evidence?

[UW70]   MM: I'm going to read one line that's on the last page. Line 123 and line 124. Let's take a second to get there [stops talking while discussants find the page]: "And from that day on, his wife was most obedient, and they lived happily ever after." So, *Maggie*, do you think, like you said, you think it's a plan. Some people think that it's a plan to scare his wife. Do you think it was a plan to make his wife obedient?

[UW71]   MAGGIE: Yes.

At [UW70], Marsha offers textual evidence that the wife was obedient thereafter. *Maggie* then asserts that this was the aim of the plan [UW71]. And what does Grace say to the evidence Marsha offers?

[UW72]   MM: I have *Parker* next on my list, but, before I go to you, *Parker*, can I just go back to Grace and see what she thinks? Do you think that it was a plan because he was scared of his wife, or did he want to make his wife obedient?

[UW73]   GRACE: I think he wanted to make his wife obedient.

Here, then, is evidence that the discussants not only are focused on a point of shared doubt about the meaning of the text (Why does the husband kill the animals?) but, in addition, have ideas about the resolution. They are also working to evaluate their ideas by developing and assessing arguments to support them, based on study of the text. Indeed, Grace's declaration at [UW73] suggests that the evidence in lines 123 and 124 has persuaded her that the husband developed the plan in order to make his wife obedient rather than to avoid mistreatment. *Parker* offers yet another motive for the plan:

[UW74]   PARKER: I think that he wanted to be like her so she'd feel, like, more secure, but actually she didn't just not feel secure but she felt scared of him because she actually thought she was going to get her head chopped off with his sword.

[UW75]   PB: He wouldn't cut her head off, do you think?

[UW76]   PARKER: I think he was just trying to make her scared.

[UW77]   MM: *Parker*, I'm really interested in what you started off saying. You said that he started off acting like that because he wanted to be like her? What do you mean by "be like her"?

[UW78]   PARKER: To make her feel more comfortable.

[UW79]   MM: To make her feel more comfortable?

[UW80]   PARKER: Or to make her feel like she's been making other people feel.

[UW81]   MM: Which one? Did he want to make her comfortable or did he want her to see how she was acting?

[UW82]   PARKER: How she was acting.

[UW83] MM: So maybe, *Parker,* he wanted to show her it's not good to be a wicked, bad person? And this is what it looks like to be a bad person, and so he wanted to teach her a lesson, maybe?

[UW84] PARKER: Yeah, maybe.

[UW85] MM: Interesting, because that's something we haven't thought about yet.

[UW86] PARKER: That's what I think . . . that's why he set up the dog.

[UW87] MM: Interesting, so that's maybe another motive he could have had behind setting up this plan.

Again, we see a participant offer a new explanation for why the husband had a plan in mind when he killed the animals. At [UW80] *Parker* seems to mean that the husband hoped to teach the wife how it felt to be treated irrationally, just as she had treated others. The plan, then, may have been aimed at showing the wife how it felt to be mistreated. Are others persuaded by *Parker*'s idea?

[UW88] GRACE: I still think it was planned!

[UW89] MM: I figured you would! [laughing]

[UW90] GRACE: Because on page, because on the last page, on line 121 . . . "Hearing this, they were all amazed and held in high esteem the youth who had tamed his headstrong wife."

[UW91] PB: What do you think the line means, then?

[UW92] GRACE: That like . . . this is . . . like they're saying it was all a plan!

[UW93] PB: Explain why you think that means it's all a plan.

[UW94] GRACE: Because it says that "the youth who had *tamed* his headstrong wife."

[UW95] PB: So, these people thought it was an okay idea that he cut off a horse's head and a dog's head and a cat's head? They thought it was a good thing?

[UW96] GRACE: I think he wanted to show her that he was crazy or something to make her be afraid of him. So she wouldn't be the one ordering him around . . . he would be ordering her.

[UW97]   PB: Okay, and I do have a question, though, about why
           people think it was okay for him . . . Why would people say
           it's not okay for her to be unruly, but it's okay for him to
           cut off horses' heads in order to tame her?

[UW98]   GRACE: Because . . . he was doing a plan to get her to calm
           down. But when she was mean and stuff, like, then she
           was, like, for real! And it wasn't a plan. She was, like, doing
           that intentionally.

[UW99]   PB: So it's different when it's for real and when you're
           pretending for a reason?

[UW100]   MM: And maybe the reason is what makes it okay. Maybe
           the fact that he was killing animals was okay because the
           reason he did it was to tame his wife. Do you think?

[UW101]   GRACE: Mmm-hmm [nodding].

Once again, Grace offers textual evidence in support of her position
that the husband was acting strategically. At [UW94] she seems to interpret the quoted lines to mean that the townspeople believe that the
husband has acted according to a plan. They call his action "taming," and
taming someone is a goal that may be reached only through deliberate,
intentional action. When Paula and Marsha question Grace as to why
people applaud the husband but reject the wife's behavior as "unruly" or
inhumane, Grace seems to accept their suggestion that the presence of
the plan to tame the wife accounts for the difference.

THE CO-LEADERS' QUESTIONS

Let us now return to the two questions that the co-leaders raised before
mixing the groups of students from Central and Sheridan schools. The
first question was: When the groups were mixed, would experience in
the discussions help participants to draw out ideas and gain insight from
each other despite differences in race, socioeconomic class, and school/
home culture? To begin with, observe that many of the discussants from
both schools spoke repeatedly.[10] Furthermore, one of the most remarkable moments of the entire project occurred about four-fifths of the way
through the conversation that we have just observed, when the following
exchange took place:

[UW102]   MM: Tracy's next. Then *Parker*.

[UW103]   TRACY: I really want to know . . . What's his name?
             [pointing to another student]
[UW104]   MM: *Arnie?*
[UW105]   TRACY: Yeah! What *Arnie* thinks. He hasn't said anything.
[UW106]   MM: Aha!
[UW107]   *ARNIE:* Let's see. . . . I think he's kind of crazy . . . because,
             well, I kind of think he's kind of . . . I think two things. He
             could be crazy or, like, the town, they got together, and,
             like, said, for the guy who married the crazy wife or the
             wild girl or whatever, and it was, like, "Dude!" Like . . .
             they had to get a town meeting or something? And . . .
             like, the father of the wild wife—
[UW108]   *JEREMY:* The wild, unruly wife . . .
[UW109]   *ARNIE:* The wild, unruly wife, like, said, "Can you help me
             tame my girl?" Maybe. But I don't know. I kind of think
             the man could be crazy.

At [UW103], we see Tracy inviting *Arnie,* who is from the visiting
school, to offer his view. Until now, *Arnie* has said nothing during the
discussion. Typically, one would expect a leader to request contributions
of participants who do not offer them voluntarily. Tracy may be asking
Arnie to speak because of a desire to show courtesy to a guest, curiosity
about his views, or even concern for his comfort in a foreign setting. It
may also be that she has learned from experience in previous discussions
that everyone should contribute to the conversation, and she therefore
encourages *Arnie's* participation. We get some ideas about Tracy's motivation as the exchange continues:

[UW110]   MM: So, Tracy, I'm gonna go back to you. What do you
             think about . . . your question was: What does *Arnie* think?
             What do you think about what he thinks?
[UW111]   TRACY: Well, it's kind of what *Maggie* was saying, and
             Grace, because, like, I think that she thinks that . . . he
             thinks that he was taming—and so does *Maggie* think that
             he [the husband] was kind of crazy, and so did *Arnie,* and I
             think that he's kind of crazy, too. And now I'm trying to
             . . . I'm thinking of what *Parker* and Grace [were] saying. I
             think [the husband] was trying to tame her to see what she

had done to other people and how it feels to be crazy . . . how does it feel when crazy people do [things] to other people.

Tracy's comment at [UW111] suggests that she hears others, including *Arnie,* agree with her initial claim that the husband is crazy when he kills the animals. And yet Tracy's struggle with the question of why the killings occur appears to be genuine, for she now entertains Grace's notion that the husband killed the animals because he was carrying out a plan. Furthermore, the reason for the plan that she offers at [UW111] seems to be that the husband intends to show the wife how it feels to be the victim of irrational behavior—much as *Parker* had argued at [UW80]. Hence it appears that Tracy asks *Arnie* for his views not simply to be polite but, rather, to make progress in resolving a question that is of concern to her.

Tracy seems to be working to "fuse the horizons," to borrow Gadamer's phrase: to reconcile the perspectives of various discussants with that offered by the text and so to understand it. She indicates that she hears several students, including *Arnie,* agree with her initial claim that the young man is crazy when he kills the animals. Yet she seems also to have heard the opposing view—that the husband is strategic rather than crazy—for she proceeds to struggle with the issue. Eventually, she concludes that she may be changing her mind, that she is beginning to think that the husband is following a plan and intends to show his wife how it feels to be the victim of irrational behavior, much as *Parker* had argued earlier.

So were the discussants in the mixed group at Central School able to draw out ideas and gain insight from one another despite differences in race, socioeconomic class, and school or home culture? The answer is yes. Tracy has asked *Arnie* for his opinion about whether the husband was irrational or strategic and then reasoned her way to a new position. Earlier, we saw *Jeremy* embrace Grace's claim that the husband had a plan and thereby explain events in the text that puzzled him. We also saw *Maggie* become persuaded by Grace and others and change her mind. And we saw Grace change her mind about the motive for the husband's plan, perhaps on the basis of *Maggie*'s argument ([UW59]–[UW69]) and the textual evidence that Marsha cites at [UW70]. In short, we have observed several instances in which discussants sought and received help from others in posing and addressing questions. Indeed, they seemed to treat the differences of opinion as resources to be pondered; Dewey might say that the differences between people—differences in race, class, and cultural background—were broken down.

Now let us turn to the co-leaders' second question: Did the discussants show tolerance and appreciate the views of others—others who appeared unlike themselves in some ways? To begin with, consider the case of Grace, a discussant from Central School. At the start of the conversation about "The Unruly Wife," she argues that the young man was not crazy but rather "smart" in creating his plan to execute the animals. *Jeremy*, who is from Sheridan, seems to begin with the question of why the young man does not get the water for himself instead of asking the animals to do it. Eventually, *Jeremy* declares: "I think that he was just setting it up," meaning that the young man was acting strategically and that he did not get the water for himself because he had a reason for killing the animals. We do not know that *Jeremy* has been persuaded by Grace's arguments, but her claim that the husband has a plan seems to help *Jeremy* explain why the youth does not get the water himself. In any event, he embraces Grace's conclusion.

Then there is *Maggie,* another student from Sheridan, who also seems to develop respect for Grace's claim that the husband acts with intent. *Maggie* begins by arguing that the young man kills the animals because he is crazy [UW41] and later acknowledges that she has "changed her mind" [UW61]. When Marsha asks *Maggie* why the husband created the plan, *Maggie* says that he wanted to make his wife obedient, not simply avoid mistreatment. Can we credit Grace with persuading *Maggie* that the husband kills the animals because he is following a plan? Perhaps, for Grace has argued the claim vociferously and persistently. At the same time, perhaps we can credit *Maggie* with persuading Grace to consider a different motive for the plan—a motive that Marsha, Grace, *Maggie,* and perhaps others seem to believe is supported by textual evidence that Marsha reads at [UW70].

Finally, there is Tracy, who, like *Maggie,* begins by arguing that the young man kills the animals because he is crazy and who later seems to change her position [UW111]. In that comment Tracy acknowledges that, much as Grace has argued, the young man may have had a plan after all. Furthermore, with regard to motive, Tracy may also have been persuaded by *Parker* that the young man wants to teach his wife how it feels to be treated irrationally.

In sum, the transcript suggests not only that students from both schools might have been persuaded by Grace's claim that the young man acted strategically but that Grace was listening to others so as to get help in developing her arguments. Perhaps Grace's determination to defend her claim—her repeated searching of the text, her own experience, and the comments of others in order to build her case—drew tolerance and respect from them. And perhaps her respect for others' views was growing all the while.

Gadamer helps us envision what seems to have happened in the conversation at Central School: "Every conversation presupposes a common language, or, it creates a common language. Something is placed in the centre, as the Greeks said, which the partners to the dialogue . . . share, and concerning which they can exchange ideas with one another. . . . In the successful conversation they both come under the influence of the truth of the object and thus are bound to one another in a new community.[11] Reflecting on the conversation about "The Unruly Wife," we see that the "something placed at the center" is the question, Why did the husband kill the animals? Much of the conversation was aimed at addressing a version of that question, namely, Did the husband kill the animals because he became irrational or because he was executing a plan? The participants identified these possible explanations for the husband's behavior. One might say that these two options became part of their "common language," that is, they were the terms that the group agreed to use in expressing the point of ambiguity that concerned them.

Eventually, nearly all came to agree that the husband killed the animals because he was following a plan. That conclusion is what Gadamer calls the "truth" of the conversation. It is the truth that the discussion revealed. As argued in Chapter 1, such a truth is absolute in the sense that it follows necessarily, given the question and the facts about the text that are agreed on. The conversation attributed the following "facts" to the story: (1) it said the wife was "crazy" [UW2], a "devil" [UW63], but the husband killed his dog, cat, and horse, which made it seem as if he was crazy [UW6]; (2) the husband cut off the head of his only horse [UW21]; (3) the cat, the dog, and the horse did not fetch and carry water [UW29]; (4) in killing the animals, the husband did more work than a lazy person would do ([UW20], [UW37]), so he was not lazy; the husband made idle threats to the wife at line 99 [UW49]. From these agreed-on facts arose the answer to the question of shared concern: the husband killed the animals because he had a plan or purpose in doing so.[12]

Now, the husband may have created his violent plan in order to scare the wife and avoid getting killed ([UW53], [UW55], [UW57]), to make his wife obedient to him ([UW69], [UW70], [UW71], [UW73]), or to teach his wife what it feels like to be treated irrationally ([UW80], [UW82], [UW111]). Agreement seems to be greatest with respect to the second of these possibilities, but the matter is not resolved definitively. There is textual evidence to support the second option, but none of them are ruled out by the facts that the discussants attributed to the text. Further discussion might reveal more about the relative merits of these possibilities.

Throughout the conversation we see students from both schools "place something at the center." That is, we see that what they say is directed at addressing their shared question. Their conversation is focused on and directed at answering it. Furthermore, via their joint efforts to do so, they are "bound to one another in a new community," as Gadamer puts it. His idea, as applied to the discussion group, seems to mean that the members become connected to one another as they identify and work to resolve the questions about the meaning of the text.

In the lines quoted above, Gadamer sounds very much like John Dewey when he talks of individuals who "refer [their] own action to that of others, and . . . consider the action of others to give point and direction to [their] own."[13] Both writers assert that a community is formed where members of a group share a purpose—perhaps that of resolving a question—about which they communicate. In the case of an interpretive discussion, that communication takes the form of dialogue in which people say things in response to one another so as to reach the goal. Answering the question—or reaching the goal—binds the people together not only because they have responded to each other in order to achieve it but because, once it is achieved, they share an understanding that they did not have before. As Gadamer puts it, they "come under the influence of the truth of the object."

So the evidence suggests that those who discussed "The Unruly Wife" drew ideas and gained insight from each other, despite differences of race, class, and culture. There is also evidence that the discussants showed tolerance and appreciation of the views of others who appeared unlike themselves in some ways.

Can we credit the success of the conversation to the participants' earlier experiences in the discussion project? In the chapters that follow, I argue that we can, at least to some extent. As a first step in that argument, let us take a closer look at three of the discussants whom we have been following.

A Closer Look at Tracy, Jeremy, and Grace

It may surprise the reader to learn that Tracy spoke only ten times in the conversation about "The Unruly Wife." In fact, she spoke fewer times on this occasion than in any previous discussion (see table 7.2). She made seven spontaneous references to the text and offered only one evaluative comment. She spoke half as often as she did in the first discussion (ten instead of twenty times) and made fewer evaluative comments (one instead of five).

These statistics, in addition to the comments that Tracy makes in the conversation we have just observed, suggest that she is speaking less and thinking and listening more by the time of the final discussion in the project. Moreover, the content of her remarks suggests that by the end she has greater understanding of how to use interpretive discussion to gain insight. Her deliberate attempt to relate the positions of several of her peers at [UW111], her request that *Arnie* share his views, and her continued searching of the text for the best resolution imply that she has learned how to go about addressing a question she wishes to resolve. That she pursued these practices even when her group had new members suggests that she recognized the utility of these efforts. Her support of Joseph's claim in the discussion of "Allah Will Provide" that the snake was working, and her contribution of textual evidence to his argument [AP30], indicate that her commitment to collaboration with others in building a text-based case has been developing over the course of the discussion project.

Jeremy likewise spoke fewer times in the discussion of "The Unruly Wife" than in the conversation about *The Giving Tree*: whereas he made thirty-eight contributions to the latter, he spoke fifteen times in the mixed group at Central (see table 7.2). Perhaps more striking is the fact that he made one evaluative comment in that final conversation, but he had made ten in discussing *The Giving Tree*. Furthermore, he made three spontaneous references to the text in that discussion and seven in the exchange about "The Unruly Wife."

Table 7.2 reveals that *Jeremy*'s contributions became increasingly text-focused. Indeed, he set the record in the discussion project for the greatest number of spontaneous references to the text when he made fifteen of them in the discussion of "Jean Labadie's Big Black Dog." The arguments he made in that discussion, in particular, suggest that experience gained over the course of the project developed his appreciation of textual evidence.

Nonetheless, it is clear that *Jeremy*'s penchant for speculating (for instance, [UW33] and [UW35]) did not disappear. Sometimes he did not clearly differentiate between the facts in the story and figments of his imagination. Not once did *Jeremy* cite a line number in the discussion of "The Unruly Wife" or in any other. Although his preoccupation with the text seemed to grow over the course of the project, vagueness in his appeals to it remained to the end.

Finally, Grace, who in the discussion of *The Giving Tree* spoke only four times and did not refer spontaneously to the text at all, participated very differently in the discussion at Central School about "The Unruly Wife." She made twenty-one comments, seven of which appealed spontaneously to the text and only one of which was an evaluative comment. Because two of her four comments in the discussion of *The Giving Tree* were evaluative, it seems safe to infer that she became more preoccupied with textual interpretation by the end of the project.

In addition, her understanding of how to go about it was perhaps the most mature of all. It was she who offered line numbers in reference to textual evidence at [UW46], [UW49], [UW90], and [UW94], and it was she who worked to develop an argument for her claim (the husband was acting according to a plan) that was based on textual evidence. She both cited relevant passages and used her interpretation to explain facts found in the story. Others seemed to recognize that the best arguments were supported by the text, but only Grace grasped that specific reference to it was more powerful than vague allusion. It is not surprising, then, that Grace succeeded in persuading others of her position.

HAROUTUNIAN-GORDON'S THREE QUESTIONS

Let us turn to the questions that I hoped to answer when the urban and suburban groups were combined. First, Did the mixed group define and pursue resolution of a query that the members shared about the meaning of the text? The answer is yes. The discussion at Central School lasted nearly an hour. That entire period of time was focused on trying to resolve the issue of why the husband killed the animals. In these excerpts, we see eight of the ten discussants participating in the conversation. The transcript reveals that all ten of the discussants spoke at least six times during the hour.[14] The questions raised by both the co-leaders and the students were directly relevant to the group's deepest point of doubt, which may explain why they were not resolved until possible resolutions had been identified and explored.[15] Hence, I infer that the discussants were focused on a query about the meaning of the text that was of concern to them.

My second question was, Would the discussants use textual evidence to address their questions? In the foregoing excerpts, we see them using evidence from the story to address their questions. In fact, it is difficult to find a comment or question, whether posed by a discussant or by a co-leader, that does not refer to the text, at least indirectly. Although only one student, Grace, made reference to line numbers, the comments by others focused consistently on events in the story and on reasoning about them. Table 6.8 reveals that there were fifty-one spontaneous references to the text in the discussion. In contrast to Discussion 1, *The Giving Tree*, which contained thirty such references, Discussion 10 shows increased preoccupation with textual evidence.

As mentioned above, however, many discussants seem content to make vague reference to events in the story without referencing them precisely. In addition to *Jeremy* (at [UW33] and [UW35]), *Parker* and *Arnie* also muse about what is taking place without appeal to words or events described in the story (the former at [UW74], [UW80], and [UW82], the latter at [UW107] and [UW109]). In doing so, they allow fantasy to take place without attempting to verify the power of the idea behind it on the basis of the text. They need to perform that verification in order to establish the facts in the text that should constrain the formation of what Gadamer calls the "object" or the idea that emerges from the conversation about the resolution of the group's shared question.

My third query was, Would the discussants work to evaluate the strength of proposed resolutions using textual evidence? Again we saw continued progress. Unlike the discussions of *The Giving Tree* and "Kaddo's Wall," the conversation about "The Unruly Wife" aimed to evaluate evidence in support of three possible resolutions of the question that concerned the group. Some agreement was reached about the answer—the husband killed the animals because he had a plan—because scrutiny of the text showed it to be the theory best supported by the evidence therein. Hence, Gadamer's "object," the idea about resolution, began to emerge from the conversation. At [UW18] *Parker* reasons to the conclusion on the basis of textual evidence and does the same thing at [UW25]. *Maggie* does likewise at [UW59]—where she reverses the conclusion she draws at [UW41]—and Tracy does so at [UW111]. Although *Jeremy* at [UW37] reaches the conclusion after some vague speculation, the facts of the story do not contradict his scenario. In Chapter 1, I noted that, according to Gadamer, the "object" of the conversation requires a "common language"—a term or phrase used by the interpreter that seems to fit the text. In the final discussion several members of the group agreed that the phrase "following a plan," rather than "crazy," fit the husband.

Of the speakers whom we see, *Arnie*, at [UW109], seems most unable to settle on a resolution of the shared question. He does not adopt the common language accepted by others as befitting the young husband. *Arnie* seems conflicted because the scenario he envisions—in which the town had a meeting and the father asked for help in "taming" his daughter ([UW107] and [UW109])—suggests a resolution that conflicts with the one that he said he believed. If the bride's father had asked the townspeople for help in taming his daughter, then the husband might have attended the meeting and subsequently created a plan. Yet *Arnie's* last statement is that the husband could be "crazy" [UW109]. Perhaps *Arnie* would have reached a resolution that was consistent with his reasoning had he grounded it in textual evidence rather than unsubstantiated speculation. As it stood, he argued inconsistently and gave himself no basis for rejecting one resolution or the other because he could neither embrace nor rule out his hypothesis.

Wittgenstein writes: "The grammar of the word 'knows' is evidently closely related to that of 'can,' 'is able to.' But also closely related to that of 'understands.' ('Mastery' of a technique.)"[16] He points out that in the sense in which we often use the word "know," it means that we are able to do something. Likewise, if we are said to "understand" X, we mean that we know what to do in order to carry out X. Although one might argue with Wittgenstein, his observation about how we use the word "know" is apt in at least some cases. Indeed, it helps us say what inhibits *Arnie:* because he does not tie his understanding of "The Unruly Wife" to the text, he cannot look at the text to see whether his idea about the town meeting has credence. He has no rules to follow, so he cannot go on. He is stuck.

Others who took part in the conversation, however, begin to show mastery of the technique of interpretive discussion because they are able to rule in and rule out claims and arguments. They also pose questions that they address about the meaning of the text and pursue their resolution. As they follow the rules, their perplexity grows and a shared point of doubt—a genuine question—is formed. Indeed, Tracy, who opened the conversation with an idea about its resolution at [UW6], was still evaluating that idea nearly one hour later [UW111]. As argued above, her closing statement may be seen as an active attempt to fuse the horizons, or render compatible the various perspectives of her peers with the perspective offered by the text. Her desire to answer the question grew because she knew how to go about testing her idea, and she did so. The same could be said of *Maggie,* Grace, *Parker,* and perhaps *Jeremy,* as well as others who were less active participants. Each time the perplexity intensified, the discussant thought about the proposed resolution with respect to events in the story: Could it explain given events or not?

So perhaps Tracy entertained the possibility that the husband was acting according to plan, as opposed to being irrational, because at [UW49] Grace addressed the issue of why the husband would create a plan that involved killing his only horse. That is where Grace argued that since everyone knows animals cannot carry water, the wife should have suspected that the killings were a ruse aimed at accomplishing some goal. Hearing that reasoning may have helped Tracy reconsider Grace's position. As a consequence, Tracy's perplexity seems to have intensified.

Further evidence that the discussion of "The Unruly Wife," which took place at Central School, shows mastery of a technique is that it meets the criteria of a good interpretive discussion. What are those criteria?

First, the discussants need to identify a shared question they wish to resolve about the meaning of a text; they did so. Second, they need to pursue its resolution at length, which involves identifying possible resolutions. It also involves testing the relative strength of the possibilities by exploring evidence in the text to see whether it is consistent with them; the discussants did both of these things. Third, they need to pursue the testing until they come to a conclusion about the resolution of their shared point of doubt given the textual evidence; they did that as well. Under those conditions, what Gadamer calls "truth" emerges.

Yet disagreement among the participants about the resolution or some aspect of it may remain at the end of a good discussion. In the present case, Grace's claim that the husband was pursuing a plan when he killed the animals seemed to gain favor with many. There was still controversy, however, about the aim of the plan: Was it to frighten the wife, make her obedient, or teach her not to act irrationally? At the end of a good interpretive discussion, it is possible to feel more perplexity than at the start, as seemed to be the case with Tracy. Then again, the group may come to consensus, and the truth of the conversation may emerge.

Now the following question arises: If, when combined, the two groups were able to work together, then to what might we attribute the accomplishment? Is it possible to give some of the credit to the leaders' and participants' experiences with discussion? In the following chapters I address that question. I reflect on the role, resources, and education of the co-leaders and relate these to the discussion experiences of the students.

CHAPTER FIVE

Learning to Question

CHAPTERS 2, 3, AND 4 show two groups of fourth-grade students learning to participate in discussion about the meaning of texts. Chapters 5 and 6 argue that their progress, at least in part, is made possible by growth in the discussion-leading skills of Marsha and Paula, the co-leaders. In the present chapter, we see how features of their preparations for discussion seem to affect the ability of both groups to form genuine questions about the meaning of the stories and pursue resolution. In Chapter 6 we explore some of the co-leaders' discussion-leading patterns, which appear to be related to their preparations for discussion. Analysis of the patterns, like exploration of the preparations, helps explain why the classroom conversations proceeded as they did.

INTRODUCTION TO THE PREPARATION FOR DISCUSSION

Before leading the discussions about each text, Marsha and Paula prepared what I referred to in Chapter 1 as a cluster of questions. The cluster identifies a point of ambiguity about the meaning of the text. That point of ambiguity is phrased as the basic question (BQ), and it is the deepest point of doubt—the question the leader wants most to resolve. In addition, the cluster identifies at least eight places in the text that seem to suggest evidence for resolution of the BQ, if interpreted in at least one way. So the cluster presents eight follow-up questions about the meaning of these passages, in addition to the BQ. All of the questions in the cluster are interpretive questions.

When Marsha and Paula told me that the first text they had chosen for the project was *The Giving Tree,* I had no objection, provided it was a discussible text. As indicated in Chapter 1, a discussible text may be any object whose ambiguity is sufficient to sustain a conversation about its meaning. In such a case, the meaning of a text seems unclear in at least one respect, yet the text offers evidence that may yield clarification.[1] If a text is discussible, then one can write a cluster of questions about it.[2] The question, therefore, was whether we could write a cluster of interpretive questions about the meaning of *The Giving Tree.*

In order to answer the question, I suggested that each of us read the story at least twice and, while reading, write questions about events in the text that seemed puzzling. The questions might concern, for example, the meaning of a word that the author uses, the motives of a character, the overall organization of the work, the evidence for a claim that the author makes—in short, anything at all in the text that the reader does not understand. It may turn out that some of the questions are answered with continued reading. Then again, there may turn out to be little or no evidence with which to address some of the questions. I suggested that, when writing the questions while reading, we not judge their quality or worry that they might be answered by the time we reach the next page. Rather, we should write them for one reason only: we have at least some curiosity about the answer.

I then suggested to Paula and Marsha that once the initial study of the text was complete—in general, literary texts should be read at least twice[3]—each of us should review the questions that we have written and identify two or three interpretive questions that were of interest to us.

After we finished the reading, the three of us met to share the questions that each of us had written about the meaning of *The Giving Tree.* The following exchange took place:

[GTd1]   s H G: Okay, what were you trying to figure out? I mean, do you have a sense of a basic problem emerging yet or . . . do you still have a bunch of questions [that seem unrelated to one another]?

[GTd2]   M M: My basic thing was this sense of happiness and love and is the tree really happy and does she really love the boy and does the boy really love the tree.

[GTd3]   PB: And my word that comes to mind has to do with almost selfishness, like selfless versus selfish love and does the boy love the tree because he gets things from the tree.

The question that first concerned Paula at [GTd3] seemed, at the time, to be an interpretive one, for it seemed to ask: According to the text, does the boy love the tree because she gives him things that he wants? In seeking evidence to use in resolving the question, one might look at the text and inquire: If the boy loves the tree because he gets things from her, why does he return to her when she is only a stump (line 40) and seems to have nothing to give? One might argue that the boy returned to the stump because he loved her though she had nothing to give. Or one might argue that the boy returned to the stump because she gave him a place to rest and so was still useful. These two interpretations of line 40 suggest different ideas about whether the boy loved the tree because she gave him things that he wanted. The evidence offered in line 40 indicates that the question, Does the boy love the tree because he gets things from her? is an interpretive question, because it cannot be resolved definitively.

Recall that in Chapter 2 I asked whether Marsha had raised an evaluative or an interpretive question when she asked Tanis whether the boy is "being selfish when he keeps taking things from the tree" [GT17]. It seemed important to find the answer, for as the discussion proceeded, participants and co-leaders introduced question after question, addressing none of them at length. I argued that the shifting of attention from one question to another may have occurred because the co-leaders introduced an evaluative question—Is the boy selfish?—that diverted attention from the text each time it was reiterated. Perhaps the attention shifted to different questions in an effort to find a way back to the text, which could be taken up again, now in relation to a new issue.

Was the question whether the boy is selfish meant to be evaluative or interpretive? If we ponder the issue in light of the cluster of questions that the co-leaders developed prior to the discussion, there seems to be little doubt, given the history of their preparation. Before we consider that history, there is one more step we need to take, and that is to review the criteria by which I evaluate a cluster of questions. The leaders were familiar with the criteria, having been introduced to interpretive discussion in a class that they had completed before the project began. The criteria are consistent with my conception of interpretation, as I explain below. Before discussing the rationale for the criteria, I present a list of them.

Criteria for Evaluating a Cluster of Questions
1. Consists of a basic question (BQ) and at least eight follow-up questions, all of which are interpretive questions.
2. All the questions in the cluster—BQ and follow-ups—are interpretive questions.
3. All the questions—BQ as well as follow-ups—are clear. They are free of technical terms (terms that could have more than one meaning and among these the intended meaning is unclear). They are free of vague phrases.
4. The follow-up questions quote a particular passage in the text, interpret the quoted words fully (that is, say no more and no less than the quoted words), and relate the quoted words to resolution of the BQ. The point of reference (page, line, or location) is included.
5. The BQ expresses the deepest point of doubt (DPD)—the question that the writer wishes most to resolve. In order to test the BQ, one reads the follow-up questions. Does resolving each one in at least one way suggest an idea about resolution of the BQ? Or do the possible resolutions that occur to one suggest that the questioner is in doubt about something other than the issue posed by the BQ?
6. All questions are follow-ups to the BQ. That is, resolving each question in at least one way suggests an idea about resolution of the BQ.
7. The BQ is in the proper form. That is, if the eight follow-up questions seem to suggest two possible resolutions, then both of these should be expressed in the BQ. If the follow-ups generally support one resolution, then the BQ should suggest that resolution. If the follow-ups suggest three or more resolutions, then the BQ should be in open form. That is, it should suggest no possible resolutions; the possibilities should be suggested by the follow-up questions. PLEASE NOTE: The form of the BQ should indicate the questioner's best guess about the resolution. If two resolutions seem equally possible, they should be expressed in the BQ. In order to determine whether a BQ should be in open form (suggest no possible resolutions), issue form (suggest two possible resolutions),

or single-possibility form (suggest one possible resolution), one must read the follow-ups and see whether they explore one, two, or more than two resolutions.

8. The cluster explores a clear point of doubt about the meaning of the text in as few words as possible. That is, the BQ is clear yet posed as succinctly as possible. The follow-up questions quote just enough to provide evidence for the suggested interpretation. The quoted words are interpreted fully but in as few words as possible.

The goal in preparing and evaluating clusters is to create a cluster that meets all of the above criteria—a tall order that generally requires three to five rounds of revision.

Rationale for the Criteria

The first three criteria specify that the questions in the cluster must be interpretive questions and clear questions. Criteria five through eight ask that the BQ express the deepest point of doubt, that the follow-up questions explore it by pointing to passages that may have implications for its resolution, and that they be expressed parsimoniously and in a form that suggests the questioner's ideas about resolution of the BQ, if possible.

The fourth criterion is critical. It asks that the follow-up questions (and the BQ, if desired) be posed with reference to a particular passage and that the question begin by interpreting the passage, that is, by saying in the questioner's words what the quoted words say. The question continues by suggesting a resolution of the BQ on the basis of the interpretation of the quoted passage. So criterion 4 is consistent with the definition of interpretation as translation and asks the questioner to make a translation before using the quoted words to explore resolution of the BQ. We will see examples of questions and clusters below. Additional examples are available in appendix B.

Now let us return to the history of the preparation for discussion of *The Giving Tree*. Paula's question about the boy's selfishness appeared in the first draft of the cluster that the co-leaders sent to me on January 11, 1997. I call the draft "Round 1." What follows is a portion of it.

The Giving Tree, Round 1

Basic Question (BQ): Why do the boy and the tree love each other?

Follow-Up Question 4: When the boy takes things from the tree (lines 20, 29, 38), is he being selfish or is he giving back to her in some way?

The reader will note that Question 4 is not in the form indicated by Criterion 4 above: it does not pose the question by quoting words, interpreting those words, and then using them to pose a resolution of the BQ. Furthermore, although Question 4 poses two possibilities—that the boy is being selfish and that he is giving to the tree—it may, in fact, instead be asking, When the boy takes things from the tree, does it show that he is selfish?—an evaluative question that would cause Question 4 to fail to meet Criterion 2. I suggest that the question may be evaluative rather than interpretive because each of the lines to which the question refers points to an instance of the boy's taking something from the tree. Line 20 reads: "And so the boy climbed up the tree and gathered her apples and carried them away." Line 29 reads: "And so the boy cut off her branches and carried them away to build his house." Line 38 reads: "And so the boy cut down her trunk and made a boat and sailed away." I see no evidence in these lines that in taking the tree's apples, branches, and trunk the boy is giving to the tree. On the basis of the lines cited, it now seems that the co-leaders may have been wondering whether the boy was acting from self-interest when he took things from the tree.

When Marsha and Paula submitted Round 1 of the questions for the cluster, however, it was not clear to me that Question 4 was evaluative. My responses to the co-leaders' questions are italicized throughout the chapter. I place parentheses around the specific words in the questions on which I comment.

Follow-Up Question 4: When the boy takes things from the tree (lines 20, 29, 38), is he being selfish or is he giving back to her in some way? *Vague. Try to relate the possibility that the boy is selfish to the problem of why the boy loves the tree and the tree loves the boy (BQ).*

In my response I am applying Criteria 3 and 6. When I say that the question is vague, I mean that I do not yet know what it is asking. When I say, "Try to relate the possibility that the boy is selfish to the problem of why the boy loves the tree and the tree loves the boy," I mean that I do not yet see how answering the question of whether the boy is selfish will help address the BQ. Hence, I ask the co-leaders to make the connection explicit in the question. I did not raise the issue of whether the question is evaluative, perhaps because I was not yet clear about its meaning.

Now consider Round 2, which the co-leaders prepared in response to my comments about Round 1. We find the following BQ and follow-up question 4:

Basic Question: Why do the boy and the tree love each other?

Follow-Up Question 4: When the text says, "I want a boat that will take me far away from here. Can you give me a boat?" (lines 34–35), does the boy ask for this because he is selfish?

The BQ is unchanged. Question 4, however, quotes a line from the text and asks about its meaning. It therefore comes closer to meeting Criterion 4, although it does not interpret the quoted words, nor does it relate them to resolution of the stated BQ. Looking at the question now, it seems more clearly than before to be an evaluative question. That is, it chooses an event described in the text—the boy saying to the tree, "Can you give me a boat?"—and asks whether the request indicates that the boy is selfish. Apparently, the criteria for judging the request selfish or unselfish are to come from the reader, for the question does not begin with the words "According to the text."

Looking at Question 4 in Round 2 persuades me that even in Round 1 it was meant as an evaluative question, although, as I say, I did not reach the conclusion until I began studying the drafts of the cluster preparation. Furthermore the evaluative question, Is the boy being selfish when he takes things from the tree? may have been the co-leaders' deepest point of doubt—the issue they wished most to resolve—rather than the stated BQ. I say this because the question was introduced in our first conversation about the text, and as we saw in Chapter 2, it was voiced repeatedly in the classroom conversations held at Central and at Sheridan, first by one leader and then by the discussants and the second leader.

So let us return to the question posed in Chapter 2: Why did the co-leaders have difficulty helping the discussants articulate an issue that, as a group, they cared to resolve and tried to address? Perhaps, as suggested, Marsha and Paula were focused on their own question and understood the discussants' comments and questions in their terms. As a consequence, they may not have tried to help each group—in particular, the group at Central School—identify a question that it wished to take up. For example, the fact that she was concerned with whether the boy was selfish may have inclined Marsha to ask Tanis whether he was selfish [GT17] after she defended her claim that the boy "wanted more stuff" by reading line 26 ("I want a wife and I want children and so I need a house. Can you give me a house?"). Does the line provide evidence of the boy's selfishness? If one has that question in mind, the line may seem to speak to it. Perhaps seeking to answer the question "Is the boy selfish?" distracted the co-leaders from hearing the questions of the discussants and thus from helping the group form a shared point of doubt.[4]

Not only may Marsha and Paula have focused on their own question, but that question seems to have been an evaluative one. As argued in Chapter 2, addressing an evaluative question does not often open the text for further study. Although one could look at the story to see what the boy did and then judge whether he was selfish, the answer to the question depends on the criteria for selfishness that the respondent brings to the discussion. To the extent that the focus shifts to discussants' or to the co-leaders' criteria for selfishness, it moves away from study of the meaning of the text. As a consequence, posing and reiterating an evaluative question may make it difficult for discussants to pursue a question about what the text is saying, for the text is shifting in and out of focus. And as we saw, the introduction of the evaluative question—Is the boy selfish when he takes things from the tree?—seemed to stop the conversation; that is, it seems to have forced the group to take up another question in order to continue the discussion.[5]

"KADDO'S WALL"

As indicated in Chapter 3, the preoccupation with evaluative questions did not end after the discussions of The Giving Tree. How did the co-leaders and the participants move from evaluating to interpreting the text? In my view, the answer, at least in part, relates to the cluster of questions that the co-leaders prepared before leading the discussion of "Kaddo's Wall" at Central School. This time, there were four rounds of revision.[6] It seems that the revisions helped the co-leaders clarify their point of doubt and their ideas about possible resolutions. In the process of revising, they struggled with textual issues that, as it happened, reappeared in the classroom. As a consequence, they may have become more focused on exploring the meaning of the story with the students, for they could further examine the evidence for their own ideas.

The co-leaders raised the issue of whether Kaddo was selfish in the early rounds of their discussion preparation:

"Kaddo's Wall," Round 1:
Basic Question: Why does Kaddo build a wall around his house?

Follow-Up Question 1: When Kaddo says, "I have so much corn in my granary that I don't know what to do with it" (line 14), does Kaddo not know what to do with the corn because he is selfish and cannot imagine giving it away? If so, does his selfishness cause him to use the surplus corn to build a wall for himself?

Follow-Up Question 2: The townspeople suggest that Kaddo give his surplus corn to the poor people who have no corn at all. When Kaddo responds, "No, that isn't a very good idea. It doesn't satisfy me" (line 31), does giving the corn away not satisfy him because he is selfish and, therefore, must have all the corn to himself? If so, is his selfishness the reason he uses all the corn to build a wall around his house?

The comments I made in response to the co-leaders are italicized. I asked first about their proposed BQ:

Hi, P and M—I think it might help to back up a bit and try to identify the point of doubt. Are you asking: Why does Kaddo build a wall around his house instead of giving his extra corn away as the people suggest? (Criteria 3 and 5)

In requesting that the co-leaders clarify the point about which they are most in doubt, I suggest an idea about something else that Kaddo might have done with his grain besides build a wall around his house. In doing so, I hope to help Marsha and Paula clarify their point of doubt—to ask themselves to juxtapose Kaddo's use of the excess corn with one that seems more plausible to them. Are they most puzzled about why Kaddo does X instead of Y? If so, the alternative should be stated so as to clarify the point of doubt and at the same time indicate the kind of resolution that is sought.

After reading Question 1, I write,

What do you mean by "selfish"? Wants to keep things for himself? Wants to get things for himself—greedy? Unaware of the condition of others? Doesn't care about the condition of others? Doesn't want to give up what he has to improve the condition of those less well off? I think if you open up the meaning of the term "selfish," you may expose more possible resolutions to your BQ. That is, your ideas about resolution should become clearer. (Criterion 5)

When I ask Marsha and Paula what they mean by the term "selfish" and suggest possible meanings, I am hoping to give them ideas with which they may return to the text and see whether it offers supportive evidence. Perhaps as they consider whether Kaddo "wants to keep things for himself" (a definition of "selfish" that I suggest) or "wants to get things for himself" (a definition of "greedy" that I suggest), they will ask whether Kaddo's actions suggest one or the other, both, or neither. In doing so, they may let textual evidence suggest the features of Kaddo's character and motives and hence focus on textual interpretation rather than evaluation using criteria from outside the text. If they find textual evidence for one or more of the suggestions, they will both clarify the question about Kaddo's character that most concerns them—that is, clarify their BQ—and arrive at ideas about the answer that are based on evidence given in the story.

The co-leaders submit Round 2 of the cluster with a modified BQ. This time, they have developed questions that aim to test three possible resolutions (Kaddo was selfish, greedy, or ignorant). My response is as follows.

P and M—I think you will get more ideas about the meaning of the passages if you try to say what they mean, in your own words, before trying to relate them to the BQ. I give you some suggestions below. (Criterion 4)

"Kaddo's Wall," Round 2:
Basic Question: Why does Kaddo build a wall around his house instead of giving away his extra corn as the townspeople suggest?

Follow-Up Question 1: When Kaddo says, "I have so much corn in my granary that I don't know what to do with it" (line 14), does Kaddo not know what to do with the corn because he does not recognize the needs of the townspeople? If so, does this ignorance explain why Kaddo builds a wall with his extra corn rather than giving it to the townspeople?

My revision: When Kaddo says, "I have so much corn in my granary that I don't know what to do with it" (line 14), does this mean that Kaddo cannot think of a use for the corn that satisfies him or that he does not know that some people are poor? If the former, does he build a wall around his house after he is told that some people are poor (lines 18–19) because he is not interested in learning about the needs of others? (Criterion 4)

I suggest a revision of Question 1 because I think my version better explains the evidence that Marsha and Paula have pointed to in the text, given what is said elsewhere. So when Kaddo remarks in line 14, "I have so much corn in my granary that I don't know what to do with it," it seems to mean that either he can't think of a use for the corn that he likes or that he doesn't know that some people are poor and need the corn to eat. The latter possibility seems unlikely because the townspeople inform him that some lack food (lines 18–19), yet he refuses to give or even lend them the corn (16–20). The quoted line, in addition to lines 16–20, gives evidence that Kaddo lacks interest in, rather than knowledge of, the fact that some people in the town are poor.

Marsha and Paula submit Round 3. The BQ remains the same as in Round 2. In Round 3, however, they seem to have moved from evaluating to interpreting the text, for they seem to have become concerned to unearth the text's criteria for evaluation. Consider, for example, Question 5 as it appears in Rounds 2 and 3:

Basic Question: Why does Kaddo build a wall around his house instead of giving away his extra corn as the townspeople suggest?

Follow-Up Question 5, Round 2: When Kaddo tells the townspeople, "My right is different from yours because I am so very rich" (lines 46–47), is Kaddo being selfish and placing his wants before those of others? If so, does selfishness cause him to build a wall instead of caring about the needs of others?

Follow-Up Question 5, Round 3: When Kaddo tells the townspeople, "My right is different from yours because I am so very
rich" (lines 46–47), does he mean that he can do what he wants
with his property or that he doesn't have to share with them because being rich makes him exempt from what is conventionally
right (right for the common people)? If the latter, does he build
a wall around his house to selfishly spite them and give them
tangible evidence that he doesn't have to give away his corn?

In Question 5, Round 2, when the co-leaders quote lines 46–47, in
which Kaddo says, "My right is different from yours because I am so
very rich," they may seem to interpret the lines when they ask, "Is Kaddo
being selfish and placing his wants before those of others?" Yet an interpretation of a quoted line should say no more and no less than the line
itself does, which in this case might be: Does it mean that Kaddo thinks
he has privileges that are unlike those of others in the town because he
has a lot of wealth? The co-leaders do not interpret the quoted lines but,
rather, immediately ask whether the lines show that Kaddo is selfish when
they say, "Is Kaddo being selfish and placing his wants before those of
others?"

On the other hand, Question 5, Round 3 offers an interpretation of
the quoted lines and, in so doing, articulates the point of ambiguity. It
asks: "When Kaddo tells the townspeople, 'My right is different from yours
because I am so very rich,' does he mean that he can do what he wants
with his property or that he doesn't have to share with them?" Marsha
and Paula make two suggestions about possible meanings, both of which
are justified by the quoted words.

By interpreting the text more closely in Round 3 than they did in
Round 2, the co-leaders begin to unearth its criteria for determining
selfishness. Question 5 seems to ask: Is the text saying that Kaddo is
selfish because it presents the wall as evidence that he believes he need
not share his corn with others? They also work to clarify their question
by explaining what they mean by "conventionally right," that is, "right
for the common people."

Likewise, if we compare Question 7 as it appears in Rounds 2 and 3,
we can again see the co-leaders moving from a preoccupation with their
own criteria for judging selfishness to criteria offered by the text:

Follow-Up Question 7, Round 2: "His grain bulged in his granary, because each season he harvested far more than he could use" (lines 5–6). Does Kaddo's granary bulge with excess grain because Kaddo is greedy and always wants far in excess of his needs? If so, does his greediness cause him to build a wall with his extra corn even though he does not need a wall?

Follow-Up Question 7a, Round 3: "His corn bulged in his granary, because each season he harvested far more than he could use" (5–6). Does Kaddo harvest more grain than he can use because he does not know what else to do with it, which implies ignorance, or because he likes to acquire more than he needs, which implies greed? If the latter, does he build a wall because he wants to have another tangible sign of his wealth?

Follow-Up Question 7b, Round 3: Does Kaddo harvest more grain than he can use because he does not recognize the needs of others, which, therefore, allows/facilitates his excessive desires, or because he likes to acquire more than he needs and is, therefore, blinded to the needs of others? (Sophie, we're working at the possible connection between greed and ignorance—does his greed make him ignorant OR does his ignorance allow/facilitate his greed?)

If we compare Question 7, Round 3 with Question 7, Round 2, we see the co-leaders again moving toward a closer reading of the text. In Round 2, they seem to focus on the words "His grain bulged in his granary" and ask whether they mean that Kaddo was greedy. In Round 3, they quote the same words but seem to focus on the additional phrase "because each season he harvested far more than he could use," for they ask: "Does Kaddo harvest more grain than he can use because he does not know what else to do with it, which implies ignorance, or because he likes to acquire more than he needs, which implies greed?" Looking at more of the words in the quoted line, they seem to find evidence for both greed and ignorance.

As Marsha and Paula work to say no more and no less than the quoted words say (Criterion 4), they get new ideas about the meaning of the text.[7] Indeed, Question 7b of Round 3 seems to arise because yet another possibility is suggested by the quoted words: that Kaddo builds a wall around his house because he is ignorant about the needs of others, which "allows/ facilitates his excessive desires." In addition, the co-leaders say that they have begun to wonder whether Kaddo's ignorance makes him greedy, or vice versa, that is, they wonder about a possible relation between the two motives.

So let us return to the question posed at the beginning of the discussion of cluster preparation for "Kaddo's Wall": How do the co-leaders and the discussants move from a focus on evaluation to a focus on textual interpretation? My claim with respect to the co-leaders is twofold. First, as they revise their cluster of questions in light of my comments and their questioning of themselves and one another, they return to study at least some of the lines in the text. As they look at the lines again, they see possible meanings that they did not see at first, and they find new evidence with which to clarify and address their questions. Hence, they become more interested in understanding what the text is saying.

Second, as they enter the classroom discussions with a clearer point of doubt and more ideas about possible resolutions, they come seeking help from the discussants: in order to resolve their BQ, they need to learn whether their interpretations of the text will bear further scrutiny. As we saw, Marsha and Paula asked the students to return to the story again and again—for example, to determine that about which Kaddo may have been ignorant, as they did with Jeremy. By directing the discussants back to the text, the co-leaders may test their interpretations and thereby gather evidence with which to address their BQ, which concerns why Kaddo builds a wall with the corn instead of sharing it with those in need. I conclude, then, that by preparing the clusters of questions, the co-leaders become focused on interpreting rather than evaluating the texts.

Now let us turn to the discussants. How does one explain the growing preoccupation with the text that they developed? In order to address the question, let us think again about the discussions of "Allah Will Provide."

"ALLAH WILL PROVIDE"

In the conversation that took place at Central, we saw Damian insist that others defend their claim that the snake was not working against textual evidence to the contrary (the fact that the bird eventually fell out of the tree, whereupon the snake devoured it). We also began to see the group forming questions of genuine concern, ones that they wished to resolve and worked to resolve. How is one to explain these changes?

Consider the first conversation that the co-leaders and I had about "Allah Will Provide," which occurred on February 6, 1997, before they prepared Round 1 of their cluster of questions. Paula seems to begin with a particular perspective on the story:

[APd1]   PB: On lines 37–38 it says, "As the snake swayed back and forth, Bou Azza realized that the bird had been hypnotized by the viper's movement." So Bou Azza realizes that the hypnosis is what kills the bird, but I think that [Bou Azza's] idea is that there was no energy expended by the snake. [Bou Azza] fell into laziness because he thought the snake was not having to lift a finger and things came to him, when in fact the snake was working. Just as when Bou Azza's wife went out and was industrious instead of lazy, she got the reward.

[APd2]   SHG: Is he [Bou Azza] lazy? Or is he trusting?

[APd3]   PB: I don't think he's a lazy person, I just think he loses his spark or whatever.

[APd4]   SHG: Well then, does he become lazy?

[APd5]   PB: Because he's trusting . . .

[APd6]   SHG: My question is: Does he become lazy or does he become trusting?

[APd7]   PB: I think I would want to explore the word "trusting."

I ask Paula to reconsider her apparent belief that Bou Azza becomes lazy because I am uncertain that the evidence justifies it. She demurs at the suggestion of laziness [APd3], but I am persistent, because I think she has been arguing the contrary [APd6]. At [APd7], she seems to mean that she might consider the possibility that Bou Azza becomes "trusting," but she wants to know what I mean by the word. I continue:

[APd8]   SHG: Let's go to line 75, where [Bou Azza] says to his wife, "I will not leave my mat, even if I die of hunger. Yesterday, I saw a serpent finding his food without working, and I have decided that if Allah fed the serpent, he will provide me with my bread." Has Bou Azza seen the snake and decided it was lazy, since it got its food without working, and therefore he [Bou Azza] will be lazy? Or, does [Bou Azza] not work because he sees that Allah took care of the snake, provided [it] with what it needed, and trusts that Allah will provide for him?

[APd9] PB: Well, my reaction to that would be: look at the author's choice of words, describing Bou Azza's new attitude. In lines 65 and 66, it says: "Bou Azza stayed in bed until noon. And he took his grass mat to the rear of the house where he sat under a fig tree." In line 73, " 'No, wife,' said Bou Azza as he stretched in the sun." And it seems to me that by giving [the] detail about staying in bed until noon, and stretching in the sun, [this] is evidence of a person who has adopted more of a lazy attitude than a trusting attitude.

[APd10] MM: Then, look on lines 105–106 on page 36: it's almost as though . . . I agree with you, that language made me think he was lazy, and also the "I'm not lifting a finger." But here he's being tempted with the gold. He made a promise to himself that he would not move, and now he could not move a finger. So it's like he's being tempted out of this trusting state, maybe.

Paula cites lines 65, 66, and 73 and argues that the details describe a lazy rather than a trusting person. Marsha starts to agree, adding, "I am not lifting a finger" [APd10], which is a paraphrase of lines 106–107, which state, "But he had made a promise to himself not to move, and now he could not lift his finger." Marsha then goes on to say that Bou Azza is tempted by the gold to abandon his trusting state. In saying this, does she mean that Bou Azza may not stir from his mat because he has promised to trust that Allah will provide for him? If so, perhaps she is beginning to see evidence for a second interpretation—that the man is trusting Allah rather than being lazy.

Before leading the discussion at Central, the co-leaders prepared a cluster of questions about "Allah Will Provide" that included two rounds. In this cluster, they raise the issue of whether Bou Azza has become lazy or trusting. My comments are again italicized.

"Allah Will Provide," Round 2:

Basic Question: Does Bou Azza (BA) become lazy, having observed the serpent's example, or does he come to trust that Allah will provide for him, as one of His creatures?—this is the BQ (for the moment) and/or: Is the pot of gold a reward for Bou Azza or, rather, evidence of Allah's care?

Follow-Up Question 4: When BA says, "I will not leave my mat even if I die of hunger. Yesterday I saw a serpent finding his food without working and I have decided that if Allah feeds the serpents, he will provide me with my bread" (74–77), is BA being lazy when he says that he will not leave his mat, or is he making a (difficult—*omit, evaluative*) promise not to move because be believes that he must trust/does trust that Allah will provide for his needs?

Follow-Up Question 5: BA "headed for home . . . with an idea in his head. . . . The serpent finds much food without really working for it, thanks to Allah" (50–55). Is BA mistaken when he assumes that the serpent did not have to work for his food? If so, is BA quick to—*draw this mistaken conclusion* (make this mistaken assumption, wishful thinking—*omit?*) because BA no longer wants to work hard and desires to be lazy?

When the co-leaders list two BQs, they indicate that they are unsure about the question they wish most to resolve. Questions 4 and 5 suggest that they see evidence for the possibility that Bou Azza becomes both lazy and trusting. Recall that they begin to explore the issue of laziness when they open the conversation at Central, asking initially about whether the snake was lazy.

Why do the discussants become more focused on textual interpretation? Why do they develop issues of shared concern? There are at least two striking parallels between the development of the co-leaders' cluster of questions concerning "Allah Will Provide" and the progress of the conversation at Central School. First, the co-leaders and the discussants were pressed to explain evidence for their claims that is found in the text. In the case of the co-leaders, the pressure came initially from me and then from themselves. The discussants were pressed to interpret the text first by the co-leaders and then by one another.

Second, the co-leaders and the discussants at Central began with a perspective on the story that seemed to change with closer scrutiny of the text. Why does the second possibility become more plausible? In the case of the discussants, the reason is Damian's insistence that those who believe the snake is not working explain why the bird became mesmerized by the swaying serpent and eventually could no longer hold on to the branch. In the case of the co-leaders, the follow-up questions developed during the preparation show that they, like the discussants, identify more and more textual evidence that suggests an alternative resolution. Look at two additional follow-up questions in Round 2 of their preparation.

> Follow-Up Question 6: When BA says, "Oh, wife, . . . if Allah saw fit to let you find such a treasure, surely he would give you the strength to carry it home" (108–110), is BA refusing to help his wife because he is lazy and does not want to get up? If so, why does the text say (105–107), "Actually Bou Azza was impressed with the thought of the gold. But he had made a promise to himself not to move," which suggests that he did not move because he trusted Allah/promised to trust Allah?
>
> Follow-Up Question 7: When BA says, "I am not going to lift a finger until Allah drops fortunes on my head the way he showered gifts on the serpent" (126–128), is this evidence that [Bou Azza] has become lazy, or that his faith in Allah is so unwavering that he will not be tempted to break his promise not to work? If the latter, is BA's faith rewarded with a pot of gold?

In Questions 6 and 7 the co-leaders quote and interpret passages suggesting to them that Bou Azza becomes lazy. As the interpretation proceeds, however, they seem to discover evidence for the possibility that Bou Azza becomes trusting.

The foregoing analysis suggests that as people begin to study the meaning of a passage in order to make a case for a particular claim, they see evidence for another interpretation that was not at first apparent. As the evidence for a competing interpretation is found, a shared concern arises: Is the correct resolution in the first theory or in the second? As study of the text produces evidence for competing resolutions, the point of doubt becomes clearer, and the interest in resolving it becomes more intense and is shared by more discussants. The questions about Kaddo's ignorance and about whether the snake was working are examples of questions about the meaning of the text that became shared concerns as the discussions generated evidence for more than one interpretation.

The role of the co-leaders in helping the discussants engage in textual analysis cannot be overestimated. Nor can the importance of clarity in the clusters of questions prepared by the co-leaders. The analysis continues with the next story that was discussed.

"JEAN LABADIE'S BIG BLACK DOG"

If the desire to study the text intensifies as people find evidence for competing claims about its meaning, and if the discovery of the contradictory evidence helps clarify the questions of concern, then perhaps we are beginning to understand how is it that one arrives at clear questions that one wishes to resolve—questions that draw one more and more deeply into the study of the text. Indeed, we get additional clues as we examine the co-leaders' experience in preparing for the classroom discussions of the French-Canadian text, "Jean Labadie's Big Black Dog." That experience seemed to affect their approach to handling the discussants in both schools, and indeed, the conversations that transpired.

Let us begin with the preparation phase. As it turned out, after one preliminary discussion of the story, I had to be out of town, so the co-leaders prepared two rounds of a cluster and led the discussion at Central School without assistance from me. Paula sent me the following e-mail message:

> Sophie, as Marsha and I mentioned in our journals, we talked earlier this week after separately attempting the first round of the cluster. We weren't sure how to proceed and "push" each other's cluster and were about to throw in the towel. But then we found two questions in my cluster (7 & 8) and one in Marsha's (8) that made us realize our issue was something larger. We moved from talking about André *only* to taking a look at the bigger picture.
>
> Our subsequent phone conversation went something like this (according to our notes): Jean is losing control of his story. Why do other people take it over? Does Jean lose control of his story when other people take it over? Who believes? Who doesn't? . . .

We were fixated on the idea of "Who owns the story, the
teller or the listener?" Then, I asked, "Did André take the story
away from Jean on purpose, or should Jean have known that
once he told it, it was no longer his?" From that, Marsha asked,
"Whose story is the big black dog?"

We decided that this was our true point of doubt and proceeded to develop our Round 2 cluster from that question.[8]

February 26, 1997—Marsha's Journal:
[Paula] and I drove together and spent most of the time talking
about the text and our game plan for leading. I was excited
about the text, especially after [our] discussion last night. In a
way that would make you proud, Sophie, we really pushed ourselves (after being so close to just accepting what we had and
hanging up the phone). There were three questions—two
in Paula's cluster and one in mine—that made us both realize
that our issue was something larger, and we weren't quite
there yet. Something [was] triggered, and all of a sudden it
started coming together. It was a great moment, and Paula and
I agreed to go back and rework our basic question . . . I was excited to see how this work would play out in the discussion.

As I read the co-leaders' messages and journal entries, I sensed a
freedom in their work on the cluster for "Jean Labadie's Big Black Dog"
that I had not perceived in the preparation for discussion of previous texts
in the project. They both speak about "pushing" themselves to think more
deeply about the story when they might have given up. One wonders why
they made the effort of their own accord. They do not address the issue
directly, but their remarks about the process give clues.

First, both say that they found questions in each other's initial clusters that suggested a topic of shared concern that neither had articulated:
the power of story to control people's thoughts. The topic was one that
both Marsha and Paula seemed to wonder about, yet they had difficulty
articulating a clear question regarding it. Hence, they worked to state the
issue in a form that expressed their deepest point of doubt, the question
they wished most to resolve.

Second, they report that they encountered frustration in trying to develop a cluster of questions to follow up one of the formulations (Marsha's

question 4). In trying to write the follow-up questions, they discovered that, as Paula put it, Marsha's question 4 "was not a solid point of doubt for us," meaning, perhaps, that although they could find passages in the text that helped them understand what different characters gained from believing the story about the big black dog, they became uninterested in the question once they found evidence to resolve it. They therefore abandoned the question since it was not a point of genuine doubt.

In sum, they seemed to know that they had a point of doubt, but they had yet to state it clearly. My guess is that the discomfort generated by the situation motivated them to work until they came to a formulation that they felt expressed their concern. In effect, they reached a state of perplexity during their discussion about the cluster of questions.

What effect did this self-generated doubt have on the class discussions of "Jean Labadie's Big Black Dog"? As we saw, the co-leaders invited the group at Sheridan to pursue an issue of its choice. They questioned the discussants in an effort to help them form a point of doubt (Was there a real dog running loose that the people saw?), then helped them pursue its resolution in spite of their belief that the question was not a genuine issue given the textual evidence. Recall how both co-leaders and discussants repeatedly confronted speakers with textual evidence, requiring them to explain the events in the story using their interpretations.

So let us return to the question of how one comes to clear questions that one wishes to resolve. I argued above that the desire to study the text intensifies as people find evidence for competing claims about its meaning. The discovery of the contradictory evidence creates questions about the meaning of the text, for one wonders, is it saying X or is it saying Y? The creation of such questions helps discussants to find a direction for the conversation—to find a question that they wish to address.[9] But review of the co-leaders' experience in preparing for the discussion of "Jean Labadie's Big Black Dog" suggests that freedom to choose an issue and support in pursuing the choice may also be important in identifying issues of concern.

By the time the co-leaders began preparing for the discussion of the fourth text used in the project, they had learned to seek and articulate points of ambiguity in the story and in their own questions. When, in conversation with one another, they identified and had the freedom to pursue the issue of who controlled the story (Did Jean, André, or nobody control it?), they responded by questioning themselves and one another further and developing a new cluster of questions that explored the issue. In doing so, they further investigated the text and clarified their question more fully as they found new evidence with which to address the problem.

And like the co-leaders, the discussants were learning to detect points of ambiguity about the meaning of the story. When they engaged in conversation that yielded issues and were given freedom to choose a question to address, they selected the option that for them provided the deeper point of doubt. In the ensuing exchanges, they returned to the text again and again to find evidence for their positions, just as the co-leaders had done during their preparation. As was true for the co-leaders, the discussants seemed to gain additional clarity about the question of concern to them as they studied the text, and their desire to resolve the issue seemed to intensify as evidence for possible resolutions was uncovered.

"THE UNRULY WIFE"

Now let us turn to the final issue in the present chapter, one that is raised by the foregoing analysis. Once a group identifies a question of genuine doubt—a shared concern—and pursues its resolution through discussion and further study of the text, how does the group learn to evaluate the strength of proposed resolutions using textual evidence? Once again, analysis of the discussion preparation, as well as a look back at the discussion of "The Unruly Wife," suggests ideas about the answer to the question.

Consider Round 3 of the cluster of questions that the co-leaders prepared for use with "The Unruly Wife." It is a good example with which to illustrate the criteria that a cluster needs to meet. The numbers in the follow-up questions refer to page numbers in the text.

> "The Unruly Wife," Round 3
> Basic Question: Does the young man become unruly, or does he act unruly because he is pretending? *OK—meets all relevant criteria; is in issue form.*[10]
>
> Follow-Up Question 1: Does the young man actually become wild and unruly given the societal expectation that husbands control their wives? When the text says that the townspeople

"held in high esteem the youth who had tamed his headstrong wife" (11), does this suggest that they approve of the youth's unruly behavior? *Relation to BQ?—Seems to explore motive for unruly behavior, not whether the young man became unruly. Criterion 6*

Follow-Up Question 2: When the young man kills the animals, does he pretend to act unruly in an effort to scare his wife into submission? If so, does he pretend because he believes that he must be in control and she must act obedient in order for them to "live happily ever after" (11)? *OK*

Follow-Up Question 3: The text says, "If at the start you don't show who you are, when later on you wish to, you'll never get too far" (11). Does it suggest that the young man must pretend to be unruly from the beginning in order to tame his headstrong wife? *OK*

Follow-Up Question 4: The text says of the young man, "He did not relish spending his life in poverty. . . . He would prefer to wed a wealthy woman" (5). Does the young man give up being courteous because he wants his wife's money? If so, does this suggest that the promise of money can make people become wild and unruly? *Relation to BQ? Criterion 6*

Follow-Up Question 5: If the young man was only acting, why does the story describe him as "angry, furious, and drenched with blood" (9), killing the only horse he had, which suggests real feelings rather than acting? Or did he need to take such action against a wife who others were convinced would "wound or kill him" (7)? *OK*

Follow-Up Question 6: When the young man says, "How I thank God you have done as you were told or else I'd have done the same to you as to the others" (9), is he showing his wife that he is glad he didn't have to carry out his threat? Does this suggest that he is only pretending to be unruly? *OK*

Follow-Up Question 7: If the young man was only pretending to be unruly, why does the text say that his wife "realized he was not joking" (9) when he killed the horse? *OK*

Follow-Up Question 8: If the young man was only pretending to be unruly, does his wife think "he would cut her to pieces if she failed to obey him" (9) because he had shown that he was capable of so doing by killing the animals? *Relation to BQ? Criteria 4 and 6*

Follow-Up Question 9: Has the young man become cruel and unruly when he kills the animals, or is he being a clever actor? If he has become a cruel person, why does he say, "I haven't been able to sleep a wink because of what happened last night" (11), suggesting that his conscience is bothering him? *OK*

The BQ seems to ask: Does the young man cut off the heads of the animals because he pretends to change his character—to "become wild and unruly"—or because his character actually changes? The question seemed clear to me. Furthermore, six or seven of the nine follow-up questions (2, 3, 5, 6, 7, perhaps 8, and 9) point to places in the text that, if interpreted in at least one way, suggest ideas about the answer and hence would be said to "follow up" the BQ. In responding to the co-leaders with regard to the cluster, I placed the phrase "OK" next to those questions, indicating that they met all relevant criteria, not merely that they followed up the BQ. So, for example, Question 6 follows up the BQ because it takes a position concerning the BQ and suggests that the young man pretends to be unruly (Criterion 6). It is also interpretive (Criterion 2) and clear (Criterion 3), and it interprets the quoted words (Criterion 4). It thus points to evidence that supports one resolution of the BQ rather than the other.

I present Round 3 of the entire cluster so that the reader may ponder its coherence. I suggest that because the BQ is clear and, indeed, provocatively phrased, indicating two mutually exclusive possible resolutions, and because six of the nine follow-up questions identify passages relevant to its resolution, we may infer two things. First, the stated BQ is a genuine point of doubt: it is a question that the co-leaders wish to resolve. The formulation of the BQ as an issue and the fact that six and perhaps seven of the nine follow-ups relate to it and suggest ideas about its answer indicate that the stated BQ is of concern to the co-leaders. Hence one might expect them to work to answer it in the classroom discussions. Even if the question had not been of interest to the students (which it was), I would expect the co-leaders to be searching the discussants' comments for ideas about its resolution.

Second, the identification of evidence that supports the two mutually exclusive possibilities indicates that the co-leaders saw justification for both and so had carefully defined the dilemma. Questions 2, 3, and 6 point to evidence suggesting that the husband was pretending, whereas Questions 5, 7, and 9 point to evidence that he was not pretending but became unruly. It seems, then, that they had identified a clear point of ambiguity about the meaning of the text, and the sheer clarity, coupled with evidence for the conflicting possibilities, may help explain why they wished to resolve it.

As it turned out, Marsha and Paula and the discussants at Central seemed to have a similar point of doubt. The latter wonder: "Was the husband crazy or was he following a plan?" This query seems like the question that concerned the co-leaders: Does the young man become unruly, or does he act unruly because he is pretending? In both cases, the point of doubt seems to be the following: Did the young man kill the animals because his character changes or because he was acting unruly for a particular reason?

If it is the case that the co-leaders and the discussants at Central had a similar point of doubt, then it is not surprising that Marsha and Paula (a) listened closely so as to hear the possible resolutions and helped participants question their value and (b) could identify relevant passages from the text. For example, careful listening on the leader's part is observed at [UW22], after Tracy asks why the husband would cut off the head of his only horse. Marsha asks Tracy to repeat the question and, after Tracy does so, Marsha asks Parker and Grace to address it. She seems to hear the question as a challenge to the strategic position, and she asks those taking that position—Parker and Grace—to focus on it.

Likewise, we see evidence of both careful listening and of the ease with which the leader pointed to relevant passages in the exchange that follows:

[UW58]   MM: I have *Maggie* and then *Parker* and then *Katie*.

[UW59]   MAGGIE: Well, I just kinda thought that maybe he did plan it. 'Cause like I said earlier he might have just killed his animals to make her really scared and he might get some new ones from her 'cause she's scared so much.

[UW60]   MM: So, *Maggie*, it sounds like you're changing your mind because, in the beginning, you were talking about [how]

you felt you agreed with Tracy when she said, "He's crazy."
But now are you changing your mind to what Grace . . . is
talking about? And *Parker,* too, he talked about this, too.
About how it was planned?

[UW61]   MAGGIE: Yes.

[UW62]   MM: Okay, then I'm going to ask you the same question:
Why did he plan this?

[UW63]   MAGGIE: Maybe because it said she was the devil and he
wanted someone to work for him and so he acted like he
was a nut case.

[UW64]   MM: So, like, was he scared of his wife?

[UW65]   MAGGIE: No.

[UW66]   MM: Like [Grace] said? Or did he want to turn his wife into
something else? [The story said] she was a devil. Did he
want to make her a different kind of person?

[UW67]   MAGGIE: Yeah, someone who'd be really scared and would
do anything that he'd say.

[UW68]   MM: What kind of person did he want to turn her into?

[UW69]   MAGGIE: Maybe to, like, someone [who] if he said, "Go get
me some water," maybe she would do that.

[UW70]   MM: I'm going to read one line that's on the last page. Line
123 and line 124. Let's take a second to get there [stops talking while discussants find the page]: "And from that day
on, his wife was most obedient, and they lived happily ever
after." So, *Maggie,* do you think, like you said, you think
it's a plan. Some people think that it's a plan to scare his
wife. Do you think it was a plan to make his wife obedient?

[UW71]   MAGGIE: Yes.

[UW72]   MM: I have *Parker* next on my list but, before I go to you,
Parker, can I just go back to Grace and see what she
thinks? Do you think that it was a plan because he was
scared of his wife, or did he want to make his wife
obedient?

[UW73]   GRACE: I think he wanted to make his wife obedient.

At [UW60] Marsha reminds Maggie of her previous position—evidence of the leader's careful listening and remembering. When Maggie

nods, indicating that her position has changed, Marsha asks about the motivation for the plan. Marsha may hear the answer as saying that the husband wants to make his wife obey him, for she reads lines 123–124, asking Maggie whether the passage is evidence for her claim. Maggie answers yes, meaning, it seems, that the evidence suggests that the husband wanted to make his wife obedient. When Grace declares that the husband "wants to make his wife obedient," she indicates that she has changed her previous position ("I think he wanted to make her scared of him"). Perhaps the evidence from lines 123–124 has persuaded her.

The foregoing analysis of the preparation for "The Unruly Wife" and the review of the excerpts from the discussion of the story that occurred at Central School suggest that the co-leaders were helping discussants work together in order to form and focus on a question that they wished to resolve and build and evaluate arguments for suggested resolutions that are based on textual evidence. We have seen instances in which co-leaders seemed to help the group by listening to what had been said and directing the discussants to places in the text that would help them construct and evaluate their arguments. The discussants, for their part, seemed to be listening to one another and, in more than one instance, changed their claims about the meaning of the text in light of the evidence and arguments that they heard.

My claim, then, is that the cluster of questions that the co-leaders prepared prior to the conversation about "The Unruly Wife" helped them both listen carefully to what was said and direct the discussants to passages in the text that helped them construct and evaluate their arguments. As we saw, the cluster was well constructed, that is, the BQ was clear, and six of the nine follow-up questions were clear and pointed to passages that, if interpreted in at least one way, suggested ideas about the resolution of the BQ.

The fact that the BQ of the co-leaders was similar to the issue raised at Central seems important, for it suggests why their interest in the comments of the participants was intense and why their listening therefore was keen. It also explains the facility of the co-leaders in finding passages that helped the discussants evaluate and defend their claims. Indeed, many of the passages referred to in the preparation were relevant to the discussion. In short, the clarity of the preparation, combined with the happy coincidence of a concern shared by the co-leaders and the discussants, helps explain why they worked together as a community of learners to explore "The Unruly Wife."

The foregoing analysis leaves us with a question, however. I have argued that changes in the co-leaders' preparations for the discussions over the course of the project help explain why the classroom conversations gradually assumed an interpretive focus, why the discussants moved from vague interest in questions to the formation of questions of genuine concern, and why, instead of speculating about possible answers, they worked together to create and evaluate arguments for suggested resolutions that are based on the textual evidence. I have not explained how a cluster of questions, prepared before the discussions with the fourth-grade students and frequently set aside during those conversations, affected the discussion-leading practices of the co-leaders. Although we have seen parallels between what happened during preparation and what took place during the discussions with the students, I have not explained how features of the preparation or experiences that the leaders had in developing them affected their discussion-leading practices.

In Chapter 6 I identify some patterns of discussion leading that Marsha and Paula developed as the project progressed. I maintain that their use of these patterns was related to features of the discussion preparations and the experiences that they had in creating them. The patterns were also related to events that occurred in the discussions themselves and the reflections that followed each one. As we will see, the journals and conversations about the experiences of preparing for and leading discussion, together with analysis of the discussion-leading practices, shed further light on the reasons why the classroom conversations assumed particular features.

CHAPTER SIX

Learning to Lead Discussion

MARSHA AND PAULA had studied interpretive discussion before the project began. They had been told that the goal was to help the group form a question about the meaning of the text and to pursue its resolution. I encouraged them to open the discussion with the BQ that they had prepared or to ask the students for their questions. In most cases, as we have seen, they picked the latter alternative.[1] As the discussants posed queries or made comments about the story, the co-leaders wrote them down. In addition, I encouraged them to ask the discussants for textual evidence that supported (or contradicted) claims about the meaning of the story. Finally, I recommended that they help all students speak at least three times during the discussion, inviting reluctant participants into the conversation.[2]

As the project progressed, Marsha and Paula developed their own discussion-leading practices, and some were repeated more frequently as they proved effective. In several cases the co-leaders seemed to happen upon these practices. The particular practices or discussion-leading patterns that I present in what follows helped create the characteristics of the conversations that we have observed.

For example, Discussions 1 and 2, which focused on Shel Silverstein's *The Giving Tree*, were characterized by the failure of the groups to come to a genuine question about the meaning of the text that the discussants focused on and worked to resolve. In Chapter 5 I argued that the co-leaders' apparent point of doubt—Is the boy in the story selfish?—was evaluative and that its repeated interjection may have deterred formation of a question that students pursued to the point of resolution. In the present chapter I identify some discussion-leading practices that seem to have arisen from the presence of the evaluative concern so that its effect on the discussion becomes more comprehensible.

Likewise, we watched as the groups began to move from evaluating the characters and events described in "Kaddo's Wall" to trying to understand the meaning of the text. Why did that transition occur? In Chapter 5 we saw how the co-leaders worked through several rounds of cluster preparation for those discussions and gradually clarified an interpretive question they wished to address. In the present chapter I examine some patterns of leading that Marsha and Paula pursued—practices seemingly related to the discussion preparation—that seemed to help the students become more focused on textual interpretation.

The conversations about "Allah Will Provide" were perhaps the first in which we saw a group move from vague interest in textual issues to the formation of shared concerns—questions they tried to resolve through extended reflection and group discussion. Although the co-leaders and the discussants continued to pose evaluative questions, the tendency to do so diminished. Once again, one wants to understand why. One reason, suggested by the analysis presented in Chapter 5, is that the more the co-leaders worked to interpret the text and the more preoccupied they became with doing so, the clearer their points of doubt became and the better they were able to help discussants form questions and pursue their resolution. We shall see below that certain patterns of discussion leading—practices that helped the questions to be formed—received more emphasis over the course of the project.

In the conversation about "Jean Labadie's Big Black Dog," the group at Sheridan seemed not only to form a shared concern but also to work on constructing a text-based argument about the resolution. It is hard to forget Parker, Kurt, Jeremy, and others crouched on the floor poring over an illustration to see how a loose dog might have run behind the barn as Jean shot his big black dog. Kurt insisted that the text supported the loose-dog hypothesis, but Jeremy remained unconvinced. Each one quoted lines from the story to make his case. Below we shall see how the co-leaders' experiences of preparing for that discussion without my assistance may have inclined them toward leading patterns that deepened the students' involvement in the construction of text-based arguments.

Finally, the analysis of the conversation about "The Unruly Wife" presented in Chapter 4 suggested that when the groups of discussants were mixed, they proceeded to interpret the story with the help of one another, much as they had begun to do earlier in the project. We saw instances in which students from the two schools worked to draw out the views of one another and help each other construct and evaluate arguments. As indicated in Chapter 5, the final version of the cluster preparation for "The Unruly Wife" was perhaps the most rigorous: the questions were clear, the follow-up questions were all interpretive, and many of them, if resolved in at least one way, suggested ideas about the resolution of the BQ. I argue below that the more rigorous cluster preparation allowed the co-leaders to pursue discussion-leading patterns that encouraged the formation of shared concerns and sustained effort to evaluate the strength of suggested resolutions.

The analysis presented in this chapter differs from that offered earlier in that the arguments are based, in part, on the quantification of the data that were collected. All ten transcripts were coded for twenty-eight patterns of discussion leading and participation. These data make it possible to identify trends in the leading and to make arguments relating the trends to the features of the discussion preparations identified in Chapter 5. Analysis of the data in relation to the features of the discussion preparations yields insight into why the discussions progressed as they did over time. The story unfolds in the pages that follow. Once again, I focus on the discussions as they took place at Central and at Sheridan.

THE GIVING TREE

To begin study of discussion-leading practices that characterized the conversations about *The Giving Tree*, let us hear the comments that the co-leaders made to me after the first discussion, which took place at Central School:

[GTd4]   MM: I went in thinking, "I don't know if this is going to work," if they'd have any questions and things, but that seemed to go. I was happy with the way the whole thing got started. [But then] a lot of it to me seemed to go around in circles. . . . And I don't even know what really ended up being a [genuine] question for the kids. I don't know if I was putting things into their mouths. Sometimes, it seemed like [it].

Paula seems to echo Marsha's last concern:

[GTd5]   PB: In some ways I fear that I fell back too much on the follow-up questions. When I wasn't sure where to go, I often would bring up a follow-up question, and I am afraid that sometimes I would try to fit what we were talking about into a follow-up question. But at the same time, I was simply trying to give it shape. If we were losing shape, I was trying to sort of bring it back.

These comments suggest that the co-leaders were, indeed, aware that the discussants at Central had failed to form a shared point of doubt about the meaning of the text and had failed to resolve, even tentatively, the issues that arose. Perhaps the question of apparent concern to Marsha and Paula—Was the boy selfish?—inclined them to raise eleven different interpretive questions in this discussion, and of the eleven, they repeated six, with thirteen total instances of repetition. At Sheridan, they raised twelve interpretive questions, three of which they repeated, with a total of eight instances of repetition.

When one compares Discussion 1 with Discussion 10—the discussion of "The Unruly Wife" that we observed—one sees a marked difference. In the latter instance, the co-leaders posed a total of six interpretive questions and repeated questions twenty-two times (see table 6.1). Indeed, they repeated two of the six interpretive questions ten times each (see table 6.9). As the discussions progressed over the course of the ten weeks, the co-leaders tended to pose fewer and fewer different interpretive questions but repeated them more frequently. The ratio of instances of repetition to distinct interpretive questions posed in the first two discussions was 0.8, compared with a ratio of 3.7 in the second discussion of "The Unruly Wife."

Table 6.1. Interpretive questions posed and repeated by group leaders*

Discussion	1 GT C	2 GT S	3 KW C	4 KW S	5 AP C	6 AP S	7 JL C	8 JL S	9 UW S	10 UW C
Number of unique IQs raised by leaders	11	12	18	5	12	7	9	7	6	6
Number of repetitions by leaders of previously raised IQs	13	8	8	7	6	9	12	12	11	22

*I use the following abbreviations in this and subsequent tables: GT=*The Giving Tree*; KW="Kaddo's Wall"; AP="Allah Will Provide"; JL="Jean Labadie's Big Black Dog"; UW="The Wild, Unruly Wife." "C" indicates that the discussion took place at Central School; "S" indicates that it took place at the Sheridan School.

What do these numbers suggest? Perhaps Marsha's sense that the first discussion of *The Giving Tree* "went in circles," or made little progress toward resolution, resulted from the large number of interpretive questions that the co-leaders asked. If students were trying to address eleven or twelve such questions in the course of a discussion lasting less than one hour, it is not surprising that they failed to progress very far toward resolution of any of them. Let us look once again at an excerpt from that first discussion at Central, during which there seem to be three issues on the floor:

[GT32]   MM: Joseph, what do you think?

[GT33]   JOSEPH: I think the boy is taking too many things from the tree because after all those things he was taking, she might not be anything. She might be gone . . .

[GT34]   MM: What line are you looking at, Joseph? Line twenty-three?

[GT35]   JOSEPH: Yeah, because it says, "And one day the boy came back and the tree shook with joy and said, 'Come, boy, climb my trunk,' and he said, 'I'm too big to climb trees,' and she . . ."

[GT36]   MM: Okay, so then Joseph, in line twenty-three, that you just read . . . do you think when it says, "the tree shook with joy" that the tree is happy because the boy came back and because she missed him, or do you think the tree is shaking with joy there because of something else?

[GT37]   JOSEPH: I think the tree is shaking with joy because he came back.

[GT38]   MM: Because he came back.

[GT39]   PB: Tanis, what do you think?

[GT40]   TANIS: I think in line one, it says, "Once there was a tree, and she loved a little boy." She probably wanted to give him stuff because she loved him.

[GT41]   MM: Oh, Tanis just said that the tree probably loved the boy.

[GT42]   TANIS: That's why she wanted to give him stuff.

As argued in Chapter 2, there are three issues on the floor: first, whether the boy is selfish (the question that Joseph seems to address at [GT 33]); second, why the tree shakes with joy (the question Marsha poses at [GT 36]); and third, whether the tree minds giving things to the boy (the question Tanis seems to address at [GT 40]). Now, in Chapters 2 and 5, I argued that repeated interposing of the evaluative question "Is the boy selfish?" by both co-leaders and students may have shifted the focus away from the text on several occasions, and new interpretive questions were introduced to shift the discussants back to interpreting the story. Indeed, that is what Marsha seems to do when, in response to Joseph's evaluative comment at [GT 33], she seems to ask at [GT 36]: When the tree "shook with joy," what evidence in the text helps explain her reaction?

I believe that Marsha was looking for a response based on textual evidence. I could be mistaken, however. During the discussion of *The Giving Tree* at Central School, there were eight instances in which it was not clear whether the leader was posing an interpretive or an evaluative question. In the discussion at Sheridan, there were fifteen such instances. By contrast, there were virtually no instances of that ambiguity in the final discussion of "The Unruly Wife."

These statistics suggest a new possibility about the skills of the co-leaders at the beginning of the project: they may not have recognized when they were posing an evaluative as opposed to an interpretive question. In addition, they may not have recognized that an evaluative question asks respondents to draw on their experience and criteria for judgment, whereas an interpretive question calls for further study of the text.[3] Perhaps because a number of the co-leaders' queries could have been addressed by evaluating rather than interpreting, one finds that thirty-five evaluative comments were made by Central students in the discussion of *The Giving Tree* and sixty-four were made by the Sheridan students in their discussion. These figures stand in sharp contrast to the figure of eighteen evaluative comments made in the final discussion of "The Unruly Wife" that was held at Central School (see table 6.2). If it is unclear whether the question posed is interpretive, there is a greater chance that the discussants will respond by evaluating rather than interpreting the text.

Table 6.2. Evaluative comments made by discussants

Discussion	1 GT C	2 GT S	3 KW C	4 KW S	5 AP C	6 AP S	7 JL C	8 JL S	9 UW S	10 UW C
Number of times discussants made evaluative comments	35	64	52	51	26	34	12	18	29	18

An excerpt from the Sheridan discussion of *The Giving Tree* from Chapter 2 is a case in point.

[GT56]   BETH: [She's] grateful and happy because she thinks she's doing the right thing.

[GT57]   PB: She's doing the right thing. Is she doing the right thing? Or is she happy [to give him things]? You know how there are two different things? I'm giving you something because I'm happy to do it, or I'm giving you something because I think it's the right thing to do.

[GT58]   ARNIE: It's the right thing to do.

[GT59]   BETH: Well, I mean, you never have . . .

[GT60]   ARNIE: [Interrupting] Because it's better to give than to receive.

[GT61]   BETH: You never have to give somebody something, but it makes you feel good that you can do that and the other person will be very grateful.

[GT62]   KATIE: It's not exactly the right thing to do, it's just that, like, it is the right thing to do but it also makes you happy. That you would actually do something. In her case I think it makes her happy because she's doing something for a boy who doesn't have anything. Like, he doesn't have a house or a boat, enough money . . .

[GT63]   WALTER: I don't feel like it would be the right thing to do because it's killing itself to make somebody have a house and a boat and it's, like, killing itself just for them.

At [GT 57] Paula seems to ask an interpretive question: According to the text, is the tree giving things to the boy because she is happy to do it or because she believes it is what she ought to do? Yet Paula adds that if one gives from a sense of pleasure, the motivation is different than if one gives from a sense of duty or obligation. In so saying, Paula plants the seed of ambiguity: Is she asking the students to interpret the text in order to discover the tree's reason for giving, as it seemed at first, or is she asking them to ponder and perhaps state the difference between the two motives, given their own experiences and criteria for judgment?

The discussants seem to hear the question as an invitation to explore the evaluative option. At [GT60], Arnie indicates that because giving is preferable to receiving, according to his way of thinking, the tree must be giving from a sense of duty. At [GT61], Beth seems to mean that the tree gives to the boy because it is gratifying to do so, perhaps because the receiver is grateful. Hence, the tree gives because of the happiness she derives from doing so. Notice that in both instances, the students are referring to their own experience, not to evidence from the text, to judge the tree's motivation. Hence, I claim that they are evaluating rather than interpreting.

Perhaps Katie comes closest to interpreting when at [GT62] she chooses facts from the text (the boy has no house, boat, or money) and then reasons that the tree acts from pleasure in helping someone who lacks things she can provide. At [GT 63], Walter evaluates the text. As argued in Chapter 2, he uses his own criterion for judgment—one should not give if doing so causes self-destruction—and reasons that the tree cannot be doing its duty in giving to the boy. Therefore, the tree must be acting from the pleasure that she gets from giving to him and making him happy.

Whereas Beth and Walter refer to events in the text in addressing Paula's question, their arguments are based on criteria that they bring to the discussion and by which they render judgment. We do not see them studying the lines to determine whether the text provides evidence for judging the tree's motivation. My claim is that Paula's question, which is not clearly interpretive, invites them to evaluate the text if they wish to do so.

So far I have argued that the failure to form a shared point of doubt and, indeed, the tendency to evaluate rather than interpret the text, may have arisen from the following causes: (1) eleven interpretive questions were posed at Central and twelve at Sheridan by the co-leaders in the discussions of *The Giving Tree,* with relatively few repetitions, so that no interpretive question was explored in depth; (2) the question of apparent concern to the co-leaders—Is the boy selfish?—was evaluative and so it took the discussants away from interpreting the text. Furthermore, it was one of several posed in the discussion that was not clearly interpretive. Perhaps, then, Marsha and Paula did not fully distinguish between interpretive and evaluative questions and the consequences of posing each. As the focus shifted between interpreting and evaluating the text, little progress was made in identifying and resolving a shared question about meaning.

Now consider another comment made by the co-leaders after that first discussion: "I don't know if I was putting things into their mouths. Sometimes, it seemed like [it]," says Marsha. And Paula laments, "I am afraid that sometimes I would try to fit what we were talking about into a follow-up question." The sense that the conversation had focused on questions of concern to the co-leaders, including ones prepared before the discussion, rather than issues of interest to the discussants may have arisen from failure to try to clarify speakers' meanings. Furthermore, this failure may have arisen, at least in part, from limitations in the discussion preparation.

The transcripts suggest that, over time, the co-leaders developed three practices that aimed to help the participants clarify the meaning of their remarks. The first was to repeat back things they said in order to confirm comprehension. The second was to identify similarities and differences between comments and questions offered by different speakers (or the same speaker over time). The third was to ask speakers directly about their meaning, for example, When you said X, did you mean . . . ? During the discussion of *The Giving Tree* at Central, Marsha and Paula followed one of these three patterns twenty-seven times.[4] In the discussion at Sheridan, they followed one of the three patterns forty-five times (see table 6.6). Table 6.4 reveals that there were twice as many attempts to repeat discussants' comments in order to confirm or clarify understanding during the discussion at Sheridan (thirty) as there were at Central (fifteen).[5]

Table 6.3. Questions asked by group leaders to clarify meaning

Discussion	1 GT C	2 GT S	3 KW C	4 KW S	5 AP C	6 AP S	7 JL C	8 JL S	9 UW S	10 UW C
Number of times leaders asked discussants directly about meaning	9	8	14	6	4	7	18	18	23	24

Table 6.4. Repetition of discussant comments by group leaders

Discussion	1 GT C	2 GT S	3 KW C	4 KW S	5 AP C	6 AP S	7 JL C	8 JL S	9 UW S	10 UW C
Number of times leaders repeated discussants' comments in order to clarify understanding	15	30	29	17	13	15	40	16	18	23

Table 6.5. Identification of similarities and differences

Discussion	1 GT C	2 GT S	3 KW C	4 KW S	5 AP C	6 AP S	7 JL C	8 JL S	9 UW S	10 UW C
Number of times leaders identified similarities and differences in discussants' remarks	3	7	14	11	15	8	11	9	19	25

Compare these figures with those from Discussion 10, the final conversation about "The Unruly Wife." In total, the co-leaders made seventy-two attempts to clarify discussants' meanings in that discussion (see table 6.6). Whereas there had been nine attempts to ask discussants directly about their meaning in the first conversation, there were twenty-four in the last (see table 6.3). Likewise, whereas there were three attempts to identify similarities and differences in what they heard during the first discussion, the co-leaders made twenty-five such attempts in the last discussion of the project (see table 6.5).[6]

Table 6.6. Clarification of discussants' meaning

Discussion	1 GT C	2 GT S	3 KW C	4 KW S	5 AP C	6 AP S	7 JL C	8 JL S	9 UW S	10 UW C
Total number of times leaders tried to clarify discussants' meaning	27	45	57	34	35	30	69	43	60	72

Thus, in answer to the question of why the co-leaders may have felt that they were "putting things into [the students'] mouths," the evidence suggests that in the first discussions Marsha and Paula made comparatively few efforts to grasp the discussants' views and questions. Furthermore, during the conversation about *The Giving Tree* at Central, they posed all the questions developed in their cluster preparation, suggesting that, as Paula had intuited, they put their questions to the students rather than trying to cultivate questions that the students might have.

Hence, we come to a major revelation of the transcript analysis: listening is critical for effective discussion leading. By "listening" I mean trying to grasp what another person intends to say. As table 6.3 indicates, the number of times co-leaders asked discussants directly about their meaning increased in Discussions 7–10 by comparison with Discussions 1–6. In Discussions 7–10 the average number of such queries is 20.75, as compared with Discussions 1–6, in which the average is only 8.0. These figures indicate that the co-leaders were working harder to listen—to understand speakers' meaning and intentions—as the project went on.[7] The importance of trying to grasp what discussants intend to say is discussed further below.

"KADDO'S WALL"

The preoccupation with evaluative questions did not end after the discussions of *The Giving Tree*, but it did diminish. How did the groups move from evaluating to interpreting the text? In Chapter 5 I made two claims. First, as the co-leaders revised their clusters of questions, they returned to study some lines in the text. In doing so, they found new evidence with which to clarify and address their questions. Hence, they became more interested in understanding the text because their questions about its meaning became clearer and more pressing. Second, as their points of doubt became more pressing, they grew more and more interested in seeking help from the discussants so as to resolve them.

So what do Marsha and Paula do in the conversation with the students, having studied the text, clarified their point of doubt, and increased their desire for help in addressing it? In order to address the question, let us look again at excerpts from the Sheridan discussion of "Kaddo's Wall," this time focusing on the discussion-leading patterns.

[KW1]   JEREMY: Well, I don't see why [Kaddo] made so much corn in the first place. He should've just made how much he needed. Then he wouldn't have a problem. Then he wouldn't have to make a wall out of it. And then when he made the wall, that's how he screwed up.

[KW2]   MM: In the beginning, Jeremy, look at what it says on lines five and six; it says that "[h]is grain bulged in his granary, because each season he harvested far more than he could use." So did he harvest more grain than he could use because—what Beth brought up—that he's greedy?

[KW3]   JEREMY: I don't know.

[KW4]   MM: Or did he harvest more grain because maybe he just thought . . . that he didn't know what else to do with it, and he's just kinda maybe an ignorant man . . . [he] doesn't realize that there are other things to do with the corn?

At [KW2] we see Marsha offer Jeremy a passage with which to evaluate the possibility that Kaddo may be ignorant rather than greedy. The practice of referring discussants to places in the story is used when the leader sees evidence that is relevant to the point under discussion. It is interesting that the co-leaders repeated the pattern of directing participants to passages in the text a total of seventeen times in the first discussion of *The Giving Tree* and four times in the second discussion of "The Unruly Wife," Discussion 10 (see table 6.7).

Table 6.7. Instances of leaders' directing participants to find specific lines or passages

Discussion	1 GT C	2 GT S	3 KW C	4 KW S	5 AP C	6 AP S	7 JL C	8 JL S	9 UW S	10 UW C
Number of times leaders offered a specific line or passage	17	6	10	5	5	4	1	4	7	4

Apparently, repetition of the pattern used in the early discussions showed the participants the benefits of finding and quoting passages that supported or contradicted their claims, for they came to do so more spontaneously as the project progressed. If one compares table 6.7 with table 6.8, one sees an increase in spontaneous references to the text by discussants and a decrease in the number of times leaders direct participants to specific passages.[8] Indeed, the students were locating textual evidence without the leaders' prompting them to do so with greater frequency as the discussions progressed.[9]

Table 6.8. Spontaneous use of the text by discussants

Discussion	1 GT C	2 GT S	3 KW C	4 KW S	5 AP C	6 AP S	7 JL C	8 JL S	9 UW S	10 UW C
Number of times discussants made spontaneous use of text	30	40	19	20	26	34	33	43	39	51

At this point in the discussion, it may seem to Marsha that the line she offers gives evidence for Jeremy's idea that Kaddo is ignorant [KW1]. But of what is he ignorant? At [KW4], Marsha suggests that he might be ignorant about what to do with excess corn. In what follows she seems to grope for an idea, and the line mentioned at [KW2] better supports Jeremy's subsequent suggestion:

[KW5]   JEREMY: . . . if he just made as much as he needed every, like, time then he could do better.

[KW6]   MM: So why, Jeremy, did he do that? Why did [Kaddo] harvest far more corn than he could ever eat?

[KW7]   JEREMY: I think because maybe he didn't . . . he wasn't a good gardener. I don't know.

Hearing Marsha's query at [KW6], Jeremy ventures that perhaps Kaddo did not know how to garden. Although at [KW7] he seems unsure about his idea, it could explain why the text says that each year Kaddo harvested more grain than he could use.

So in answer to the question of how the groups develop a focus on textual interpretation, the foregoing suggests that because leaders draw repeated attention to the text, eventually the discussants do likewise. Yet the growing focus on textual interpretation may also be a consequence of yet another discussion-leading practice:

[KW8]   PB: Well, Walter, I have a question for you. You said if you were Kaddo . . . that you would have given some of your corn away? Would you have given some of your corn away because you're a generous person and you just would want to share with others, or would you have given your corn away because you realize that someday you might need their help in return?

[KW9]   JEREMY (Interrupting): Yeah! Except I don't . . . and that would be the good thing to do at the same time.

[KW10]   WALTER: Yeah, well, because . . . if I were Kaddo, I'd have millions of pieces of corn, but I'd just give it up . . . give them away.

[KW11]   PB: So, hold on one second, Jeremy . . . [Walter], so would you, simply because you were wealthy, say, "Well, I'm just a generous person. I have so much that giving some away, I won't feel it?" Or might you be thinking, "Wow, what if I don't have all this forever and I might need their help some day?"

[KW12]   WALTER: Yeah!

[KW13]   PB: Is [it] one or the other?

[KW14]   WALTER: Well, because if you give it away then you might
           need their help because . . . let's say you don't give it away
           and you run out of corn, then they. . . . and they don't like
           you so they don't want to help you.

[KW15]   PB: And [the story] said that Kaddo knew he couldn't go to
           those people, right?

As indicated in Chapter 3, Paula may be trying to help Walter imagine
Kaddo's reasoning at [KW11]. Although the question is evaluative, Paula
seems to intend that it open up thinking about the text, for she follows
Walter's evaluative comment at [KW14] with reference to the story [KW15].
Here is an instance of a leader's directing attention back to the text so
as to test which idea best fits the evidence about Kaddo. It makes use of
evaluative thinking to advance textual interpretation.[10]

"ALLAH WILL PROVIDE"

What patterns of discussion leading do the co-leaders follow to bring the
groups to a shared point of doubt about the meaning of the text that they
work to resolve? I suggest four in the section that follows, three of which I
have mentioned already. Again, these patterns seem to arise because the co-
leaders have studied the text and clarified a point of doubt, which increases
their desire for help with textual interpretation from the discussants. Indeed, over the course of the project, we observed increasing interest in
listening to the participants and understanding what they mean. Furthermore, the listening of the co-leaders seemed to become more perceptive.

Let us look again at excerpts from the discussion of "Allah Will Provide," in which a genuine shared question appears to arise for the first
time in the project. We return to Central School and to Damian, this time
focusing on the practices of the co-leaders:

[AP17]   DAMIAN: I have a question. I wanted to ask . . . I don't
           think. . . . I think the snake was working real hard.

[AP18]   MM: Wait, you do or don't?

[AP19]   DAMIAN: I do.

[AP20]   PB: So we have a new opinion here . . . that the snake is
           working hard. Tell us about that.

[AP21]   DAMIAN: I think the snake is working hard because he tried to hypnotize . . . if . . . he wasn't trying to hypnotize him, why did the bird fall out . . . of the tree? If he wasn't working, if it was just being, like, a snake, why did the bird fall out of the tree?

At [AP18] Marsha asks Damian directly about his meaning (a pattern mentioned above). At [AP20] Paula repeats back Damian's position as she has heard it (a pattern mentioned above) and notes that it is different from the view of the snake that has been defended thus far (a pattern mentioned above). Paula, in saying "Tell us about that," may be asking Damian to give a justification for his view. In doing so, she shows that she has heard a different idea, and she asks for the group to focus on it. Damian responds to the request, pointing to an event in the story that seems to corroborate his position [AP21]. The responses that the co-leaders give in the next segment of the discussion help accomplish the formation of the shared concern:

[AP24]   PB: Sounds to me like we're starting to have a split between what people think. Some of us are thinking that the snake was working hard and it was a part of his nature to hypnotize animals to get food. Other people were saying, "I don't know if he was working hard, he was just swaying his body." Is there anyone who hasn't spoken yet who wants to say whether they think the snake was working hard or not? Joseph?

[AP25]   JOSEPH: I think, I think the snake was working hard because can't nobody just hypnotize something like quick, it takes time.

[AP26]   CYNTHIA: I've changed my mind. I agree with Joseph. Because it does take time to hypnotize somebody because sometimes people look like, "What are you doing?" [puts an incredulous look on her face] and they start gettin' like [sways head back and forth] and then they start falling asleep, but it does take time.

[AP27]   PB: Okay, Tracy, how 'bout you?

[AP28]   TRACY: I agree with Joseph too. [laughter]

[AP29]   MM: Everyone's agreeing with you, Joseph!

[AP30]   TRACY: Because sometimes people be like, "You can't hypnotize me," but then when they get ready they just start going with the flow. And I want to go back . . . when Joseph was saying about the hypnotizing and stuff? I want to add something on to it about the hypnotizing. He was right when the snake had to work hard for his food because sometimes the bird was ready to fly but he couldn't move! And then he was thinking he could get away. But then he started going with the flow with the snake, so that's why I think the bird got ate.

[AP31]   DAMIAN: Those three still didn't answer my question. Why did they think, if the bird was . . . if y'all [looking at the discussants directly] said the snake was just being a snake by moving around, why did the bird get hypnotized and fall and he [the snake] ate him?

At [AP24], Paula states the two opposing views that have now been voiced about the issue of whether the snake was working. She then asks for others who have not yet spoken to choose sides. In doing so, she sets up the dilemma for further clarification—a new pattern that seems to evolve from the practice of identifying similarities and differences between speakers' views. As discussants opt for one resolution or the other, they need to defend their choices. Each speaker seems to recognize this fact, for, as argued in Chapter 3, Joseph justifies his position on the basis of his personal experience with hypnotism [AP25]. Likewise, Cynthia appeals to personal experience in siding with Joseph at [AP26]. Paula asks Tracy for her view at [AP27], and Tracy begins by agreeing with Joseph on the basis of personal experience but then shifts attention back to the text [AP30]. In pointing to an event in the story—that the bird wanted to fly away but was mesmerized and unable to move—Tracy solidifies the dilemma as a textual issue. She thereby opens the door for Damian to reassert his question to Tracy, Cynthia, and Grace, which he does at [AP31]. Indeed, it was Damian who first formed the question as an issue about the meaning of the text [AP21].

I submit that the co-leaders are becoming more careful listeners. They inquire about the speakers' meanings, and they identify similarities and differences in the positions that they hear (see table 6.5). They underscore differences in points of view when they hear them, thereby drawing attention to the difference in perspective and setting up the opportunity to evaluate the strength of the possibilities. As the conflicting interpretations become articulated, the co-leaders encourage the participants to take positions, a move that requires them to defend their choices. Gradually, the discussants come to see that textual evidence is the most persuasive evidence, and the appeal to it becomes more spontaneous. Hence, the shared point of doubt about the meaning of the text is formed.

"JEAN LABADIE'S BIG BLACK DOG"

As argued in Chapter 5, the opportunity to choose an issue to pursue may help people develop and work to address genuine questions. We saw that in preparing for discussion of "Jean Labadie's Big Black Dog," the co-leaders, without prodding from me, pushed themselves to refine the cluster of questions until they had identified a basic question that interested them. The experience of finding and then working to answer a question of great interest may have inspired them to formulate a plan for helping discussants do likewise, for that is exactly what they do, again of their own accord. The following excerpt from Paula's journal lays out the plan:

> PB's Journal—February 26, 1997;
> We decided:
> Four questions [from the discussants at the start] would be a good amount before we went back and asked how they wanted to tackle them;
> *Show* them what we [are] doing, so that everyone is very sure of where we [are] in the discussion;
> Slow it down and be more deliberate;
> Help them navigate, showing them what is going on along the way, summarizing at intervals;
> If we change course, give them notification;
> Talk about the issues *they* were interested in, even if [the issues] seemed "off course" to us.

When Paula says, "Four questions would be a good amount before we went back and asked them how they wanted to tackle them," she makes explicit a discussion-leading strategy that she and Marsha have pursued from the beginning of the project: opening the conversation by asking the discussants for questions that they have about the story. Paula does not explain why they decided to hear four questions and then ask the group to determine the next move. Perhaps they felt that hearing four comments or questions at the start would give everyone an idea of the group's initial interests.

Did the co-leaders follow their plan? And what, exactly, do its various injunctions mean? In order to address these questions, let us look again at some excerpts from the discussion of "Jean Labadie's Big Black Dog" that took place at Sheridan School (Discussion 8). In doing so, we gain insight into not only the meaning of the plan but also how the co-leaders followed it by using established discussion-leading patterns to help discussants develop a genuine question and ideas about the resolution and to evaluate the strength of the possibilities, given the textual evidence.

The discussion transcript shows that the conversation at Sheridan began as follows:[11]

[JLi] MM: I'm going to explain what we're going to do. . . . Hold on. We're going first of all to raise hands. Like we always do. And when we call on you, then you talk. But before we start our conversation, our discussion about "Jean Labadie's Big Black Dog," we're just . . . going to get some things on the floor. So we're going to take about four or five comments, questions, if you guys are confused. General things. We're going to stick them out there and let everybody have a chance who wants it. And then we'll kind of go back to them and review what they are and then we'll decide what we all want to talk about. How does that sound?

At [JLi] Marsha explains to the discussants how they will proceed, perhaps "help[ing] them navigate," as Paula put it in her statement of their plan. Marsha also follows the plan in telling the group that they will listen to four or five comments or questions and then decide how participants wish to proceed.[12]

The transcript shows that the discussion began with five comments or questions from the participants. Then Marsha made the following statement:

[JLii]　　　MM: I'm just going to go over our comments, things we've come up with. We're just laying stuff on the floor. . . . The first comment, by Beth, was that she thought Jean was ignorant. Walter said he was confused about that cut, and if the dog wasn't real, what explains how he [André] got that cut on his hand? Parker said, related to what Walter was talking about . . . or actually Parker, you said that you don't get the story. Because at first, it was talking about chickens and all of a sudden it starts talking [about] a big black dog and we never come back to the chickens and find out who's stealing Jean's chickens. Then, Jeremy, you said, just like Parker, that you don't get the story. And if there wasn't any big black dog, how come people were seeing it? And Daphne said that she didn't get it either, and there was no real dog there so in the end, he [Jean] just shot the air, it doesn't make sense. I'm kind of seeing something that a lot of people are interested in and that is whether or not— is this big, black dog real?

[JLiii]　　UNIDENTIFIED STUDENT: Yeah, that's a good question!

[JLiv]　　KATIE: He's not!

The co-leader repeats five comments that she has heard and then asks the group what it wants to talk about, much as their plan for leading the discussion enjoined the co-leaders to do. Instead of simply asking the group what it would like to discuss or how it wishes to proceed, however, Marsha suggests a question for consideration—a question that she seems to have heard in what several of the discussants have asked. Perhaps the issue of whether the big black dog that the people see is a real dog is one that Marsha identifies when she hears Walter say he was "confused about that cut" and ask why, if the dog wasn't real, André got a cut on his hand. Perhaps she also identifies it when she hears Jeremy asking, "If there wasn't any big black dog, how come people were seeing it?" Likewise, when Marsha hears Daphne say that "there was no real dog there so in the end, he just shot the air . . . it doesn't make sense," the issue seems to be the same: if the dog is made up, how do we account for facts in the story that seem to imply the presence of a real dog, namely, André's cut, people seeing the dog, people saying that the dog is gone when Jean shoots into the air?

The comment from the unidentified student at [JLiii], coupled with the fact that Katie proceeds to address it, suggests that Marsha's suggested question is a concern that several in the group share. Indeed, the remainder of the discussion focuses on it, and the controversy about it becomes intense, as we have seen. Soon after the discussion begins, Parker presents what I have called the "loose-dog hypothesis":

[JL1]   MM: So Parker just threw out another option. . . . Maybe there's just a big, black dog running free and [it] just happens to be coming along whenever they're talking about it. And so people think that's the big black dog. Kurt, I've got you next on my list.

[JL2]   KURT: Uh, I think the dog isn't real . . . Jean Labadie's dog . . . but I think there might be a loose black dog, like Parker said.

[JL3]   PARKER [delighted]: Yeah?

[JL4]   PB: Well, if that's so, if there is this big, black dog that was loose, how come at the very end of the story Jean gathers all the townspeople and he shoots this big black dog? And you see the picture—there's no big, black dog there—and he shoots it. And it says, "And everyone agreed that the dog was gone for good." So maybe this is a question for Kurt and Parker.

As argued in Chapters 3 and 5, Marsha and Paula may be unconvinced that the people see the dog die because Jean shoots a loose dog that is running around. Indeed, there is little textual evidence to support the loose-dog hypothesis. Nevertheless, Paula returns to the hypothesis at [JL4]. The videotape of the discussion shows her pointing to a picture of Jean pulling the trigger of a gun while there is no evidence of a dog present. She seems to ask: If the big black dog is a loose dog running about, why do we see Jean pointing a gun and shooting at nothing? And why, after he does so, do the people agree that the dog is gone?

In so saying, Paula not only pursues a topic initiated by the discussants—the loose-dog hypothesis—but she seems to follow yet another injunction of the co-leaders' plan: "slow [the discussion] down and be more deliberate," meaning, it seems, ask the group to look at textual evidence and interpret it in relation to claims that are made. Here, Paula asks Kurt and Parker to look at a particular passage and explain its meaning, given their loose-dog hypothesis. Kurt responds to Paula's question with textual evidence, followed by an interpretation of the quoted words:

[JL5]   KURT: Well, on page 177, lines 311 and 312, it says, "Jean Labadie lifted his gun to his shoulder, pointed it at nothing, and pulled the trigger." So he didn't shoot anything.

Although Kurt responds, the co-leaders seem unconvinced that he has explained the evidence and related it to his hypothesis, for they keep asking him to do both things:

[JL6]   MM: But, Kurt, it says everyone agreed that the dog was gone.

[JL7]   KURT: That's what I don't get.

[JL8]   MM: And earlier it says, if you guys are following along, I'm on, line, like [lines] 309 and 310[on page 177]. And it says, "See how he runs with his big red tongue hanging out. And everyone saw the big black dog."

[JL9]   KURT: Yeah, I don't get it.

[JL10]   PARKER: Well maybe, like, the dog . . . was right next to where he was shooting.

[JL11]   PB: Okay, so you still think that there is a dog.

[JL12]   PARKER: Like, next to . . . like behind the barn. . . . Jean Labadie didn't know that, like, a dog was behind the barn.

[JL13]   JEREMY: Wait! Wait! I . . .

[JL14]   MM: Hold on a second, Jeremy, I see hands, remember, but I don't hear, like, "Oh! Oh! Oh!" Kurt, what do you think? Do you agree with Parker or—you pointed out that there was nothing there but everyone saw it?

Notice how effectively the co-leaders combine discussion-leading patterns in order to help discussants clarify their point of doubt and evaluate ideas about its resolution using textual evidence. At [JL6] Marsha presses Kurt about the meaning of the textual evidence to which he has drawn attention. At [JL8] she points to further evidence. At [JL7] and [JL9], Kurt admits perplexity. When Parker offers the loose-dog hypothesis at [JL10], he seemingly responds to Kurt's avowed state of perplexity. Paula repeats Parker's idea back to him and asks him to explain and defend it at [JL11].

Responding at [JL12], Parker may elaborate the loose-dog hypothesis in order to explain what Kurt did not, namely, how people could see the dog and agree that he was gone after Jean shot at nothing. Perhaps, suggests Parker, the people saw an actual dog near Jean. In so saying, Parker confirms Paula's understanding of what he has said and explains his idea in more detail. At [JL14] Marsha asks Kurt whether his position is similar to or different from Parker's. He says there may be a loose dog near Jean, since the illustration shows no dog and yet says that everyone saw the dog. By following discussion patterns that they have developed, both the listening and the questioning of the co-leaders seem to become more persistent and perceptive.

As argued above, once a passage that is in need of explanation has been exposed, the argument about its interpretation can become intense. So "slowing [the discussion] down" may involve not only citing a relevant passage and relating it to a claim but also making a close interpretation of it and perhaps assessing the strength of the interpretation. One makes a "close interpretation" by saying, in one's own words, no more and no less than the quoted words say. In this way points of ambiguity in the text can be exposed, which may cause controversy to intensify.[13]

In the excerpt that follows, the discussion unearths ambiguity about the meaning of the phrase "he shot at nothing." Again, the leaders follow the discussion-leading patterns that they have developed to help discussants to evaluate the loose-dog hypothesis:

[JLv]   JEREMY: Well, I think . . . [the story] said that he [Jean] shot at *nothing* 'cause he saw nothing. [So] then how would he shoot next to a big black dog [and see nothing]?

[JLvi]   MM: So what are you saying, Jeremy?

[JL17]   PARKER: But he could be shooting right next to a barn.

[JL18]   MM [to Jeremy]: What do you think about Parker's option, then?

[JL19]   JEREMY: But then how . . . would [Jean] see the big black dog if [the story] says he shot at nothing? He shot at nothing and everybody else saw the big black dog? Maybe there was a wild one. But he [Jean] said he saw nothing.

[JL20]   KURT: It didn't say he saw nothing.

[JL21]   MM: He pointed at . . . he pointed at nothing.

[JL22]   KURT: It said he shot at nothing.

[JL23]   JEREMY: Well, then, that's the same thing. He pointed at
              nothing. He shot at nothing.

At [JLvi] Marsha asks Jeremy to clarify his meaning. At [JL18] she asks him to agree or disagree with Parker, which is another form of identifying similarities and differences between positions. At [JL21] Marsha repeats the line from the text: "He pointed at nothing." By asking discussants directly about meaning and about the similarities to another's position, as well as by quoting the text, she helps the discussants expose the ambiguity: If Jean pointed the gun (or shot) at nothing—the meaning is the same, says Jeremy at [JL23]—could it be that he saw a dog, as Kurt maintains [JL20]?

[JL36]   JEREMY: [Jean] could have seen it but he didn't.

[JL37]   KURT: [Jean] could've seen it but pretended like he didn't.

[JL38]   JEREMY: Aw, [Jean may have thought:] "I see a dog but I
              don't want to kill it." He said he wanted to kill it.

[JL39]   KURT: No, he didn't.

[JL40]   JEREMY: Yeah, he said, "I'm going to end this," so he shot
              at nothing.

[JL41]   MM: You know what, hold on, Jeremy. I want to ask you a
              question, then. What do you think? What are you saying?

[JL42]   JEREMY: I'm saying there's no black dog. Maybe there
              would've been, but not at that part. Maybe those people
              are complete idiots.

[JL43]   MM: Well, then, Jeremy . . . why do people see the big
              black dog?

[JL44]   JEREMY: I know: because [the story] said he shot at
              nothing.

[JL45]   MM: So why do people see [the dog]? Is it because, like
              Brian said [earlier in the discussion], because [Jean is] a
              powerful storyteller who could hypnotize people?

[JL46]   JEREMY: [no response, chin in his hands, stares at the
              floor]

At [JL36] Jeremy acknowledges that, given the quoted words, it is possible that Jean could have seen the dog, but he asserts that, in fact, he did not see it. Although Jeremy recognizes the possibility that Kurt has identified—that one could point at nothing yet see something—he does not believe that Jean did so. Again arguing on the basis of textual evidence at [JL40], Jeremy maintains that since the story said that he wanted to kill the dog, Jean would have pointed the gun at the dog if he had seen it. At [JL41] Marsha asks Jeremy directly about his meaning. In doing so, she may help him step away from the issue of whether Jean wants to kill the dog and return to the question that the group has been trying to answer: Is there a loose dog running around? Jeremy seems to take her question in that way, for that is the question he answers at [JL42].

The co-leader reacts to Jeremy's response by reiterating the interpretive question that Jeremy needs to answer [JL 43]. He seems to recognize that if he rejects the loose-dog hypothesis and maintains there is no loose dog running around when Jean shoots the gun, then he needs to explain why the text says, "Everyone saw the big black dog." Marsha's combination of clear, perceptive listening and persistent questioning seems to help Jeremy recognize the question that he needs to answer. He has offered an idea at [JL42], namely, "Maybe those people are complete idiots." Marsha offers another suggestion at [JL45]. He embraces neither idea, and one has the sense that he may be genuinely befuddled about the answer to Marsha's question.

The foregoing analysis reveals that Marsha and Paula followed their plan for helping the discussants identify and pursue questions that were of genuine concern to them. Furthermore, they executed the plan by following patterns of discussion leading that we have watched them develop, including repeating back what discussants say, working to identify similarities and differences that they hear in the discussants' positions, asking discussants about their meaning, asking them to provide textual evidence for their claims, and reiterating interpretive questions that keep the issue before the group in focus.[14] By following their plan, the co-leaders helped the discussants in the same way that they had helped themselves identify a genuine question of shared concern. In both cases, they worked to understand the deepest point of doubt—the question they wished most to resolve—and then pursued its resolution by following the discussion-leading patterns in effective combinations.

Marsha and Paula continued to follow their plan in the discussions of "The Unruly Wife." As they did so, participants not only identified questions of interest about the meaning of the text but also worked together to construct and evaluate arguments made in support of possible resolutions—something we did not see Kurt and Jeremy do, or do with grace, in the preceding excerpts.

I conclude the present chapter with a look at some excerpts from the discussion of "The Unruly Wife" that took place at Central School—the last discussion in the project and the one for which the co-leaders mixed the two groups of students. How did preparation of the cluster, coupled with use of discussion-leading patterns, help the discussants progress in the way they did?

"THE UNRULY WIFE"

In order to address the issue, we begin by recalling that the cluster of questions prepared for this story was, for the most part, clear and well constructed. The following excerpts from the discussion suggest that certain discussion-leading practices may help explain the success of the discussion. And the clarity of the preparation seems, once again, to have affected the choice and application of the discussion-leading patterns.

The first series of exchanges occurred at Central after the discussants had begun to wonder whether the husband cut off the heads of the animals because he was crazy or because he was following a plan:

[UW38]   MM: We'll go to *Maggie*.
[UW39]   MAGGIE: Well, since what *Parker* and Troy said, about why he would cut off his only horse's head, well, maybe he would scare his wife so much so she might get him another horse.
[UW40]   MM: So *Maggie,* do you think that it was part of his plan, like . . .
[UW41]   MAGGIE: No, I think he was crazy.
[UW42]   MM: You think he was crazy like Tracy said in the beginning? So you don't think, like Grace said—he's been setting this up all along. You think the guy's just nuts.
[UW43]   MAGGIE: Umm-hmm [nodding affirmatively].

At [UW40] Marsha asks Maggie about the meaning of her statement in relation to the question of whether the husband was crazy or following a plan when he killed the animals. At [UW42] Marsha presses Maggie about the implications of her statement, repeating back to Maggie what she has said and asking her whether she sides with Tracy or with Grace. In doing so, she helps Maggie clarify her stand with regard to the shared point of doubt. The conversation continues:

[UW44]   GRACE: I still think it was all a plan.

[UW45]   MM: Tell us why.

[UW46]   GRACE: Because when [the husband says to the wife] on line 99, "How I thank God you have done as you were told or I would have done to you what I've done to the others," I don't believe that.

[UW47]   PB: If you were [the wife]?

[UW48]   MM: You wouldn't have believed what?

[UW49]   GRACE: I wouldn't have believed when he said on line 99. I wouldn't have believed that because . . . why would he chop off the neck of his only horse? So I still think it was all a plan, because if it wasn't a plan, then he wouldn't have chopped off the head of his horse and his cat and his dog. Because they can't carry water and they . . . it's silly for you to think they can carry water. So I think his wife shouldn't have believed that.

[UW50]   MM: His wife shouldn't believe what? That he would have killed her?

[UW51]   GRACE: Mmm-hmm [nods].

[UW52]   MM: She should not have believed him? Okay, so you think that it was all planned and that he. . . . Why do you think he was doing this plan, though, Grace? You think it's all a plan, but why?

[UW53]   GRACE: Because he probably didn't want to get killed.

[UW54]   MM: He didn't want to get killed? So was he scared of the wife, or did he want to turn the wife into something else?

[UW55]   GRACE: I think that he was scared of her at first but then I think he wanted to make *her* scared of *him*.

[UW56]   MM: Why would he want her scared of him?

[UW57]   GRACE: So that he wouldn't get killed by her bad temper.

Each comment made by the leaders in the excerpt printed above conforms to one or more of the discussion-leading patterns that they have developed. At [UW45] Marsha asks Grace to explain her position, which in the context means: defend your claim. Grace goes immediately to the task, citing textual evidence and analyzing it [UW46]. Both co-leaders ask Grace about her meaning (at [UW47], [UW48], and [UW50]). In the latter instance, Marsha also repeats back what she has understood Grace to say, seeking confirmation of comprehension. At [UW52] Marsha poses another interpretive question to Grace—one she needs to answer in order to establish her claim that the husband was following a plan in behaving as he did. In doing so, Marsha engages Grace in evaluating her position. At [UW54] Marsha repeats back the idea Grace has offered and asks her whether she means X or Y. At [UW56] Marsha again asks Grace to elaborate her reasoning—an invitation to clarify her position.

As indicated above, Marsha and Paula asked for clarification or repeated discussants' comments in order to clarify their meaning forty-seven times (see tables 6.2 and 6.3) during the discussion of "The Unruly Wife." Twenty-five times they posed questions aimed at identifying similarities and difference between positions (see table 6.5). If we add together the number of times co-leaders worked to clarify the meaning of what was said by asking discussants what they meant directly, repeating back what they said, or questioning the similarities and differences between positions, we find that they posed questions of clarification a total of seventy-two times (see table 6.6). In the excerpt that follows, we see another pattern that may have played an important role in helping the discussants reach their shared point of doubt and work together to form and evaluate possible resolutions using textual evidence:

[UW58]   MM: I have *Maggie* and then *Parker* and then *Katie*.

[UW59]   MAGGIE: Well, I just kinda thought that maybe he did plan it. 'Cause like I said earlier he might have just killed his animals to make her really scared and he might get some new ones from her 'cause she's scared so much.

[UW60]   MM: So, *Maggie*, it sounds like you're changing your mind because, in the beginning, you were talking about you felt you agreed with Tracy when she said, "He's crazy." But now are you changing your mind to what Grace . . . is talking about? And *Parker*, too, he talked about this, too. About how it was planned?

[UW61]   MAGGIE: Yes.

[UW62]   MM: Okay, then I'm going to ask you the same question: why did he plan this?

[UW63]   MAGGIE: Maybe because it said she was the devil and he wanted someone to work for him and so he acted like he was a nut case.

[UW64]   MM: So, like, was he scared of his wife?

[UW65]   MAGGIE: No.

[UW66]   MM: Like [Grace] said? Or did he want to turn his wife into something else? [The story said] she was a devil. Did he want to make her a different kind of person?

[UW67]   MAGGIE: Yeah, someone who'd be really scared and would do anything that he'd say.

[UW68]   MM: What kind of person did he want to turn her into?

[UW69]   MAGGIE: Maybe to, like, someone [who] if he said, "Go get me some water," maybe she would do that.

[UW70]   MM: I'm going to read one line that's on the last page. Line 123 and line 124. Let's take a second to get there [stops talking while discussants find the page]: "And from that day on, his wife was most obedient, and they lived happily ever after." So, *Maggie,* do you think, like you said, you think it's a plan? Some people think that it's a plan to scare his wife. Do you think it was a plan to make his wife obedient?

[UW71]   MAGGIE: Yes.

[UW72]   MM: I have *Parker* next on my list but, before I go to you, *Parker,* can I just go back to Grace and see what she thinks? Do you think that it was a plan because he was scared of his wife, or did he want to make his wife obedient?

[UW73]   GRACE: I think he wanted to make his wife obedient.

At [UW60] Marsha reminds Maggie of her previous position, again distinguishing it from the position of some of the others. When Maggie acknowledges that her view has changed, Marsha repeats the interpretive question that she had previously asked Grace [UW62]. Indeed, in the discussion of "The Unruly Wife" at Central, co-leaders repeated interpretive questions a total of twenty-two times (see table 6.1).

What is the effect of repeating interpretive questions in a discussion? When Marsha asks first Grace and then Maggie what the plan was intended to accomplish, she reminds them that the interpretation they offer—that the husband acted according to a plan—needs to be defended. If he acted strategically, then, says Marsha, one needs to describe the conditions that the plan aimed to bring about. The repeating of an interpretive question is a call to make or examine an argument: if one claims that the husband killed the animals in order to set up some desired state of affairs, then one needs to describe what that state of affairs was, using textual evidence.

As argued in Chapter 5, Marsha may take Maggie's answer to mean that the husband creates and executes a plan because he wants to make his wife obey him. I drew that inference because Marsha responds to Maggie by reading lines 123–124 and asking her whether the passage provides evidence for her claim. Maggie says yes, meaning, it seems, that the text suggests that the husband wanted to make his wife obedient. Grace seems to concur; the husband "wants to make his wife obedient," she says, indicating that she has changed her previous position, having been persuaded, perhaps, by the textual evidence found in lines 123–124.

The discussants at Central tried to respond to interpretive questions twenty-three times over the course of the discussion. Furthermore, they spontaneously appealed to evidence in the text fifty-one times (see table 6.8). It appears, then, that by repeating interpretive questions frequently, the co-leaders may have helped the genuine question take form by asking the discussants to look at it from various perspectives, as provided by the text.

In order to test the truth of the possibility, let us take one more step and ask: Of the six interpretive questions that the co-leaders asked in the discussion at Central, which ones were repeated, and how many times was each repeated? Table 6.9 tells the story.

Questions 1 and 5 received the most attention; the co-leaders posed each of them ten times. The similarity between Question 1 and Question 5 is also noteworthy: Question 1 asks whether the young man's behavior is planned, and Question 5 questions the motivation for such a plan. So not only is the discussion focused around two interpretive questions, but these questions are closely related to one another. Hence, the question of whether the husband is crazy or acts according to a plan is explored in depth.

Table 6.9. Frequency of reassertions of interpretive questions posed by leaders in Discussion 10

QUESTION	REASSERTIONS BY LEADER	REASSERTIONS BY DISCUSSANT	TOTAL REASSERTIONS
1. Does the husband kill the animals because he is irrational ("crazy") or because he is following a plan and pretends to be irrational?	10	7	17
2. Why do you think the young man told the animals to fetch water?	0	1	1
3. Based on the actions he has taken, is the young man lazy?	1	0	1
4. Does the story ever say the wife thought the young man was nice?	0	0	0
5. If you think it is a plan, then what was the husband aiming to accomplish?	10	10	20
6. Do you think the young man was pretending because he didn't want to be poor?	0	2	2

The importance of repeating interpretive questions is dramatized when we look once more at the following exchange, which took place near the end of the discussion:

[UW103]   TRACY: I really want to know . . . [pointing to *Arnie*] What's his name?

[UW104]   MM: *Arnie?*

[UW105]   TRACY: Yeah! What *Arnie* thinks. He hasn't said anything.

[UW106]   MM: Aha!

[UW107]   ARNIE: Let's see. . . . I think he's kind of crazy. . . . Because, well, I kind of think he's kind of . . . I think two things. He could be crazy or, like, the town, they got together, and, like, said, for the guy who married the crazy wife or the wild girl or whatever, and it was, like, "Dude!" Like . . . they had to get a town meeting or something? And . . . like, the father of the wild wife—

[UW108]   JEREMY: The wild, unruly wife . . .

[UW109]   ARNIE: The wild unruly wife, like, said, "Can you help me tame my girl?" Maybe. But I don't know. I kind of think the man could be crazy.

[UW110]   MM: So, Tracy, I'm gonna go back to you. What do you think about . . . your question was: "What does *Arnie* think?" What do you think about what he thinks?

[UW111]   TRACY: Well, it's kind of what *Maggie* was saying, and Grace, because, like, I think that she thinks that . . . he thinks that he was taming—and so does *Maggie* think that he [the husband] was kind of crazy, and so did *Arnie,* and I think that he's kind of crazy, too. And now I'm trying to . . . I'm thinking of what *Parker* and Grace [were] saying. I think [the husband] was trying to tame her to see what she had done to other people and how it feels to be crazy. . . how does it feel when crazy people do [things] to other people.

At [UW103] and [UW105], Tracy seems to ask Arnie a question that has become, for her, a genuine question: Did the husband kill the animals because he was crazy or because he was following a plan? She, rather than the co-leaders, repeats the question that they have asked ten times and in doing so invites a discussant who has not yet spoken to enter the conversation.[15] Having done so, at [UW111] Tracy works to resolve her point of doubt by reflecting on others' ideas. As argued in Chapter 4, she attempts to "fuse the horizons," or reconcile the perspectives of her peers with that offered by the text.[16]

So if it is the case that Tracy has formed a genuine question, then perhaps the co-leaders have helped her, and indeed, others, by repeating the question, by seeking clarification of responses to it, by asking for and offering textual evidence in order to defend claims, and by asking discussants what they now think about their claims, given what they have heard. These, then, are patterns of discussion leading that seem to help shared concerns take form in a group. They also help discussants identify possible resolutions and test their efficacy. As the interest in the question deepens, the students seem to become more open to the ideas of others in order to form and evaluate their positions. People seem to discover their need for the help that the thinking of others can provide. And so we see Tracy asking Arnie, a child whom she had just met, what he thinks about the issue. We see a learning community form as people work together to cultivate a shared question and an "object," or idea about its resolution. As we see the object beginning to emerge, we recall the words of Gadamer quoted at the end of Chapter 1: The partners in the conversation "come under the influence of the truth of the object and are thus bound to one another in a new community."[17]

CHAPTER SEVEN

Implications for Educators

THE CASE STUDY that we explored in Chapters 2–6, though small in scope, has implications for education in the twenty-first century. It provides evidence that participation in interpretive discussion, or discussion about the meaning of texts, can develop the habits and skills needed to cultivate questions. Thus it can help discussion participants identify interests, that is, things they wish to know. It can teach them how to pursue investigation—how to explore a text to find points of ambiguity and evidence with which to address the ambiguities. And as they pursue investigation, they develop habits of reflection, including those of listening, speaking clearly, and patiently relating what is said, heard, and read about the point of doubt so as to clarify and resolve it. It can also teach them how to participate in a community—how to listen to the ideas of others, work to understand them, relate them to their own ideas and interests, and hence to tolerate and appreciate others who have different perspectives and may come from racial, cultural, economic, or religious backgrounds that differ from their own.

The benefits of interpretive discussion have been well recognized. In Chapter 1, I mentioned the Great Books Foundation, which publishes texts and helps people learn to engage in Shared Inquiry, the center of which is what I have been calling "interpretive discussion." In addition, Mortimer Adler developed the Paideia program, which, like Shared Inquiry, engages students in discussion about the meaning of texts.[1] Adler's program was an outgrowth of the program for liberal arts education that he developed with Robert Maynard Hutchins at the University of Chicago in the 1930s.[2] The Philosophy for Children Program, housed at Montclair State University, develops its own texts, which are used to engage children in philosophical thinking.[3] *Questioning the Author*, described by Isabel Beck et al., also employs textual interpretation.[4] Although discussing the meaning of the text plays somewhat different roles in these various programs, it is important in all of them.

The contribution of the present volume is threefold. First, it provides a theoretical foundation for the practice of interpretive discussion and hence helps identify its assumptions, features, and anticipated effects. Second, it offers empirical evidence for claims about some of these effects. And although further research is needed to test the claims more broadly and to discover more about the consequences of participation in discussion, the findings of the case study lend direction to that testing. Third, it has implications for the kinds of experiences that educators need to have in order to successfully engage their students in interpretive discussion. Indeed, even with undergraduate and graduate students it is no easy task to be an effective leader of such conversations. It is to the implications for teacher preparation that I now turn.

The evidence taken from the case study suggests that educators need four kinds of experience if they are to lead interpretive discussions well. First, they need to practice leading, perhaps as part of a teacher preparation program, for as we saw, by the end of the project, Marsha and Paula were more successful in helping discussants come to a shared point of doubt and in pursuing its resolution than they were at the beginning. The opportunity to lead ten discussions (five texts and five clusters of questions) appears to have been critical to that progress.

Second, the case study suggests that educators need opportunities to prepare clusters of questions about the meaning of texts. In order to lead effectively, they need to develop a set of questions that clearly expresses their deepest point of doubt about a text's meaning. It takes patience, practice, and guidance to prepare clear questions, and a teacher education program, for example, can offer opportunities to both lead and prepare to lead interpretive discussions.

Third, educators need to reflect on the interpretive discussions that they lead and in which they participate, as the case study implies. We saw several instances in which reflection contributed to change in subsequent performance, as when Marsha and Paula, having pondered their discussion of *The Giving Tree* at Central, made greater effort to question the students at Sheridan about the meaning of their remarks. Likewise, following the plan for leading the discussions of "Jean Labadie's Big Black Dog," a plan that the co-leaders developed through reflection, gave the students more control over the topic of conversation and led to greater involvement in it.

Fourth, the evidence presented in this volume suggests that educators need to participate in interpretive discussions—to work with a leader and other discussants to define and address questions of shared interest. As was the case with Tracy, we can expect discussants to become engaged in and eventually initiate patterns that their leaders adopt.

In what follows, I take up each of the four activities—leading, preparing to lead, reflecting on, and participating in interpretive discussion. I explain some benefits of including them in a program that prepares people for teaching kindergarten through grade twelve and beyond. Along the way, I raise and address related issues. I do not suggest that these activities should replace classroom observation, student teaching, the study of discipline-specific teaching methods, or courses in the foundations of education. Rather, I describe how the Master of Science in Education program at Northwestern University, a fairly traditional program, weaves the study and use of interpretive discussion into its courses. I offer Northwestern as an illustration, not a model.

INTERPRETIVE DISCUSSION AS PART OF TEACHER EDUCATION: ONE EXAMPLE

The Master of Science in Education program at Northwestern University requires candidates for the degree to complete fifteen graduate courses. Each course lasts for ten weeks. Three of the courses focus on the development of what we call a "Master's Project," a research project that tries to resolve a question that has been defined by the candidate about teaching and learning practice. Other required courses include discipline-specific methods of teaching, a practicum (opportunities to observe in schools and reflect on those observations), student teaching, and courses about the foundations of education, including philosophy of education, social contexts of education, and psychology (child and adolescent development and learning as well as educating exceptional children). In addition, the students take learning sciences courses that explore the design of learning environments and the use of technology in teaching and learning situations.

When Paula and Marsha were in the program (1996–1997), they led one interpretive discussion as part of their course work. If it had not been for their Master's Project, they would have had only this one discussion-leading experience. Hence, more recently we have offered our students several chances to prepare clusters of questions, lead discussions in a practicum setting or with peers, and reflect on them. Let me describe some of these opportunities.

Research and Analysis I: Discussion and Question Development is the first course in the Master's Project sequence. It is usually a large class. For example, in the fall quarter of 2004, ninety-nine students were enrolled. I divided them into eight groups of twelve to thirteen each and engaged seven alumni of the program, all experienced educators who practice interpretive discussion, to work with me as section leaders. I led one section myself. Most of the sections were heterogeneous with respect to the academic discipline and grade level that the group members planned to teach.[5]

Each week, the seven section leaders and I met to discuss the text that the candidates would converse about in the following week. After reading the text and writing questions individually, we brought two interpretive questions (ones that we wished to resolve) to the meeting. We read our questions aloud and worked to identify common interests. In doing so, we arrived at a shared question. The question served as the Basic Question candidate for our cluster. After the meeting, each section leader wrote two follow-up questions for the BQ candidate. One member of our group revised the follow-up questions as needed so that they were clear and suggested ideas about resolution of the BQ. The latter was often revised to better express our deepest point of doubt.[6] I reviewed the draft of the cluster, and the other section leaders assessed my comments and suggested modifications.[7] The revision process, which was conducted by email, continued during the week. Before leading discussions in our sections, we reviewed the "final" version of our cluster together. During the first four weeks of the course, the section leaders led the discussions with their groups, having prepared to lead these sessions as described above.

For the fifth class meeting, the students in the class were asked to submit a cluster of questions about the meaning of a text that they wished to discuss with students in a classroom where they were observing. Group members in each section worked in pairs as co-leaders. Each pair identified a text for discussion that met the following criteria: (1) it passed the cluster test, that is, the co-leaders were able to write a cluster of questions about its meaning that met the criteria presented in Chapter 5; (2) it fit into the curriculum of the students whom at least one of the co-leaders was observing;[8] and (3) it met the approval of the mentor teacher at that observation site.

Once they selected the text, the co-leaders presented a copy of it, together with the cluster of questions that they had prepared, to the section leader. The section leader read the text and queried the co-leaders about the meaning of their questions so as to promote clarity. Just as Marsha and Paula worked through several rounds of cluster revision with me, the co-leading pairs revised their clusters several times with the help of their section leaders. When the section leader judged that the deepest point of doubt (BQ) and the follow-up questions met the criteria, the co-leaders were free to hold the discussion in the practicum setting.

Research and Analysis I offers our teacher candidates one opportunity to prepare for and lead an interpretive discussion. But one experience is not sufficient. Hence I also ask them to lead discussion in other courses.[9] One of these is Philosophy of Education, a class of one hundred students or more. Again, I divide the group into sections of twelve to fourteen people each and engage our alumni to work as section leaders. During the course, the candidates themselves lead class discussions with their peers. Every week a different pair of co-leaders in each section, with the assistance of the section leader, develops a cluster of questions about the meaning of the text under discussion. The section leaders, for their part, meet with me each week to prepare to assist the student co-leaders.

How do I work with the section leaders? As with Research and Analysis I, we come to our instructional team meeting with questions about the text under discussion, and together we develop a candidate for the BQ. The question is offered to the pairs of co-leaders, who sometimes choose to develop a cluster that explores its resolution. Sometimes the co-leaders choose a different issue altogether, depending on their interests. In either case, the section leader reviews drafts of the cluster, asking questions of clarification. I, as the course instructor, assist with the reviews.[10] The student co-leaders, having revised their clusters, lead the discussion in their sections, while the section leaders and I provide support during the class.[11] Afterward, the co-leaders post a written reflection on their experiences, identifying useful patterns and suggestions about preparation or leading. I respond to each reflection, often focusing on the issues raised.

Despite the challenging nature of the texts that are used in the course, co-leaders seem to be well prepared to listen to the questions of their peers, help them identify a shared point of doubt about the reading, and work toward resolution. Preparation of the section leaders in the instructional team meetings is critical, for as we discuss the texts and identify possible BQs, the section leaders become familiar with the text and are able to help the co-leaders develop their clusters of questions during several rounds of revision.

LEADING INTERPRETIVE DISCUSSION

What Is to Be Learned from Leading Interpretive Discussion?
Leading the first interpretive discussion is a soul-turning experience for many people. Until they find themselves in the position of the leader, they only vaguely glimpse the need for careful preparation and attentive listening. As questions, comments, and ideas swirl quickly around them, leaders rapidly discover that the time-consuming process of question revision pays off: they are able to locate passages of interest, hear ambiguities and points of doubt in discussants' remarks, and discern similarities and differences in their positions. Although, as the case study suggests, it takes time to develop the patterns that effective leaders follow, the desire to possess them is greatly enhanced by that initial discussion-leading opportunity. The following comment was posted by one person after the first co-leading experience: "I got a much, much greater appreciation for the whole idea of interpretive questions. . . . I didn't really understand their power until I had to lead a discussion. Digging deep into the text . . . in turn, learning more about the text throughout this digging, refining my questions, the collaboration with others, all of these things made this process really meaningful. Now I see this as such a great tool that can be used in so many educational contexts."[12]

The evidence from the case study suggests that leading interpretive discussions is useful to educators for at least four reasons. First, those who lead may develop effective discussion-leading patterns as they discover for themselves which ones are productive, given particular conditions. I had advised Marsha and Paula to set up queues of speakers, to repeat back the comments and questions that they heard, to call for textual evidence, and to summarize the progress made in forming and addressing questions, but my suggestions gained acceptance only as they proved useful. Furthermore, interpreting rather than evaluating the text, identifying similarities and differences in what people said (a step that often functioned as a means of summarizing what had been said), limiting the number of interpretive questions posed, repeating a very few often, and asking discussants directly about their meaning were all patterns that the co-leaders evolved through their experiences of leading (see Chapter 6, tables 6.1, 6.3, 6.4, 6.5, and 6.6).

Second, by leading discussion, people can learn to listen effectively, as every leader needs to do in order to help discussants develop a genuine question and pursue its resolution. In Chapter 6 I argued that over time, Marsha and Paula became better able to hear participants' questions, ideas, and points of ambiguity. Furthermore, they listened more perceptively by following the effective discussion-leading patterns that were evolving.

Third, leading discussion may teach people how to question as it teaches them to listen. The case study suggests that the most provocative questions posed by the co-leaders came when they were working to understand the discussants' remarks and asked about their meaning and implications. Think, for example, of the time Marsha questions Jeremy about why Kaddo harvested more corn than he could use. Her question arises after Jeremy says, "I don't see why he [Kaddo] made so much corn in the first place. He should have just made how much he needed" [KW1]. Marsha asks whether Jeremy thought Kaddo was greedy, as Beth had suggested earlier. When Jeremy says he does not know, Marsha suggests that perhaps Kaddo is "a kinda ignorant man"—an option she seems to have heard Jeremy suggest, although he may not have heard it in his own words. Marsha's ability to question Jeremy seems to follow from her ability to grasp and explore his intended meaning.

Or think of Paula when she questions Kurt and Parker about their so-called loose-dog hypothesis in the Sheridan discussion of "Jean Labadie's

Big Black Dog." At [JL4] she confronts them with evidence that counters their hypothesis, saying: "Well . . . if there is this big, black dog that was loose, how come at the very end of the story Jean gathers all the towns-people and he shoots this big black dog? And you see the picture—there's no big, black dog there—and he shoots it. And it says, 'And everyone agreed that the dog was gone for good.'" The evidence to which Paula points kept many, including Kurt, Parker, Walter, and Jeremy, in a state of aporia throughout the discussion as they worked to explain it.

Fourth, experience with leading teaches people to manage discussant participation. For example, how might a leader encourage participants who are reluctant to speak or persuade eager respondents to listen carefully? The case study data indicate that in each of the ten conversations, every discussant present spoke at least twice. Yet as table 7.1 shows, the rate of participation was not even, although there was progress toward that goal. I call the goal "equal air time," meaning that all the participants, excluding the leaders, make about the same number of comments and speak for about the same length of time in the discussion.

The average number of comments made by the leaders and the discussants in each of the ten conversations is shown in table 7.1. Over time, the number of speakers within 50 percent of the average at Central increased from two of seven in Discussion 1 to seven of eight in Discussion 7. At Sheridan, the participation did not even out as much: five of nine were within 50 percent of the average in Discussion 2, and that proportion was unchanged in Discussion 8. When the groups were mixed, only three of nine were within 50 percent of the average in Discussion 9, and six of ten were within 50 percent of the average in Discussion 10 (the discussion we observed).

Table 7.1 suggests what many believe to be true from personal experience: it is not always easy to achieve equal air time, even when the group is small. The mixed groups were in fact "new" groups, so it is not surprising that some spoke more than others. But the challenge of equalizing participation at Sheridan remained throughout the project. Of the comments made by the co-leaders in Discussion 8 (Sheridan), 31 percent were group-management comments—setting up a queue of speakers, organizing votes, quieting some so others could speak, for example—and 28 percent were attempts to clarify meaning. In Discussion 7 (Central), 23 percent of the leaders' comments were aimed at managing the group, and

33 percent aimed to clarify meaning. So the co-leaders spent 10 percent more time working to manage the group at Sheridan, perhaps because some, like Jeremy, were eager to speak much of the time.

Table 7.1. Average participation by school and by discussion

Central School	GT (1)	KW (3)	AP (5)	JL (7)	Overall
Co-leader comments (average)	44	90	44	105.5	70.9
Discussant comments	13.1	16	8.2	19.3	14.2
Discussants within 25% of average	1	5	2	1	
Discussants within 50% of average	2	7	6	7	
Number of discussants	7	9	9	8	
Sheridan School	GT (2)	KW (4)	AP (6)	JL (8)	Overall
Co-leader comments (average)	83.5	43.5	58.5	76	65.4
Discussant comments	22.1	11.9	17.7	20.8	18.1
Discussants within 25% of average	3	3	2	1	
Discussants within 50% of average	5	4	5	5	
Number of discussants	9	9	7	9	
Mixed group			UW (9)	UW (10)	Overall
Co-leader comments			134.5	108	121.3
Discussant comments			21.4	18.2	19.8
Discussants within 25% of average			1	4	
Discussants within 50% of average			3	6	
Number of discussants			9	10	

Often, experience in the group, along with efforts on the part of the leader, helps discussants move toward equal air time. Table 7.2 shows changes in the rate of participation for the four students in the case study whom we have watched most closely. Notice that Grace and Kurt spoke more frequently as the project progressed, whereas Jeremy and Tracy spoke fewer times. It seems that Jeremy and Tracy were choosing to listen more often, and Grace and Kurt were choosing to speak more often.[13] Perhaps each came to new appreciation of certain patterns of participation as the project progressed.

Table 7.2. Change in rate of participation of individual discussants

Central School	GT (1)	KW (3)	AP (5)	JL (7)	UW
Grace					
Spontaneous use of text	0	4	2	4	7
Evaluative comments	2	6	2	0	1
Total comments	4	11	7	13	21
Tracy					
Spontaneous use of text	9	6	7	8	7
Evaluative comments	5	6	4	1	1
Total comments	20	20	17	26	10
Sheridan School	GT (2)	KW (4)	AP (6)	JL (8)	UW
Jeremy					
Spontaneous use of text	3	7	17	15	7
Evaluative comments	10	14	4	2	1
Total comments	38	28	32	32	15
Kurt					
Spontaneous use of text	absent	0	2	4	7
Evaluative comments	absent	1	1	1	3
Total comments	absent	4	9	30	34

The reader may wonder why equal air time is desirable. Should not a teacher accept the fact that some students naturally talk more than others? Perhaps, but consider the following argument. Everyone in the group needs to learn the patterns required for textual interpretation. So everyone needs to raise questions and identify points of ambiguity in a text, formulate resolutions based on textual evidence, construct arguments in support of resolutions, evaluate the strength of arguments (their own and those of others), clarify questions and statements, listen to the questions and positions of others—especially difficult when these challenge their own thinking—and persevere in the face of complexity, confusion, and frustration. If group members speak for roughly the same amount of time, the discussion gives them equal opportunity to engage in the verbal aspect of these practices.

For example, raising questions requires people in a discussion to speak. Indeed, coming to a shared point of doubt requires that all participants enter the conversation, either voicing their questions or responding to those of others. We have seen Paula and Marsha learn to start the discussion by taking questions from several people, then asking others to respond or add to the list, and, finally, requesting that members choose the issue they wish to pursue. Optimally, all group members will contribute to such a decision. Likewise, constructing and evaluating arguments requires people to speak. They must cite relevant places in the text, offer interpretations, and draw inferences about the implications of their interpretations. Furthermore, to ask for and make clarifications also requires people to speak. In short, many of the goals one has for discussants in an interpretive discussion can only be met if they speak, and speak repeatedly.

Equally important to all the above activities is listening. For example, forming a shared concern goes beyond stating questions at the start of the discussion, for it is a clear question, expresses a genuine point of doubt, and is shared by others in the group. There is no way to arrive at such a question except by listening to the questions and comments of other discussants, as well as voicing one's own. Likewise, arguments cannot be evaluated until they have been heard and understood.

We have watched the co-leaders and the discussants who participated in the case study become better at speaking clearly and convincingly and at listening perceptively. If students are speaking for about the same amount of time, then they are listening for about the same amount of time as the others, and the opportunity to learn the patterns of textual interpretation is about the same for everyone.

A further advantage of equal air time is that if discussants speak for about the same amount of time, then at least in theory, the interests and the perspective of each person can be shared with all, and the group has access to more ideas than it would if only a few do most of the talking. As equal air time begins to prevail, fewer are left unheard, and everyone has access to a greater diversity of viewpoints and ideas.

Let me take up one more issue that may concern the reader: the amount of time the leader of an interpretive discussion speaks. I have just finished arguing for equal air time. Yet as indicated in table 7.1, in all ten discussions Marsha and Paula spoke more times than did any of the discussants. Some might maintain that one goal is to eliminate or minimize teacher talk.[14] Is that a goal of interpretive discussion? And if I am advocating equal air time, why should that goal not apply to the leaders as well as the participants?

The evidence from the case study suggests that Marsha and Paula needed to talk in order to follow effective discussion-leading patterns. That is, they needed to repeat back what they heard so as to grasp and clarify intended meanings, they needed to ask directly about meaning, they needed to identify similarities and differences in what they heard, they needed to pose questions, they needed to ask for textual evidence to support claims, and they needed to help participants locate evidence. By following these patterns, the co-leaders helped discussants develop shared questions and respond to one another in order to move toward resolution.

Over time, as we saw, some of the discussants began to follow these patterns themselves so that eventually one would expect the leaders to speak less frequently in the discussion. Often that happens. I believe, however, that leaders speaking less often should come as a natural consequence of the group's maturity. Indeed, that maturation may come more quickly if the leader speaks as much as necessary when the group first forms in order for it to reach the primary goal—that of forming and pursuing resolution of a shared point of doubt.

Co-Leading Discussion

Marsha and Paula worked as co-leaders in their discussion project. Together, they selected the texts and prepared clusters of questions, working to detect points of ambiguity and vagueness in their queries. While leading the discussions, they helped each other repeat back speakers' remarks, relate them to one another, identify points of ambiguity as well as similarities and differences, and question participants about their views. Keeping track of ideas that arise in discussion is one of the greatest challenges, and two people can learn to support one another in the endeavor. Frequently, we saw Marsha question discussants about an issue that had been posed by Paula, and vice versa. We also saw them help one another listen to and remember what had been said. The case study suggests, then, that teacher candidates should work as co-leaders in learning to lead discussion.

The reader might respond that learning to co-lead is not appropriate for novice teachers because they will be responsible for leading discussion by themselves much of the time once they hold positions in academic settings. I do not deny that they will need to work as solo leaders, but consider the following argument: working as a co-leader, both in preparing for and in leading discussion, teaches people to identify common interests, work together to reach the objectives, and use the actions of one another to define next steps, if not long-term courses of action. For example, the aim of the co-leaders may be to clarify the question that is of greatest concern to themselves or to the group, or it may be to help a discussant find evidence to support a claim. As co-leaders, they work together to reach the objective. Think, for instance, of Marsha's journal entry about preparing a cluster of questions for "Jean Labadie's Big Black Dog":

> [Paula] and I drove to [Central School] together and spent most of the time talking about the text and our game plan for leading. I was excited about the text, especially after [our] discussion last night. In a way that would make you proud, Sophie, we really pushed ourselves (after being so close to just accepting what we had and hanging up the phone). There were three questions—two in Paula's cluster and one in mine—that made us both realize that our issue was something larger, and we weren't quite there yet. Something [was] triggered, and all of a sudden it started coming together. It was a great moment, and Paula and I agreed to go back and rework our basic question. . . . I was excited to see how this work would play out in the discussion.

When Marsha says, "There were three questions—two in Paula's cluster and one in mine—that made us both realize that our issue was something larger, and we weren't quite there yet," she indicates that the three questions told them they had a shared concern that neither had articulated. I have argued that the presence of that shared but vaguely articulated doubt caused them discomfort and moved them to keep working toward clarification (see Chapter 5). Here is an instance in which the actions of the other—the questions that the other wrote—were used to work toward a new, more satisfying expression of their shared question.

Co-leading also presents the discussants with instances of people working together to achieve shared goals, for example, defining their actions using the actions of the other. Also visible are the moments when difference in the leaders' perspectives helps them reach a goal. Co-leading shows the discussants two people helping one another to discover something that, perhaps, is unknown to both.

Furthermore, when people begin to teach by themselves, they may find a co-leader in another teacher, a parent, a student, an administrator, or a community member. The requirements for the task are these: (a) the co-leaders read and study the material; (b) the co-leaders write questions about the meaning of the text, questions that are brought to the meeting in which the two leaders prepare the cluster of questions; (c) the co-leaders prepare a cluster of questions together, questioning each other until the point of doubt and the eight follow-up questions are clear; (d) during the conversation with the participants, the co-leaders work together to help them form and address a point of genuine doubt about the meaning of the text. Because co-leaders need no further credentials, they may be easier to locate than one might imagine.

Finally, the evidence from the case study suggests that co-leading may help people learn patterns of textual interpretation more fully than if they prepared for and led discussions by themselves. This is because co-leaders push each other to question, listen, and clarify ideas to an extent that those working alone may not achieve. Both Marsha and Paula learned to question the text, work toward clarifying their points of doubt, and follow discussion-leading patterns that helped discussants define questions and explore texts in order to resolve them. Both co-leaders became skilled at writing down what discussants said, linking ideas to one another, identifying similarities and differences, and hearing a shared point of doubt in the discussants' remarks, thereby helping create conditions under which it became possible to hear a challenging point of view.

PREPARING TO LEAD INTERPRETIVE DISCUSSION

If education programs offer people opportunities to lead interpretive discussion, then the programs need to support the preparation for those opportunities. As argued in Chapter 5, the clearer the cluster of questions that co-leaders developed prior to leading, the more effective they seemed to be in helping the discussants form and pursue a shared point of doubt. In preparing and revising the clusters of questions, leaders identify points of doubt about the meaning of texts that they care to resolve. They also locate passages that address the points of doubt, and in doing so, start down the path of resolution. And as they work to meet high standards of clarity and precision toward which the criteria for evaluating the cluster direct them, they develop the ability to express their questions clearly—to ask what they want to ask. They ready themselves for conversation that will engage others in seeking meaning.

Now, as the first step in preparing for discussion, the co-leaders must select a suitable text. So let us return to the topic of text selection and continue the exploration of it that was begun in Chapter 1.

Selecting Texts for Discussion
Any item with enough ambiguity to permit questioning of its meaning may be a suitable text for interpretive discussion. Hence the text may be a story or other work of fiction whose meaning is unclear. It may be a work of nonfiction as well. Or it may be an object such as a relic or artifact (Stonehenge, a totem pole, or implements unearthed on archeological digs). It may be a data set, a film, a photograph, a painting, a musical composition, or an example of architecture. In fact, nearly any item may be a text suitable for interpretive discussion, provided that the leader can develop at least one cluster of questions (a Basic Question and eight follow-up questions, all interpretive) about its meaning.

In general, a text is delimited in some way and hence may be examined as to its features and properties. A text might be an object that those practicing a discipline choose to investigate so as to learn more about it and, perhaps, about how knowledge of it can illuminate current ideas and beliefs. For example, scientists have long pondered whether the planet Mars supported microbial life at one time. Because water is required for life on Earth, scientists have studied Mars for evidence of water. Using telescopes, unmanned probes, and the laws of chemistry and astrophysics as they are currently understood, scientists have studied the planet and seen reflections that may have come from ice or geological formations suggestive of erosion by water. Mars rovers have examined soil and rocks where evidence of salts and mud were found. Does the evidence support the claim that there was once water on Mars? The answer to the question has implications for the issue of whether Mars at one time supported life.[15] For people knowledgeable enough to raise questions about it, Mars can serve as a rich text.

A text can also consist of multiple objects—objects that, if taken together, suggest questions and resolutions that otherwise might not arise. For example, a group studying American history might ask: Why did Americans decide to declare independence from England in 1776? The final version of the Declaration of Independence seems to be based on grounds of popular consent—the will of the people. Earlier drafts, however, emphasize particular abuses of the king of England—abuses that are mentioned but not emphasized in the final document.[16] Hence resolution of the question may vary depending on the drafts of the Declaration that one consults, and a well-defended resolution may require study of draft material as well as the published version.

Because a text that is suitable for interpretive discussion must be one in which the questioner finds ambiguity, it follows that the questioner is able to raise questions about its meaning that may be answered in more than one way, based on the evidence it provides.[17] Some texts are more ambiguous than others, meaning both that they offer multiple points of ambiguity and that they provide evidence for addressing the ambiguities that they raise. Such texts may be highly suitable for discussion, and teachers need practice in identifying sufficiently ambiguous texts.

Let us consider mathematics. Are there texts that are suitable for discussion in the areas of geometry, algebra, and trigonometry, for example? Indeed, is it possible to have an interpretive discussion at all in mathematics? If so, are there discussable texts suitable for elementary as well as high school students? Answering these questions requires time and practice in evaluating candidates for texts in the fields of mathematics. I have held interpretive discussions about sections of Euclid's *Elements* with high school students and adults.[18] Two teacher candidates in the program at Northwestern University led discussions about the drawings of M. C. Escher in a seventh-grade mathematics classroom.[19]

And yet the question remains: Can mathematics teachers lead interpretive discussions about texts that have a "right" answer—a resolution that the teacher knows and calls correct? The answer, I believe, is yes. If the text is a mathematics problem whose solution can be reached in multiple ways, then one may discuss which way is preferable, given the textual evidence or other specified criteria. The literature concerning mathematics education offers examples of students discussing strategies—that is, trying to determine the best ones—for addressing mathematics problems of many sorts.[20] In addition, some mathematical questions may have multiple answers, given textual evidence, and surely discussion is possible in these cases. Still, the question is worthy of reflection by mathematicians and mathematics teachers. So I leave further commentary on it to others.

As indicated in Chapter 1, the best test for ambiguity that I know is the cluster test. In selecting a text, leaders are sure it is discussable if they can write a cluster of questions about it. In attempting to do so, leaders discover whether there are at least eight places that suggest ideas about the answer to the problem of most concern—the BQ. If there are, they can be assured that the text is discussable, for they know there is at least one problem about its meaning that they can address with others by studying at least those eight places.

The cluster test is not the only one that a text must pass, however. In addition, it should be developmentally appropriate for the discussants and should suit curricular aims. Educators can benefit from repeated opportunities to select discussable texts that fit a variety of situations.

Preparing Clusters of Questions

Sometimes people question whether they can engage a group in an interpretive discussion without preparing clusters of questions about the meaning of the text beforehand. After all, cluster preparation takes time, and teachers often feel pressed for time. Isn't there a shortcut?

Given the data that the case study provides, as well as personal experience, I conclude that the answer to the question is no. Although teachers can ask questions about meaning without preparing clusters—questions they are given by a teacher's guide, colleague, or an expert, for example—they are not thereby prepared to lead discussion. This is because if they have not tried to address the questions by sifting through the evidence that the text provides, identifying possible resolutions, testing the strength of candidates for resolution against counterevidence as well as corroborating evidence, and clarifying the point of doubt they wish to resolve, they are not prepared to lead discussion. Since they have not worked to understand the text in this thorough way, they lack resources that the development of a cluster generates. What are those resources?

First, the questioning of themselves and the discussants that we watched Marsha and Paula carry out as the case study progressed came as a result of following patterns that are sometimes hard to follow. It is not always easy to accurately repeat back what has been said in effort to help others clarify their intended meanings. It is not always easy to help them identify points of ambiguity in the comments of one another and in the text. It is not always easy to pose possible meanings of discussants' remarks to help them specify the intended meaning. It is not always easy to accurately recite the similarities and differences between speakers' comments, to locate textual evidence that supports or refutes claims, or to listen to a perspective that challenges one's own. Forming a cluster of questions before the discussion heightens leaders' motivation to follow these patterns even when it becomes challenging to do so, for their well-cultivated point of doubt supplies them with curiosity that sustains their patience and effort, as we have seen.

Second, though leaders might get lucky in that an issue of interest to several participants arises easily—as happened in the discussion of "The Unruly Wife" at Central School—such a question must be cultivated if it is to sustain the discussion. That is, possible resolutions must be identified and tested to see whether they, given their implications, explain events in the text. Becoming familiar with the work, as one does in preparing a cluster of questions, furthers one's understanding of it and improves one's ability to locate relevant passages.

Now, precisely because it is demanding and time-consuming to develop a clear cluster of questions, that effort may sustain many activities that extend beyond the interpretive discussion itself, for the discussion may open participants to questions and interests that they continue to pursue after the conversation ends. And the understanding of the text that the teacher has gleaned from cluster preparation may prove a valuable resource to the students as they pursue their investigations.

The above notwithstanding, let me add that it may be appropriate for a group to work together to develop a cluster of questions. If, for example, the text is new to leaders as well as discussants, each person might write questions while reading, identify the interpretive questions, and share those that are of most interest with the others. If there is a shared point of doubt, then see if it is possible to write eight follow-up questions for it. If it is indeed possible to find eight (or even seven) places in the text that, if interpreted in at least one way, suggest ideas about resolution of the shared concern, then much will be learned about the meaning of the text in making the discovery. Other goals of interpretive discussion, such as helping members work together to form and evaluate arguments, may be met as well.

PARTICIPATING IN INTERPRETIVE DISCUSSION

It is difficult to lead an interpretive discussion if one has not been involved as a participant. By working with others to identify a shared point of doubt under the guidance of a well-prepared leader, one begins to comprehend the aim of the conversation. One also begins to envision how the aim is achieved, for, having felt the shared point of doubt take shape, one is in a position to identify and evaluate the effectiveness of various discussion-leading patterns in bringing it about.

Evidence from the case study indicates that as people participate in interpretive discussions, they begin to practice at least some of the patterns that the leaders follow, suggesting that one begins learning to lead while participating as a group member.[21] Recall, for example, how, as the project progressed, the co-leaders offered the discussants fewer references to textual evidence (see table 6.7), while discussants spontaneously appealed to the text with greater frequency (see table 6.8). As was the case with the co-leaders, at least some discussants became more focused on defending their claims with textual evidence.

Likewise, evidence from the case study presented in Chapter 2 suggests that at the start of the project, discussants as well as the co-leaders had difficulty distinguishing between interpretation and evaluation of the text. Discussion participation helps one develop a feeling for the difference. Indeed, discussants made fewer evaluative comments as the project continued (see table 6.2), suggesting both that they felt the difference between interpretation and evaluation and that over time their focus became more strongly oriented toward interpretation.

Furthermore, table 6.9 shows that in the discussion of "The Unruly Wife" that we observed, leaders repeated the following question ten times: Does the husband kill the animals because he is irrational ("crazy") or because he is following a plan and pretends to be irrational? The discussants reasserted the same question seven times. The co-leaders asked what the husband aimed to accomplish with the plan (question 5) a total of ten times, and participants reasserted that question another ten times. The pattern of raising the same interpretive question repeatedly was followed with greater frequency by discussants as well as leaders as the project progressed. Having discovered the efficacy of a practice, a discussant may initiate it if given the opportunity to lead the discussion.

In accordance with these findings, we offer students in the Master of Science in Education program opportunities to participate in many interpretive discussions. These discussions occur in the three courses of the Master's Project sequence, in Philosophy of Education, in Social Contexts of Education, and in psychology classes such as Childhood and Early Adolescent Development and Learning and Adolescent Development. In addition, students in practicum and student teaching seminars regularly analyze the meaning of texts where the "texts" are problematic situations encountered in school settings. Through conversation a shared point of doubt emerges, and facts in the situation are examined in light of that query. Here, however, the goal of the conversation is sometimes to identify appropriate next steps, given the resolution of the deepest point of doubt.[22]

REFLECTING ON INTERPRETIVE DISCUSSION

The data from the case study suggest that in addition to leading, preparing for, and participating in interpretive discussions, leaders need opportunities to reflect on their discussion experiences. In Chapter 1 I indicated that reflection should focus on the "accomplishments" of the discussion—accomplishments with respect to building a community of learners and the content of the conversation. We have observed Marsha and Paula reflecting on both of these topics. In what follows we look at reflections provided by students and section leaders who have led, prepared for, and participated in interpretive discussion in the Master of Science in Education program at Northwestern. What have been their responses to these opportunities?

Student Responses to Discussion Leading

Below, I consider survey data collected in 2003–2004 as well as comments posted online after discussion experiences. The surveys were administered at the conclusion of the courses in which people had the opportunity to lead, prepare for, and participate in interpretive discussion. The questions were open-ended: respondents were asked to comment on all the activities in the course, including those related to discussion. Categories of response were created when reviewing the data. Where several people made the same comment, we set up a category to reflect that view. The reader should bear in mind that with respect to table 7.3, a respondent may have made more than one comment.

Table 7.3. Student feedback about discussion leading

	FALL 2003 COURSE 406	FALL 2004 COURSE 406	SPRING 2004 COURSE 413	SUMMER 2004 COURSE 402
Number of respondents	67	83	96	51
Positive comments				
Interesting/useful	46	37	59	19
Beneficial to have co-leader	0	1	11	1
Negative comments				
Rigid/contrived	3	0	1	1
Need more support/ explanation	1	1	5	2
Problems with co-leader	0	0	5	0

The data presented in the table suggest that leading interpretive discussion is a popular activity, which in turn suggests that the candidates felt successful in their efforts to do so. For each course, there were fewer negative than positive comments. Furthermore, many respondents volunteered that discussion leading was useful or interesting. The following, for example, was posted to the online discussion board shortly after a discussion in the Philosophy of Education class:

> As [a co-leader], I took notes on the discussion. I just recorded what people were saying. Sometimes it was hard to keep up, but having a computer really helped; I thought periodically about the progress we were making either toward or away from [resolution of] the BQ; I tried to make sure people were sup-

porting their ideas with text; I tried to steer the discussion
back to the BQ when it got away from [the BQ]; I tried to
make sure all terms were defined; I summarized once or
twice where we were, where we had come from.[23]

Candidate Responses to Preparing Clusters of Questions
How do teacher candidates respond to opportunities to prepare clusters
of questions? Table 7.4 summarizes data from the 2003–2004 school
year. The survey item they were given was open-ended. It read: Please
comment on the activity of preparing a cluster of questions. The categories presented in the table were created on review of the data in attempt
to summarize them.

Table 7.4. Student feedback about cluster preparation

	FALL 2003 COURSE 406	FALL 2004 COURSE 406	SPRING 2004 COURSE 413	SUMMER 2004 COURSE 402
Number of respondents	67	83	96	51
Positive comments				
Interesting/useful	28	31	40	6
Good preparation for discussion leading	10	0	6	4
Helpful to understand text	5	1	7	2
Negative comments				
Too much work/tedious	2	1	24	5
Rigid/contrived	7	2	3	0
Repetitive/busywork	0	0	4	7

Perhaps the most striking thing about table 7.4 is that twenty-four
responses indicate that preparing to lead discussion was "too much work/
tedious" in course 413, The Philosophy of Education, in which candidates
led discussions about Plato's *Republic*, Rousseau's *Emile*, and Dewey's
Democracy and Education. So although there were fifty-three remarks to
the effect that developing the clusters was interesting and helpful in that

course, the lack of comfort with the process was apparent. Three of the five section leaders agreed with the assessment.

What to do? In the spring of 2005 we hit upon the idea of assigning two helpers from the section to each co-leading team. These helpers would aid the co-leaders in refining their questions, and question review took place online so that others in the section could participate. After the co-leaders posted their clusters of questions to the online discussion board, the helpers would question them in an effort to clarify the deepest point of doubt and the follow-up questions. The section leaders then read the third or fourth round of cluster preparation and directed my attention to difficulties that remained. Hence the task of clarifying clusters of questions was shared by a larger group—the co-leaders, two helpers, the section leader, and myself—thereby lessening the burden on the section leaders and co-leaders. In addition, acting as helpers gave the candidates another opportunity to refine their ability to detect ambiguity and clarify questions.

Class members and section leaders have endorsed the addition of helpers to the preparation phase. In the spring of 2006, a candidate in the philosophy of education course posted the following comment to the online discussion board in reflecting on the experience of preparing clusters of questions: "The one thing that I found to be the most helpful in the preparation process was receiving feedback from the helpers and the TA [section leader]. Our helpers did a great job of helping us to clarify and revise our ideas. After you and your co-leader spend so much time immersed in the text and your own questions, it was helpful to get another perspective."[24] As was true of Marsha and Paula, the writer seems to have become engaged in the experience of preparing clusters of questions in spite of the challenges it entailed. The contributions of those reviewing the rounds of preparation seems to have been greatly appreciated.

Candidate Responses to Participating in Discussion

Course evaluations indicate that engaging in interpretive discussions is a popular activity. For example, when asked to comment on the aspects of Research and Analysis I (Course 406) that were most useful, forty of the sixty-seven respondents surveyed in 2003 mentioned participation in interpretive discussion. Likewise, forty-one of those who responded to the survey of the Philosophy of Education class (Course 413), conducted in the spring of 2004, offered the same comment. When asked directly about participation in discussion, fifty-eight people in that class said that they enjoyed the experience, and ten more made favorable comments about the section leader.

Response to the activity of preparing to participate in discussion was more complicated. Each week, class members were asked to read the text and write questions about its meaning as they read, much as the instructional team did in preparing for its meetings and as Marsha and Paula had done. After rereading the text and reflecting on the questions they had written, the students selected two interpretive questions from the list in which they had particular interest. Next, they were to phrase each question with reference to a particular passage that, if explored, suggested ideas about its resolution. Students were asked to quote and interpret the relevant passage in phrasing the question and then to use the interpretation to suggest a resolution (see Criterion 4 of the criteria for evaluating a cluster of questions listed in Chapter 5). They brought to class two questions worded in the prescribed format.[25]

As analysis of the case study data has emphasized, it is not easy to write clear interpretive questions that explore a point of genuine doubt. Indeed, some candidates objected to the assignment, as table 7.5 indicates.

Table 7.5. Comments about preparation of interpretive questions

	FALL 2003 COURSE 406	FALL 2004 COURSE 406	SPRING 2004 COURSE 413	SUMMER 2004 COURSE 402
Number of respondents	67	83	96	51
Positive comments				
Helpful to understand text/prepare to participate in discussion	11	9	29	16
Negative comments				
Rigid/contrived	11	10	16	0
Need more support/ explanation	7	9	6	11
Repetitive/busywork	6	3	5	7

Two of the most frequently aired complaints were that the process of preparing the interpretive questions was "rigid/contrived" (37 of 297 responses received in 2003–2004) or "repetitive/busywork" (21 responses). I surveyed the section leaders in those courses to see whether they agreed with the complaints.

Of the fourteen section leaders who replied, eight disagreed with the assertion that writing interpretive questions is "rigid/contrived." One of the six who agreed with the candidates wrote that the process would seem that way if writing interpretive questions is "seen as a rote system of quoting text without relation to a larger issue." Another wrote: "When [candidates] don't take [writing interpretive questions] seriously, they can be artificial."

Nine of the section leaders disagreed that writing interpretive questions is "repetitive/busywork." One of the five who agreed with the candidates commented, "Could be repetitive, but this does not mean that it is not valuable." Another stated that "when students do not have an understanding of the process" writing the questions may seem "repetitive/busywork."

Under what conditions do people find it meaningful to write interpretive questions in preparation for discussion? By comparing information presented in tables 7.3, 7.4, and 7.5, one can see that in three of the four courses surveyed in 2003–2004, the number of positive comments about question preparation increased when the activity occurred in the context of cluster preparation, as opposed to preparation for participating in discussion. In the case of Research and Analysis I (Course 406), the frequency of positive responses more than tripled (forty-three and thirty-two [table 7.4] compared to eleven and nine [table 7.5]); in the case of Philosophy of Education (Course 413), it was nearly double (fifty-three [table 7.4] compared to twenty-nine [table 7.5]). In addition, the number of comments to the effect that question preparation was "rigid/contrived" or "repetitive/busywork" decreased when the questions were written in the context of cluster preparation: there were twelve responses of "rigid/contrived" in the four classes surveyed (table 7.4) rather than thirty-seven (table 7.5) and eleven responses of "repetitive/busywork" in the four classes surveyed (table 7.4) rather than twenty-one (table 7.5).

It appears, then, that developing interpretive questions in preparing for discussion leading rather than discussion participation changes the meaning of the activity. Why might that be? The section leaders asked questions or made comments to help clarify the questions that the students prepared for discussion participation. When they were preparing to co-lead discussion, however, students found the activity of writing the questions more social, and the increased opportunity for dialogue may have been enjoyable. Perhaps most salient is the fact that when preparing to lead discussion, there was a clear purpose for working to clarify the questions: the anticipation of leading discussion about the meaning of the text that they were exploring. By identifying an underlying BQ for which each interpretive question in the cluster suggests an idea about resolution, one sees its relationship to a larger issue, that is, one sees how working to clarify the questions can advance the project of resolving the BQ and better understanding the text. Once people are faced with the challenge of co-leading a discussion about the meaning of a text, the purpose and value of clarifying interpretive questions become clear.

Conclusion

AS MANY have recognized,[1] "Questions that are genuine questions, that don't have pre-specified answers, and evaluations that validate students' contributions, are going to create a different kind of classroom discourse and a different level of engagement."[2] When the authors speak of "genuine questions, that don't have pre-specified answers," they would seem to include questions that students wish to resolve—ones for which neither students nor teachers have definitive resolutions. When they speak of "evaluations that validate students' contributions," they refer to teacher responses that affirm students' efforts to address such questions. Accordingly, the authors suggest that when students are expected and helped by teachers to form and address genuine questions, the content of classroom conversation will change, and students will become more closely involved with academic activity than is often the case in schools today.

In this book I have argued that participating in interpretive discussion can help students cultivate genuine questions. They do so by finding points of ambiguity in texts, constructing and evaluating arguments to resolve them, clarifying questions and statements, listening to challenging perspectives, and thus coming to understand things they do not know and want to find out. Furthermore, we have seen students and teachers alike persevering with these tasks in the face of confusion, fatigue, and frustration. The data from the case study, as well as those gathered subsequently from polling people in the Master of Science in Education program at Northwestern University, suggest that participating in interpretive discussion can engage people in reflection. It can, as the authors quoted above say, "create a different kind of classroom discourse and a different level of engagement."

Hence it behooves us to explore the possibility of integrating interpretive discussion into the teaching of academic subjects at the elementary and secondary levels as well as in higher education. And it behooves us to explore the possibility of preparing educators to lead interpretive discussion and thereby engage students in the activities of cultivating questions and interpreting texts. Furthermore, the challenge is especially pressing today, at the dawn of the twenty-first century. Why is that so?

There are at least three reasons. First, the new millennium opened with a mandate from Washington, D.C., that no child be left behind. Under the provisions of the education statute, the measure of success is scoring well on standardized tests that are identified at the state and the national levels. Failure to achieve standards of adequate yearly progress in reading and mathematics, as measured by the tests, can result in the dismissal of principals and faculty, and indeed, in school closings.[3] And as Zumwalt notes, "test preparation and 'teaching to the tests' have driven the curriculum, even in schools that should have no fear of failing."[4] Serious critique of the No Child Left Behind Act will continue.[5] Although the goal of educating every child is a worthy one, the data from the foregoing case study encourage us to explore a focus that can help students and their teachers pursue the activities of questioning and textual interpretation, which, as we have seen, are both engaging and productive.

Second, now, more than at any time in the past, success in life demands that we communicate with one another despite differences of race, culture, economic and political background, and religious persuasion. Not only has technology opened opportunities for easy contact with others around the world, but many communities find that they have become more diverse. We cannot so easily maintain the ambivalence toward difference of which Austin Sarat speaks.[6] As we have seen, learning to treat difference as a resource for finding and addressing shared concerns is something that participation in interpretive discussion engenders.

Finally, there is the issue of equity—the opportunity for all students to develop the ability to question, interpret, and reflect on both what they know and what they want to find out. The writer W. E. B. Du Bois argued that institutions of learning must encourage "Freedom of Spirit," which requires the freedom to question. Through questioning comes discipline and understanding of oneself, he maintained. These follow from taking the initiative to form and answer the questions, try things out, and identify the consequences of the trials.[7] Du Bois made his argument in a speech given at Fisk University in 1924 in which he hoped to persuade its leaders and alumni that black people who had been enslaved would never gain the knowledge, skills, and habits of mind needed to compete successfully with whites unless Fisk encouraged its students to question.

The equity that Du Bois was seeking has not yet been achieved.[8] The evidence from the case study supports his claim that cultivating questions and pursuing their resolution develops the patience and the will to study—what he seems to mean by "discipline." Should not education offer all students the opportunities they need to develop discipline and self-understanding and thus become free and productive members of society? And should not the preparation of teachers focus their attention on the art of turning the soul, helping them develop the skills and dispositions needed to practice the art?

APPENDIX A

DISCUSSANT PARTICIPATION

Table A.1. Number of comments by discussant, Central School
discussions*

DISCUSSANT	GT (1)	KW (3)	AP (5)	JL (7)
PB	39	78	49	79
MM	49	102	39	132
Cynthia	22	14	11	14
Damian	absent	24	4	absent
Ethan	12	6	absent	13
Grace	4	11	7	13
Jason	absent	12	5	26
Joseph	8	26	12	21
Sonya	absent	18	9	11
Tanis	24	13	6	30
Tracy	20	20	17	26
Troy	2	absent	3	absent
Unattributed				
("child," "chorus," etc.)	1	2	1	2
Total number of comments	181	326	163	367

*I use the following abbreviations in this and subsequent tables: GT=*The Giving Tree;* KW="Kaddo's Wall"; AP="Allah Will Provide"; JL="Jean Labadie's Big Black Dog"; UW="The Wild, Unruly Wife." "C" indicates that the discussion took place at Central School; "S" indicates that it took place at Sheridan School. The numbers in parentheses refer to discussion number.

Table A.2. Number of comments by discussant, Sheridan School discussions

DISCUSSANT	GT (2)	KW (4)	AP (6)	JL (8)
PB	57	48	50	49
MM	110	39	67	103
Arnie	24	2	17	7
Beth	22	11	26	12
Brian	10	7	6	15
Daphne	6	absent	absent	4
Jeremy	38	28	32	32
Katie	43	28	absent	40
Kurt	absent	4	9	30
Maggie	15	3	absent	absent
Parker	15	13	12	31
Walter	26	11	22	16
Unattributed ("child," "chorus," etc.)	20	8	3	8
Total number of comments	386	202	244	347

Table A.3. Number of comments by discussant, mixed-group discussions

DISCUSSANT	UW (9)	DISCUSSANT	UW (10)
PB	118	PB	82
MM	151	MM	134
Beth (S)	32	Arnie (S)	8
Brian (S)	18	Grace (C)	21
Cynthia (C)	11	Jeremy (S)	15
Damian (C)	absent	Katie (S)	29
Daphne (S)	35	Maggie (S)	26
Ethan (C)	4	Parker (S)	30
Jason (C)	8	Sonya (C)	16
Joseph (C)	47	Tanis (C)	21
Kurt (S)	34	Tracy (C)	10
Walter (S)	4	Troy (C)	6
Unattributed	4	Unattributed	0
Central students (5)	70	Central students (5)	74
Sheridan students (5)	123	Sheridan students (5)	108
Total	466	Total	398

CLUSTER OF QUESTIONS FOR *THE GIVING TREE*

In the clusters that follow, my comments are printed in italics. I indicated that a question was OK when it met all the criteria for evaluation (see Chapter 5).

ROUND 1 WITH SHG'S COMMENTS

Basic Question: Why do the boy and the tree love each other?—*OK*

Follow-Up Questions:

1. Does the tree love the boy because the boy needs her (17–20, 27–29, 36–38, 52–53)?—*here, I would quote the line that gives you evidence for your suggestion: E.g., when the text says, "And so the boy cut off her branches . . . And the tree was happy (28–30)," does it mean the tree was happy because it could give something to the boy that he needed? If so, does the tree love the boy because giving the boy what he needs makes her happy?* When the boy leaves (22–31), is the tree unhappy because she misses the boy's company or because she thinks the boy doesn't need her anymore?—*Again, quote lines to give evidence. Actually, this is probably a separate question—why the tree is unhappy when the boy leaves. It needs to be worded in a way that relates it directly to the BQ.*

2. Does the tree love the boy because she is able to give to him (*The Giving Tree*, 17–20, 27–29, 36–38)?—*quote specifically. A possible revision, given the idea developed in question 1: if the tree loves the boy because giving him things he needs makes the tree happy, why is she unhappy when the boy cuts down her trunk (39)? (If the question is changed in this way, does the first part of the question—set off above—add anything?)*

3. Does the tree love the boy because the boy loves her (7–8)? If the boy loves her, why does he keep going away (11, 22, 31)?—*Quote relevant passage and pose question.*

4. When the boy takes things from the tree (20, 29, 38), is he being selfish or is he giving back to her (in some way?)—*Vague. Try to relate the possibility that the boy is selfish to the problem of why the boy loves the tree and the tree loves the boy.*

5. Does the boy keep coming back to the tree because he needs something (16, 25, 34, 50) or because he misses/needs her?—*The missing is coming up for a second time. You might quote lines which suggest he misses the tree and relate his missing the tree to his loving her to develop this possibility. Does the boy return, line 40, because he misses the tree or because he needs something? If the former, is it because he misses his giving friend? Someone who loved him?*

6. Does the boy only realize that he loves the tree as an old man (43–51) or does he realize it all along?—*Try to quote evidence that he has this realization; relate to BQ.*

7. Does the boy love the tree because the tree is happy each time he returns (23, 32)?—*Add: If so, why does the text say, "I am sorry, boy, said the tree, but I have nothing left to give you," which suggests she is not happy to see the boy?*

8. Is the tree happy because the boy has returned (55) or because it is still able to give the boy something—a quiet place to sit and rest?—*Relate to BQ: if the latter, does the tree love the boy because she is able to give him what he needs once again?*

—*New idea I have had: if their reasons for loving each other change, does the boy come to realize the tree, in giving what she had, was loving him, which brings him back to the tree and makes him love her in a new way? ("After a long time, the boy came back again," 40).*

ROUND 2 WITH SHG'S COMMENTS

Basic Question: Why do the boy and the tree love each other? *OK.*

Follow-Up Questions:

1. When the text says, "And so the boy cut off her branches and carried them away to build his house . . . and the tree was happy" (28–30), does it mean the tree was happy because it could give something to the boy that he needed? If so, does the tree love the boy because giving to the boy what he needs makes her happy? *OK—relates to BQ directly; provides evidence for suggestion.*

2. If the tree loves the boy because giving him the things he needs makes her happy, why does the text say, "And the tree was happy . . . but not really" (39) when the boy cuts down her trunk? *OK—ditto. Any ideas about resolution?*

3. When the text says, "And the boy loved the tree . . . very much and the tree was happy" (7–8), does it mean that tree was happy—*how about: does it mean that the tree loved the boy because he loved her, which made her happy?*— because the boy loved her? If so . . . SHG—we're stuck and confused!!!— *Why do you need "if so"? You have quoted a line which suggests possible resolution to the BQ (that the tree loves the boy because he loved her, for his loving her made her happy!) I think you're okay.*

4. When the text says, "I want a boat that will take me far away from here. Can you give me a boat?" (34–35), does the boy ask for this because he is selfish—*meaning: wants/expects tree to give him her trunk? Or because he loves the tree and knows it always wants to give him things?—Relation of this question to BQ? Need to make this explicit.*

5. When the text says, "And after a long time the boy came

back again" (40), does the boy return because he misses the tree or because he needs something? If he returns because he misses the tree, does he miss the giving friend who loved him?—*Add: and if so, does the boy love the tree because she loved him?*

6. In returning to the tree as an old man who says, "I don't need very much now" (50), does the boy do so because he still needs one more thing—a stump to sit on—or because he misses the tree? If the latter, does the boy love the tree for reasons beyond its giving?—*Good; such as?*

7. Does the tree love the boy because he keeps returning, needing something?—*add: and giving the boy things he needs makes the tree happy?* If so, why does the text say, when the boy again returns, "I am sorry, Boy, said the tree, but I have nothing left to give you" (41), which suggests it is not happy to see the boy? Is the tree not happy to see the boy because she thinks she has nothing more to give him?

8. When the text says, "Well, an old stump is good for sitting and resting. Come, Boy, sit down. Sit down and rest" (52–53), is the tree happy because the boy has returned or because she is still able to give the boy something? If the latter, does the tree love the boy because she is able to give him what he needs once again? *OK*

You have made progress. Notice that my main suggestions had to do with filling in your reasoning in detail so that your interpretation of the text in relation to the BQ becomes explicit. See 3, 5, 6, and 7.

CLUSTER OF QUESTIONS FOR
"JEAN LABADIE'S BIG BLACK DOG"

In the clusters that follow, my comments are shown in italics. I indicated that a question was OK when it met all of the criteria for evaluation (see Chapter 5).

ROUND 2 WITH SHG'S COMMENTS

BQ: Whose story is the story of the big black dog?—*meaning: Do Jean and André control people with their stories of the big black dog, or do the stories control all those who hear and contribute to them? (You may be able to improve upon this. But I hope this begins to further clarify the point of doubt.)*

Follow-Up Questions:

1. When Jean says, "Have you seen my big black dog, André?" (165), does the author want the reader to believe that Jean—who originally creates the story of the big black dog—controls André with the story? *(You might find a better quotation)—(omit?—is the storyteller originating the story)?* If so, does being the storyteller make it Jean's story?—*Here, it seems to me, you are asking whether Jean has control of the story as its creator, right? Hence my suggested revision of the BQ.*

2. When André says, "Yes, yes, I do see him now," (167), is this

evidence that Jean is drawing André into the story—and
making him believe it, so that Jean is in control of André?
Or is André beginning to control Jean by contributing to
the story himself? If so, why does the text say, "Jean was
pleased" (p. 167)—*(Omit, as it seems to add no new meaning—does the story still belong to Jean, or does the story now
belong to BOTH of them?) [To the reader: I now think the
co-leaders were correct in adding the part I told them to omit,
as it relates directly back to their BQ.]*

3. When André says, "I saw your big black dog in the road"
   (167), as a storyteller, is Jean pleased that André believes his
   story, or pleased that he—André—is getting involved in it—
   meaning: getting involved in creating it? If the latter, is Jean's
   annoyance due to the fact that André's involvement is
   (omit—not passive—but is) making it André's story, which is
   taking control away from Jean? *(You might want to quote
   168—". . . He was also annoyed . . .")*

4. When André says, "Someone will surely mistake such a fast
   dog for the *loup-garou*" (168), is he doing this so that the
   story no longer will involve only Jean and André? Is involv-
   ing others a way for André to take the story away from Jean,
   or to share it?—*meaning of "share it"? I would work with this
   question further (good quotation) and relate it more explicitly to
   the new BQ.*

5. The text tells us that André says of the dog, "Everyone is
   afraid of him," and that "Jean was angry" (169). When André says this, is he attempting to spread Jean's story or to
   reshape the story as his own? Is Jean angry because he has
   lost control as the storyteller, or because André is telling it
   to others? *(and Jean intended it as a story for André only?)—
   good start; rework in line with suggested BQ?*

6. When André says, "But today on the road he growled and
   snapped at me" (169), does this suggest that André *(as the
   listener/storyteller)* is taking the dog out of Jean's yard and
   setting him loose? If so, is this "setting loose" a metaphor
   for unleashing the story in the villagers' imagination

because the dog is now a threat to them? —(Whose story is it now? Why?) —*vague; sounds like a "teacher" question!) Again, I'd rework in light of altered BQ.*

7. When the villagers see the big black dog "running behind (the) house," "running around the corner of the store," and "running through the graveyard" (173), are they adding to Jean's story [or] to André's story, or are they creating a story of their own? If the latter, does this imply that Jean and/or André have lost control of the story? —*Yes, here you seem to have evidence for the story itself having the control, not the tellers.*

8. When Jean says, "There, it is done. That is the end of my big black dog. Isn't that true?" (177), is this evidence that Jean is asking others to believe HIS story? Or is he asking them to change THEIR story? —*Meaning? Is Jean trying to regain control of the story by adding the dog's death to it? Can he do this only if the people believe, which suggests that he cannot create the story alone, but that everyone—tellers and hearers—must agree on the story? If they agree, do they thereby persuade themselves of the truth of a certain story and give that story power over them?*

NOTES

PREFACE

Epigraph. H-G. Gadamer, *Truth and Method,* ed. Garrett Barden and John Cumming (New York: Crossroad, 1985), 429.

1. The Great Books Foundation uses the phrase "Shared Inquiry" to refer to a very similar approach. See *Shared Inquiry Handbook: A Basic Guide for Discussion Leaders and Participants* (Chicago: Great Books Foundation, 2007). The foundation, located in Chicago, publishes the Junior Great Books series.

2. L. Darling-Hammond and J. Bransford, eds., *Preparing Teachers for a Changing World: What Teachers Should Learn and Be Able to Do* (San Francisco: Jossey-Bass, 2005).

3. C. Tracey, "Listening to Teachers: Classroom Realities and NCLB," in *NCLB Meets School Realities,* ed. G. Sunderman, J. Kim, and G. Orfield (Thousand Oaks, Calif.: Corwin/Sage, 2005). The author states that teachers surveyed in Fresno, California, and Richmond, Virginia (1,445 responses to a survey sent to 1,866) in 2004 indicated that they "thought they needed . . . an end to an excessive focus on tests that distorts and narrows the educational process" (103).

4. D. Kuhn, *Education for Thinking* (Cambridge: Harvard University Press, 2005), argues that school learning experiences shape one's conception of learning: "Based to a large extent on their own school experiences, children form conceptions of what learning is about that may well last a lifetime. The prevailing emphasis on standardized test preparation and performance . . . makes one likely conception of learning that of drilling arbitrary information into memory to pass tests" (17). I will argue that a focus on cultivating questions can develop a conception of education that

values the habits and products of reflection and hence offers a vision of learning that differs from that of memorizing facts.

5. See, e.g., R. P. Dennis and E. D. Moldof, eds., *Becoming Human,* vols. 1 and 2 (Chicago: Great Books Foundation, 1977).

6. The Spencer Foundation is located in Chicago, Illinois.

7. *Junior Great Books,* Series 3, First Semester; Series 5, Second Semester; and Series 4, Second Semester (Chicago: Great Books Foundation, 1992). These stories also appear in the 2006 edition of *Junior Great Books,* Series 3–5.

CHAPTER ONE: INTRODUCTION TO INTERPRETIVE DISCUSSION
Epigraph. R. Strier, *Resistant Structures: Particularity, Radicalism, and Renaissance Texts* (Berkeley: University of California Press, 1995), 25.

1. Plato, *Meno,* in *Collected Dialogues of Plato,* ed. E. Hamilton and H. Cairns, trans. W. K. C. Guthrie (Princeton: Princeton University Press, 1961), 71B.

2. Plato, *Meno,* 80B, where Meno, too, confesses that he does not know what virtue is.

3. Plato, *Meno,* 79E, where the question finally confronts Meno with his state of perplexity and opens him to seek understanding of Socrates' claim that learning takes place through recollection.

4. In the *Republic,* Socrates describes "dialectic" as the means by which understanding is constructed. See, e.g., *The Republic of Plato,* 532–534, ed. and trans. Allan Bloom, 2d ed. (New York: Basic, 1958).

5. M. Heidegger, *Early Greek Thinking,* trans. D. F. Krell and F. A. Capuzzi (New York: Harper and Row, 1975), 61. Heidegger writes: "To gathering belongs a collecting which brings under shelter. . . . The safekeeping that brings something in has already determined the first steps of the gathering and arranged everything that follows." Heidegger seems to mean that the gathering has been done with a purpose in mind and that that purpose orders what is gathered and in what way. Seeking is like gathering in that what is unknown guides the search and how its object is understood.

6. I. L. Beck et al., *Questioning the Author: An Approach for Enhancing Student Engagement with Text* (Newark, Del.: International Reading Association, 1997).

7. J. T. Bruer, *Schools for Thought: A Science of Learning in the Classroom* (Cambridge: MIT Press, 1993).

8. M. Lampert and D. L. Ball, *Teaching, Multimedia, and Mathematics: Investigations of Real Practice* (New York: Teachers College Press, 1998); M. Lampert, *Teaching Problems and the Problems of Teaching* (New Haven: Yale University Press, 2001).

9. A. S. Palinscar and A. Brown, "Reciprocal Teaching of Comprehension-Fostering and Comprehension-Monitoring Activities," *Cognition and Instruction* 1 (1984): 117–175.

10. A. S. Palinscar and B. G. Ladewski, "Literacy and the Learning Sciences," in *Cambridge Handbook of the Learning Sciences,* ed. K. Sawyer (New York: Cambridge University Press, 2006).

11. R. D. Pea, "The Social and Technological Dimensions of Scaffolding and Related Theoretical Concepts for Learning, Education, and Human Activity," *Journal of the Learning Sciences* 13, no. 3 (2004): 423–451.

12. D. C. Edelson and B. J. Reiser, "Making Authentic Practices Accessible to Learners: Design Challenges and Strategies," in *Cambridge Handbook of the Learning Sciences,* ed. K. Sawyer (New York: Cambridge University Press, 2006).

13. L. B. Resnick, *Education and Learning to Think* (Washington, D.C.: National Academy Press, 1987).

14. B. Rogoff and J. Lave, *Everyday Cognition: Its Development in Social Context* (Cambridge: Harvard University Press, 1984); B. Rogoff, *Apprenticeship in Thinking: Cognitive Development in Social Context* (New York: Oxford University Press, 1990).

15. A. H. Schoenfeld, ed., *Mathematical Thinking and Problem Solving* (Hillsdale, N.J.: Lawrence Erlbaum Associates, 1994).

16. The tradition has many adherents; an early representative is L. M. Rosenblatt, *Literature as Exploration* (New York: Modern Language Association, 1995). Others are mentioned in the notes that follow.

17. E. D. Hirsch, *Validity in Interpretation* (New Haven: Yale University Press, 1967), 129, argues that understanding precedes interpretation. That is, interpretation becomes necessary when understanding comes to a stop— when there is something in the text that is not understood. Gadamer uses the term "interpretation" more broadly, as we shall see.

18. For a convincing argument, see J. Kertscher, " 'We Understand Differently if We Understand at All': Gadamer's Ontology of Language Reconsidered," in *Gadamer's Century: Essays in Honor of Hans-Georg Gadamer,* ed. J. Malpas, U. Arnswald, and J. Kertscher (Cambridge: MIT Press, 2002).

19. H-G. Gadamer, *Truth and Method,* ed. Garrett Barden and John Cumming (New York: Crossroad, 1985), 347–350.

20. Ibid., 350.

21. Ibid., 94. See page 94 for a description of play and also pages 99–108, where the concept of play is related to representation, transformation, and interpretation.

22. Now, likening the act of understanding the meaning of a text to playing a game did not originate with Gadamer. Indeed, he himself argues that Plato's concept of "dialectic" has the character of play. See, e.g., H-G. Gadamer, "Plato's Unwritten Dialectic," in Gadamer, *Dialogue and Dialectic: Eight Hermeneutical Studies of Plato,* trans. P. C. Smith (New Haven: Yale University Press, 1980), 154–155. In the Platonic dialogues, the text that was being discussed was not written. Interpretation of the text, however, employs a back-and-forth movement that follows the rules of conversation and argumentation.

23. Gadamer, *Truth and Method,* 266.

24. Ibid., 325–326.

25. M. Heidegger, *What Is Called Thinking?* trans. J. G. Gray (New York: Harper and Row, 1968), 14, writes, "To learn means to make everything we do answer to whatever essentials address themselves to us at a given time. Depending on the kind of essentials, depending on the realm from which they address us, the answer and with it the kind of learning differs." The "essentials," it seems, are aspects of the situation that draw particular responses, including questions, from us; what we "learn" consists of the answers to these questions. My interpretation of the quoted words draws on the example of the carpenter that Heidegger gives on p. 15.

26. In Chapter 7 I consider the possibility of the students' and discussion leaders' preparing for discussion together by writing questions about the text and reading them to one another. Doing so may bring them to a shared point of doubt—something the group does not know and wishes to find out through further study of the text.

27. H. R. Jauss, *Question and Answer: Forms of Dialogic Understanding* (Minneapolis: University of Minnesota Press, 1989), 213.

28. W. Iser, *The Act of Reading: A Theory of Aesthetic Response* (Baltimore: Johns Hopkins University Press, 1980), 97. Iser describes how one's question or "interest" directs one's understanding of the text.

29. J. Grondin, *Introduction to Philosophical Hermeneutics*, trans. J. Weinsheimer (New Haven: Yale University Press, 1994), 28.

30. *An Introduction to Shared Inquiry: A Handbook for Junior Great Books Leaders*, 4th ed. (Chicago: Great Books Foundation, 1999), 42–44.

31. D. Donoghue, *The Practice of Reading* (New Haven: Yale University Press, 1998), cites Stanley Cavell's reading of Shakespeare's *Macbeth* as an example of "disinterested" reading, explaining that "nothing he says about the language of *Macbeth* could be used for any ideological purpose" (70). Apparently, Cavell was engaged in textual interpretation when he wrote the essay: he was trying to understand the play's meaning rather than evaluate it or use it for a purpose beyond the text.

32. Donoghue, *Practice of Reading*, 97.

33. Donoghue sides with Gadamer, Iser, and Fish and against Richards, Hirsch, and others who argue that interpreting the meaning of a text is determining the author's intended meaning. S. Fish, *There's No Such Thing as Free Speech . . . And It's a Good Thing, Too* (New York: Oxford University Press, 1994,) 182–183; I. A. Richards, *Principles of Literary Criticism*, ed. J. Constable (New York: Routledge, 2001), 28; Hirsh, *Validity in Interpretation*, 255. There are complex issues related to the debate that go beyond the scope of the present text. In grounding my vision of interpretation in Gadamer's hermeneutic orientation, I side with him on the issue. Hence, I assume a broad vision of what may be questioned and what may call for interpretation.

34. Fish, *No Such Thing*, 182–183. Fish argues that interpretation, defined as translation, proceeds on the assumption that the content of the text is not

random, that the text has intention, although the intention of the text may not be the author's intention. I accept that position as consistent with the orientation of interpretive discussion.

35. Heidegger, *What Is Called Thinking?* 17, would seem to agree when he says: "Whenever man is [drawn into the enigmatic], he is thinking. . . . All through his life and right into his death, Socrates did nothing else than place himself into this draft, this current, and maintain himself in it. This is why he is the purest thinker of the West." The first goal of leaders and discussants, as it was for Socrates, is to find questions that are of concern to them. And these questions arise from not only what one encounters but from that with which the encounter is made—one's beliefs and thoughts.

36. Iser, *Act of Reading*, 118–119.

37. Gadamer, in *Truth and Method*, describes the dialectic, or back-and-forth, movement as taking place between the parts of the text as these are studied, and the idea about the overall meaning of the text. His view is similar to Iser's: what is remembered and what is expected contribute to the reader's sense of the whole. What is encountered in the study of any given point in the text is related to what is both remembered and expected and may result in a modification of either: "This process of construing is . . . governed by an expectation of meaning that follows from the context of what has gone before. It is also necessary for this expected meaning to be adjusted if the text calls for it" (259).

38. Iser, *Act of Reading*, 118–120.

39. P. Grice, *Studies in the Way of Words* (Cambridge: Harvard University Press, 1989), 26, argues that participants in a conversation (or authors of texts) are expected to observe the "cooperative principle," which means, roughly, that they will, at any given point, say what is required, given the goal of the discourse. Grice seemingly would maintain that observation of the cooperative principle renders consistency a goal of discourse, for how can cooperation—such as that needed for building a house—be achieved if the discourse is not consistent?

40. W. E. Empson, *Seven Types of Ambiguity* (1930; New York: New Directions, 1947 [1st U.S. ed.]), 1.

41. These include the following: first, the word or grammatical structure is effective in several ways at once (ibid., 2); second, the word or phrase could, from a logical or grammatical point of view, have several meanings (48–49); third, two ideas, both relevant to a context, are referred to by one word, as with a pun (102); fourth, two or more possible meanings are in conflict but combine to offer a more complex idea on the part of the author (133); fifth, an author discovers his own idea in the act of writing, and a term comes to mean more than one thing by the end (155); sixth, a statement says nothing because of tautology, contradiction, or irrelevance, and the reader is left to invent statements about meaning that conflict with one

another (176); seventh, possible meanings, given the context, show a
fundamental division because they are in conflict (192).

42. M. M. Bakhtin, "Discourse in the Novel," in *The Dialogic Imagination*,
trans. and ed. C. Emerson and M. Holquist (Austin: University of Texas
Press, 1981), permits further insight into the sources of ambiguity in a text
when he writes: "At any given moment of its historical existence, language
is heteroglot from top to bottom: it represents the co-existence of socio-
ideological contradictions between the present and the past, between dif-
fering epochs of the past, between different socio-ideological groups in the
present, between tendencies, schools, circles and so forth, all given a bodily
form. These 'languages' of heteroglossia intersect each other in a variety
of ways" (291). These comments pertain to oral as well as written language.
Bakhtin seems to mean that because statements are the consequences of
mixing expressions and ideas from many sources, they express contradictions that arise from the mixing. In preparing clusters of questions, the
interpreter-translator identifies points of contraction—lifts them out of the
text, so to speak—by bringing to bear his or her own beliefs, which are
themselves the product of heteroglossia.

43. I recommend, as the Great Books Foundation has, that leaders prepare a
question set or "cluster" of at least eight interpretive questions. The concept of a "cluster" is discussed extensively in Chapter 5. For the Great
Books Foundation's presentation of the concept, see *Introduction to Shared
Inquiry*, 58–62.

44. L. Wittgenstein, *Philosophical Investigations I*, 3d ed., trans. G. E. M.
Anscombe (New York: Macmillan, 1958), sec. 7.

45. Gadamer, *Truth and Method*, 445–446.

46. Wittgenstein, *Philosophical Investigations I*, e.g., secs. 150, 151; Gadamer,
Truth and Method, 96.

47. Grice, *Studies in the Way of Words*, describes conversational rules, many of
which are followed in an interpretive discussion. See, e.g., 24–40, which
describe rules of conversational logic. These are conventional rules related
to the cooperative principle described in note 39 above and are followed
where operative.

48. Bakhtin, "Discourse in the Novel," 282, in the spirit of Gadamer and
Wittgenstein, adds that when understanding is achieved, it is because
a question has been answered.

49. Plato, *Republic*, 518b–d.

50. Plato, "Theaetetus," in *Collected Dialogues of Plato*, ed. E. Hamilton and H.
Cairns, trans. F. M. Cornford (Princeton: Princeton University Press, 1961).
"Theaetetus" is said to be from the late period of Plato's dialogues, written
before his third trip to Syracuse, where he was called in as a political
consultant, probably between 370 and 361 B.C. The dialogue opens with
a conversation between two people who have known both Socrates and

Theaetetus. One of the two records the conversation between Socrates and Theaetetus, and the other person listens as a slave reads it aloud.

51. Plato, *Theaetetus*, 150a–151e.

52. Gadamer, *Truth and Method*, 269.

53. Ibid., 351.

54. J. Lave, "Situated Learning in Communities of Practice," in *Perspectives on Socially Shared Cognition*, ed. L. Resnick, J. M. Levine, and S. T. Teasley (Washington, D.C.: American Psychological Association, 1991).

55. See, e.g., J. Piaget, *Six Psychological Studies*, trans. A. Tenzer, ed. D. Elkind (New York: Vintage/Random House, 1968), essay 1, "The Mental Development of the Child."

56. For example, J. Fodor, *The Language of Thought* (New York: Crowell, 1975), 27 and passim.

57. Wittgenstein, *Philosophical Investigations I*, secs. 224, 241–242. See also secs. 1–7, in which Wittgenstein explores the ways in which conventions of word use are taught. Wittgenstein says that we may follow a rule blindly (sec. 219), but that when we follow it, we "know how to go on" (secs. 150–155).

58. J. Lave and E. Wenger, *Situated Learning: Legitimate Peripheral Participation* (New York: Cambridge University Press, 1991), esp. 94–105.

59. Ibid., 93.

60. Ibid., 50.

61. Lave, "Situated Learning," 67.

62. Ibid.; Gadamer, *Truth and Method*, 267.

63. J. Dewey, *Democracy and Education* (New York: Macmillan, 1916), 87.

64. Ibid.

65. A. Sarat, "The Micropolitics of Identity/Difference: Recognition and Accommodation in Everyday Life," in *Engaging in Cultural Differences: The Multicultural Challenge in Liberal Democracies*, ed. R. Shweder et al. (New York: Russell Sage, 2002), 397.

66. R. Shweder, "What About Female Genital Mutilation?" in *Engaging in Cultural Differences: The Multicultural Challenge in Liberal Democracies*, ed. R. Schweder et al. (New York: Russell Sage, 2002), 247–248.

67. Gadamer, *Truth and Method*, 445–446.

68. Anthropologists such as Richard Shweder offer a perspective on cultural practices that are foreign to Westerners (see, e.g., note 65 above); that perspective enables them to raise new questions. Without perspective, the questions would not arise.

69. Here we hit upon another hotbed of controversy. E. D. Hirsch, for example, argues that the only correct interpretation of a text is that which conveys what the author meant to say (*Validity in Interpretation*, 207). Gadamer, on the other hand, argues that there may be many correct interpretations and that correctness depends not on grasping the author's intent but on viewing the text in terms of the questions posed about its meaning. For further

discussion of Gadamer's view of truth, see the interesting essay by Jens Kertscher, "'We Understand Differently if We Understand at All,'" 135–156.

70. Modern theories of learning such as those described in the learning sciences literature have many points in common with the interpretive discussion approach. For example, the paper by J. Andriessen, "Arguing to Learn," in *The Cambridge Handbook of the Learning Sciences*, ed. R. K. Sawyer (New York: Cambridge University Press, 2006), describes argument development as a means of learning by people in a group.

71. Gadamer, *Truth and Method*, 341.

CHAPTER TWO: FINDING A SHARED CONCERN: THE PROJECT BEGINS

1. The names of all participants in the case study, including those of the two co-leaders, have been changed.

2. I quote a description of that conversation presented by the co-leaders in their unpublished master's project, completed and submitted in August 1997.

3. The Urban/Suburban Northwestern Consortium Project, begun in 1996–97, gradually expanded to include most of the teacher candidates in our program. The consortium, which includes several public and private urban and suburban K–12 schools, was funded by a grant from the Joyce Foundation in Chicago from 2000 to 2004.

4. The abbreviation stands for Illinois Goal Assessment Program. IGAP has since been replaced by other standardized tests.

5. For example, B. Glaser and A. Strauss, *The Discovery of Grounded Theory: Strategies for Qualitative Research* (New Brunswick: Aldine Transaction, 1967, reprinted 2006), 2; A. Strauss, *Qualitative Analysis for Social Scientists* (Cambridge: Cambridge University Press, 1987); M. Miles and A. Huberman, *Quantitative Data Analysis*, 2d ed. (Thousand Oaks, Calif.: Sage, 1994); A. Strauss and J. Corbin, *Basics of Qualitative Research: Grounded Theory Procedures and Techniques* (Thousand Oaks, Calif.: Sage, 1990); A. Strauss and J. Corbin, *Basics of Qualitative Research: Techniques and Procedures for Developing Grounded Theory* (Thousand Oaks, Calif.: Sage, 1998).

6. M. Cochran-Smith and S. Lytle, *Inside/Outside: Teacher Research and Knowledge* (New York: Teachers College Press, 1993), 43.

7. I. Harris, "What Does 'The Discovery of Grounded Theory' Have to Say to Medical Education?" *Advances in Health Sciences Education* 8 (2003): 49–61.

8. I quote from classroom discussions and interpret the excerpts with reference to questions about discussion patterns that were followed by both the leaders and the participants. The patterns were uncovered as the investigation proceeded. For a system of transcription that marks intonation and gesture, see A. S. Pihlgren, "Socrates in the Classroom: Rationales and Effects of Philosophizing with Children" (Ph.D. diss., Stockholm University, 2008).

9. All quoted passages are from S. Silverstein, *The Giving Tree* (New York: Harper and Row, 1964). This quotation is from line 1 (pages are unnumbered; line numbers are given).

10. Ibid., lines 7–8.

11. Ibid., line 21.

12. Ibid., lines 34–35.

13. Ibid., line 39.

14. Ibid., lines 41–52.

15. Each contribution to the dialogue is numbered for ease of reference. The numbering runs consecutively and begins anew with each text to permit referencing across discussions and chapters.

16. N. M. Sanders, *Classroom Questions: What Kinds?* (New York: Harper and Row, 1966), 2.

17. The meaning of "personal experience" is explored in the remainder of the present chapter. L. M. Rosenblatt, *Literature as Exploration,* 5th ed. (New York: Modern Language Association, 1995), discusses the role of personal experience in making interpretation. For example, at 78 and passim, she argues that personal experience plays a role in text interpretation. See also L. M. Rosenblatt, *The Reader, the Text, the Poem: The Transactional Theory of the Literary Work* (Carbondale: Southern Illinois University Press, 1994) at, e.g., 186. I concur, and indeed I argue, with Gadamer and Rosenblatt, that readers draw on personal experience in coming to understand a text. When people evaluate a text, however, they use personal experience to provide the criteria for evaluation. When they interpret a text, the criteria for judging claims about its meaning come from the text, as it is interpreted.

18. See, e.g., S. Haroutunian-Gordon, *Turning the Soul: Teaching Through Conversation in the High School* (Chicago: University of Chicago Press, 1991), 118–131. In my account of the evaluative discussion between Mrs. Prince and her students about premarital sex, the teacher asks whether the students believe that people should have sexual relations before they marry. In so doing, she interrupts the discussion about the meaning of *Romeo and Juliet* in order to explore the students' views of the issue. Their views are expressed with reference to criteria that they hold on the basis of their personal experiences.

19. Here is an example of the drive to build a consistent interpretation of which Iser speaks. The move that Paula makes at [GT28] illustrates the way observing Grice's "cooperative principle" (see Chap. 1, n. 39) moves those participating in a conversation to work toward consistency.

20. From a Wittgensteinian perspective, posing interpretive questions in the context of an interpretive discussion points the way in which the conversation is to continue. One who responds appropriately to the questions knows "how to go on" according to the rules of discussion (*Philosophical Investigations I,* 151) and will answer by making interpretations of the text, not evaluating it.

21. "Spontaneous use of the text" refers to any attempt by a discussant to use specific passages in the text to ask a question, answer a question, or comment on another discussant's answer, without being prompted to do so by a leader. The discussant must use a specific text reference, even if he or she does not cite an exact line number in so doing.

22. At some moments interpretive questions can sound like evaluative questions, and vice versa. I point out examples as we encounter them in pages that follow.

23. These excerpts show why interpretive discussion may be said to be an example of a language game, because we see how language and action are woven together by rules that players follow.

24. Silverstein, *Giving Tree,* lines 20–21.

CHAPTER THREE: FINDING A SHARED CONCERN: THE PROJECT
CONTINUES

1. H. Courlander and G. Herzog, "Kaddo's Wall," in *The Cow-Tail Switch and Other West African Stories* (Austin, Tex.: Holt, 1947).

2. Plato, *Meno,* 84A.

3. Here Paula, who is struck by Walter's remark, tries to query him about his assumptions: Would he give away his corn because of generosity or because of concern for the future? Once Walter's beliefs and reasoning are clear, the group may return to the text to see if there is evidence that Kaddo reasoned similarly or held the same assumptions. One might say that Paula is trying to understand Walter's "fore-conceptions," as Gadamer calls them—the tacit beliefs that he would hold if he were in Kaddo's circumstances. Much as Gadamer argues, querying assumptions begins when something in the text (in this case, Walter's statement) draws our attention (see Chapter 1).

4. R. Gilstrap and I. Estabrook, "Allah Will Provide," in *The Sultan's Fool and Other North African Tales* (New York: Holt, Rinehart, and Winston, 1958).

5. Ibid., 35.

6. If questioned further, Grace might maintain that although she said, "Yes, I think he [the snake] was working trying to get the bird to fall down out of the tree," she did not mean that the snake was working hard. It is possible that she did not change her mind after all.

7. Gilstrap and Estabrook, "Allah Will Provide," 34.

8. H-G. Gadamer, *Truth and Method,* ed. Garrett Barden and John Cumming (New York: Crossroad, 1985), 259.

9. See Chap. 1, text accompanying n. 38.

10. N. Carlson, "Jean Labadie's Big Black Dog," in *The Talking Cat and Other Stories of French Canada* (New York: HarperCollins, 1952).

11. Ibid., 163.

12. Ibid., 166.

13. Ibid., 172.

14. Ibid., 176.

15. Wittgenstein, *Philosophical Investigations I*, sec. 151.

16. R. Strier, *Resistant Structures: Particularity, Radicalism, and Renaissance Texts* (Berkeley: University of California Press, 1995), 4, writes: "An insight that explains or illuminates a great deal in a text . . . does not have to explain everything and be everywhere valid. [One should avoid] the moment when resistance in the text is overcome rather than acknowledged." Although Jeremy appears perplexed and perhaps dissatisfied that he cannot explain all the facts, it is clear that he acknowledges his obligation to try to reach the goal, as do others such as Kurt and perhaps Parker. It is also clear that Jeremy acknowledges his failure rather than denying it, much as Strier seems to urge.

CHAPTER FOUR: MIXING THE GROUPS

1. D. J. Manuel, "About What Happened to a Young Man Who Married a Very Wild and Unruly Wife," in *Spanish Stories (Dual-Language)*, trans. A. Flores (1960; repr. New York: Dover, 1987), 4–11.

2. The last classroom conversations involved in the project took place on March 17 and 18, 1997. The conversation at Central occurred on March 18.

3. The title of the story is abbreviated to "The Unruly Wife" in the analysis that follows in the present chapter and thereafter.

4. Manuel, "Unruly Wife," 7, lines 29–30.

5. The names of the participants from Sheridan School are italicized in the present chapter.

6. Manuel, "Unruly Wife," 7, lines 50–51.

7. Italicization in this sentence expresses the speaker's emphasis.

8. In so saying, Grace returns to the very fact that Tracy pointed out and argues for the opposite conclusion: when Tracy questions the killing of the horse, she seems to reject the idea that it is a carefully planned action. Grace, however, seems to insist that killing the horse is not the act of a crazy person in this instance. As Marsha seems to recognize, however, the burden is on Grace to explain what the husband hopes to accomplish with such a plan.

9. Here again, we may be seeing an instance in which the drive for consistency is moving the reflection, in accordance with Iser.

10. See table A.3 in appendix A, which shows the number of times each participant spoke in the discussion.

11. H-G. Gadamer, *Truth and Method*, ed. Garrett Barden and John Cumming (New York: Crossroad, 1985), 341.

12. I call these "agreed-on facts" because they were justified, either by reasoning or by pointing to the text, and no one objected to them.

13. J. Dewey, *Democracy and Education* (New York: Macmillan, 1916), 87.

14. See appendix A, table A.3.

15. See table 6.9, which indicates the interpretive questions that were raised

by participants or leaders and the number of times that the questions were repeated.

16. L. Wittgenstein, *Philosophical Investigations I*, 3d ed., trans. G. E. M. Anscombe (New York: Macmillan, 1958), sec. 150.

CHAPTER FIVE: LEARNING TO QUESTION

1. My definition of a "discussable text" implies that some texts, at least for some readers, are not discussable. In so saying, I do not mean that the reader is not interpreting while perusing these texts—quite the contrary, as argued in Chapter 1. For a given reader, however, some texts contain either few obstacles to interpretation (D. Donoghue, *The Practice of Reading* [New Haven: Yale University Press, 1998], 80), and some, although they contain obstacles, or points of ambiguity, as I call them, provide little evidence for resolving them. In both cases, it is difficult to discuss the works, and I would call them "non-discussable," at least for that reader.

2. As explained in Chapter 1, my approach is grounded in the assumption that every reader can and does make interpretations—by which I mean translations—when reading. The process of preparing the cluster of questions makes the experience of interpretation a conscious process that can be discussed with others, evaluated, and modified. It makes interpretation into a social experience over which one has control, much as Donoghue has noted (*Practice of Reading*, 106).

3. The second reading may accomplish several things. First, it may change one's perspective on particular passages, for with the second reading, one has initial grasp of the whole. Second, the questions about the meaning of the text which have begun to form may direct the reading down paths that were not followed initially. Often, one sees evidence for resolution of the questions that was not apparent on the first reading. In short, points of ambiguity are both clarified and addressed on the second reading.

4. W. Iser, *The Act of Reading: A Theory of Aesthetic Response* (Baltimore: Johns Hopkins University Press, 1980), 17–18, argues that building a consistent interpretation is the work of every reader. A question that one raises about the meaning of the text is a way into understanding it, provided that one can find evidence in the text with which to address the question. Relating the evidence to resolution of the question yields an interpretation—an understanding of the text with respect to that query. The cluster of questions that they prepared suggests that the novice co-leaders were seeking a consistent understanding of the boy's character, given the facts provided by the story. Their goal of making a consistent interpretation may have interfered with that of helping the discussants to do likewise.

5. See appendix B, which presents two rounds of cluster preparation for *The Giving Tree* with my comments and questions.

6. Excerpts from the four rounds of preparation for "Kaddo's Wall" are presented in the text that follows.

7. What follows is a response to the sentence reprinted above from an alumna, section leader, and teacher who uses interpretive discussion in her classroom: "As human beings with a variety of different experiences, we tend to 'project' our assumptions, our definitions, our opinions onto the written word if we do not carefully read the quoted words—'no more, no less.' It happens almost subconsciously until the discipline of interpretive discussion draws our attention to these 'prejudices.' For me, this was the most useful lesson that linked interpretive discussion and encouraging/seeking to understand diversity of thought in discussion." Pers. comm. (Spring 2004).

8. See appendix C, Round 2 of the preparation for "Jean Labadie's Big Black Dog," with my comments.

9. My analysis of the data supports Iser's claim that the goal of making a consistent interpretation drives the inquiry and that questions are generated as material in the text thwarts that effort (see note 4 above).

10. See the description of the criteria for evaluating clusters of questions presented above, where I distinguish between questions in the form of issues and single possibilities and open questions. The latter do not suggest ideas about possible resolutions of the question, whereas issue questions suggests two, and single-possibility questions suggest one.

CHAPTER SIX: LEARNING TO LEAD DISCUSSION

1. The discussion of "Allah Will Provide" at Central School opened with neither the prepared BQ nor discussants' queries. Apparently, the students did not raise their hands to pose questions or make comments once the reading of the story concluded. Paula begins with an evaluative question that, apparently, was of interest to her.

2. Participants may be encouraged to enter the conversation by (1) requesting that they interpret a passage, (2) asking them whether they agree with an interpretation that has been given, or (3) asking them to find textual evidence that might support a claim, for example.

3. As noted above, it is not always so easy to distinguish an interpretive question from an evaluative one. If one is aware of the different kinds of responses that each type elicits, however, then one is likely to modify the question until the kind of response that is intended is clearly communicated.

4. There were cases in which the co-leaders repeated discussants' comments and thus questioned their grasp of the speaker's intention. We coded such instances as attempts to understand the speaker's meaning.

5. The increased effort to help speakers clarify meanings during the Sheridan discussion may have occurred as a consequence of the reflections on the conversation about *The Giving Tree* quoted above.

6. The increase cannot be explained by saying that Discussions 9 and 10 were longer than Discussion 1.

7. Table 6.2 indicates a jump in the number of times leaders queried discussants about their meaning in the first conversation about "Kaddo's Wall" (Discussion 3). That discussion focused on the meaning of the terms "self-ish" and "greedy." Preparation for the discussion had drawn the leaders' attention to these terms, which may have affected the subsequent classroom discussion. The sustained querying of speakers' meanings did not take place until the last four discussions in the project, as table 6.2 indicates.

8. As indicated above, "spontaneous reference to the text" refers to any instance in which a discussant makes a specific text reference without being prompted to do so by the co-leaders. The spontaneous reference can be used to either ask or answer a question, make a comment, or evaluate another discussant's comment. The key is not how the text is used, but that the leaders do not prompt the discussant for the text reference (e.g., by asking, "Can you tell us where that happened?"; "What makes you think that?"; "What line are you talking about?").

9. J. Lave and E. Wenger, *Situated Learning: Legitimate Peripheral Participation* (New York: Cambridge University Press, 1991), 113–117, argue that those who participate as apprentices can learn from their interactions with the mature members and gradually incorporate the practices of the latter into their own patterns of action, although they may reject some of the practices. In fact, Lave and Wenger's perspective helps explain what happened to the discussants and the co-leaders participating in the project. In the present instance, the generally productive practice of referring to textual evidence is repeated by the discussants with increased frequency—a testimony to the efficacy of limited peripheral participation.

10. As indicated above (see Chapter 3, note 3), here Paula explores what Gadamer calls "fore-conceptions"—the tacit assumptions or beliefs with which Walter approaches the circumstance in which Kaddo finds himself. The practice of investigating tacit beliefs and assumptions was repeated ten times over the course of the discussions.

11. The excerpts from the discussion about "Jean Labadie's Big Black Dog" that were not quoted in Chapter 3 are identified with roman rather than arabic numerals, so as to preserve the numbering given in Chapter 3.

12. It may now be clear why I find Gadamer's understanding of interpretation as translation so useful: it is in trying to say, in one's own words, what the text says that one discovers points of ambiguity and hence the beginnings of genuine points of doubt. And these, if cultivated, may be productive in an interpretive discussion.

13. I should point out that in order to repeat back to the students what they said in opening the discussion, Marsha and Paula took notes as people spoke and then read from their notes. In so doing, they followed a pattern they had practiced previously. Marsha's suggestion of a question to pursue based on what she has heard, and Katie's eagerness to address it, suggest that Marsha's listening was continuing to grow more perceptive.

14. All of these discussion practices make it possible to follow Grice's cooperative principle. By repeating back what discussants say, working to identify similarities and differences heard in the discussants' positions, and asking discussants about their meaning, the co-leaders help themselves and the discussants understand what has been said. As a consequence, the communication means more, because people understand it. By asking discussants to provide textual evidence for their claims and by reiterating interpretive questions that help the shared concern to form and keep it before the group, the co-leaders help discussants pursue an issue so that an "object" or idea about resolution can emerge from the conversation, and perhaps what Gadamer calls a "truth" (see Chap. 1, n. 67 and accompanying text).

15. Here, then, is a striking consequence that seems to have arisen from the limited peripheral participation of the discussants: Tracy calls on Arnie, which is a move typically made by the discussion leader. At first an inexperienced discussant, Tracy has observed and participated in a practice that she then initiates in an effort to resolve the question of concern to her.

16. See Chapter 4.

17. H-G. Gadamer, *Truth and Method,* ed. Garrett Barden and John Cumming (New York: Crossroad, 1985), 341.

CHAPTER SEVEN: IMPLICATIONS FOR EDUCATORS

1. M. J. Adler, *Reforming Education: The Opening of the American Mind* (New York: Macmillan, 1977); M. J. Adler, *The Paideia Proposal: An Educational Manifesto* (New York: Macmillan, 1982); M. J. Adler, *Paideia Problems and Possibilities: A Consideration of Questions Raised by the Paideia Proposal* (New York: Macmillan, 1983).

2. For a history of the Adler-Hutchins era at the University of Chicago, see M. Mayer, *Robert Maynard Hutchins: A Memoir* (Berkeley: University of California Press, 1993); H. S. Ashmore, *Unreasonable Truths: The Life of Robert Maynard Hutchins* (Boston: Little, Brown, 1989).

3. See, e.g., M. Lipman, *Thinking in Education,* 2d ed. (Cambridge: Cambridge University Press, 2003); G. B. Matthews, *Philosophy and the Young Child* (Cambridge: Harvard University Press, 1980).

4. I. L. Beck et al., *Questioning the Author: An Approach for Enhancing Student Engagement with Text* (Newark, Del.: International Reading Association, 1997).

5. Two sections were grouped homogeneously: one group was planning to teach at the elementary level (grades K–9), and the other intended to work as administrators in higher education. Each of these sections included about thirteen people.

6. Each week, a different section leader led the development of the preparation.

7. During the ten-week course, our instructional team prepared for and led

our sections in discussions of the Italian film *Il Postino*, directed by Michael Radford (U.S. release: Blue Dahlia Productions, Miramax Pictures, 1995), A. N. Whitehead's *The Aims of Education and Other Essays* (New York: Free Press, 1929), Plato's *Meno*, my *Turning the Soul: Teaching Through Conversation in the High School* (Chicago: University of Chicago Press, 1991), and Donald Schön's *Educating the Reflective Practitioner* (San Francisco: Jossey-Bass, 1987). These texts, read in the order listed, were chosen because they explore the following related topics: (1) the complexity of student-teacher relations (*Il Postino*); (2) the role of interest in learning (Whitehead); (3) the role of teacher and student in helping one another to question (Plato); (4) the cultivation of questions in a group discussion (Haroutunian-Gordon); (5) the similarities and differences between the teacher as discussion leader and the teacher coach (Schön). Over the years that I have taught the course, titles of the texts have varied, but the list given here is an effective combination for orienting students toward enduring and pressing questions related to teaching and learning.

8. In the case of those in the higher education administration group, the text was a dataset, document, case study, or other text that interested people at the site where one of the co-leaders worked or was completing an internship.

9. Other instructors in the program also ask students to lead discussion. I am describing their work with it in the courses that I regularly teach because I am most familiar with these opportunities.

10. Each section leader sends me the cluster of questions that the co-leaders have developed. I respond to specific questions and in that way assist with the resolution of preparation issues raised by the section leader. For example, I might be asked to read through the entire cluster to see if I think that the stated BQ expresses the deepest point of doubt that the co-leaders wish to address. Or I might be asked how to modify a question so as to clarify it further. My comments are then posted online.

11. For example, we try to help the co-leaders question discussants about their meaning, repeat what is said, identify similarities and differences in perspectives, state the shared points of doubt that have been voiced, and seek textual evidence for claims.

12. Posted to the online class discussion board by a student after co-leading a discussion in Philosophy of Education, Spring 2006.

13. Table 7.2 reveals other interesting patterns in participation. The number of evaluative comments made by these participants declined over the course of the project, except in Kurt's case. Indeed, the decline in the frequency of Jeremy's evaluative comments is most dramatic; it falls from ten in the discussion of *The Giving Tree* to one in the discussion of "The Unruly Wife." In three of the four cases (all but Tracy's), the number of spontaneous references to the text increased, and indeed, Tracy's remained high throughout the project. The changes in participation patterns that these figures

reveal may arise because participants are learning that some ways of responding are more efficacious than others. Indeed, as argued in Chapter 6,
the co-leaders seemed to modify their discussion-leading patterns for
much the same reason.

14. See M. K. Wolf, A. C. Crosson, and L. B. Resnick, "Accountable Talk in
Reading Comprehension Instruction," published by the Center for the
Study of Evaluation, National Center for Research on Evaluation, Stan-
dards, and Student Testing (Los Angeles: University of California, 2006).
The authors state a common goal of the methods called Questioning the
Author (Beck et al.), Reciprocal Teaching (Palinscar and Brown), and Col-
laborative Reasoning (C. A. Chinn and R. C. Anderson, "The Structure of
Discussions That Promote Reasoning," *Teachers College Record* 100, no. 2
[1998]: 315–368): "Ultimately, the students take responsibility to lead the
dialogue as they develop into increasingly independent readers" (2).

15. T. Tokano, ed., *Water on Mars and Life* (Berlin: Springer, 2005); M. Hanlon,
The Real Mars (New York: Caroll and Graf, 2004), esp. 42–55, 208–219;
P. Cattermole, *Mars: The Mystery Unfolds* (Oxford: Oxford University Press,
2001), esp. 163–165; D. M. Harland, *Water and the Search for Life on Mars*
(Berlin: Springer, 2005); T. Encrenaz, *Searching for Water in the Universe*,
trans. B. Mizon (Berlin: Springer, 2007); M. H. Carr, *Water on Mars* (New
York: Oxford University Press, 1996).

16. Multiple drafts of the Declaration of Independence were made available to
me by the Great Books Foundation. It published the final version of the
document in 1955.

17. I am indebted to Richard Strier for reminding me that texts may be found
ambiguous (and hence discussable) by some but not by others. That is
because questions depend not simply on what is in the text but also on the
beliefs, concepts, and terms with which the questioner interprets it.

18. S. Haroutunian-Gordon and D. S. Tartakoff, "On the Learning of Mathematics Through Conversation," *For the Learning of Mathematics* 16.2 (1996):
2–10.

19. Two teacher candidates, the fall quarter of 2004.

20. M. Lampert, "When the Problem Is not the Question and the Solution Is
not the Answer: Mathematical Knowing and Teaching," *American Educational Research Journal* 27 (1990): 29–63; A. H. Schoenfeld, "On Mathematics and Sense-Making: An Informal Attack on the Unfortunate Divorce of
Formal and Informal Mathematics," in *Informal Reasoning and Education*,
ed. J. Voss, D. Perkins, and J. Segal (Hillside, N.J.: Erlbaum, 1990); A. H.
Schoenfeld, "What Do We Know About Mathematics Curricula?" *Journal
of Mathematical Behavior* 13.1 (March 1994): 55–80; A. H. Schoenfeld,
"Reflections on Doing and Teaching Mathematics," in *Mathematical
Thinking and Problem Solving*, ed. A. H. Schoenfeld (Hillside, N.J.:
Erlbaum, 1995).

21. The observation is consistent with Lave and Wenger's view of the

advantages that can accrue to those involved in legitimate peripheral participation. For example, the discussants participate in only a few of the leader's activities (e.g., trying to evaluate arguments on the basis of textual evidence). Yet, engaged as they are in interpretive discussion, discussants also observe behaviors of the leaders and the consequences of those behaviors. They see not only possible courses of action but also conditions and consequences of pursuing them.

22. W. Parker, "Friends and Strangers: Speaking and Listening in Classroom Discussion," in *Listening in Context: Challenges for Teachers,* ed. S. Haroutunian-Gordon and L. J. Waks, forthcoming as a special issue of *Teachers College Record.* Parker distinguishes between "seminars," which aim to understand the meaning of texts, and "deliberations," which aim to identify appropriate action. Discussions in the Northwestern practicum and student teaching seminars frequently have both goals.

23. Posted to online class discussion board by a student in Philosophy of Education, Spring 2006.

24. Posted to the online discussion board, Spring 2006, after co-leading a discussion.

25. For example, if the text is Plato's *Republic,* one might ask: Would Plato say that leaders need to ask discussants to explore issues one at a time? If so, would Plato support the practice because he says "justice is the minding of one's own business" (433b), meaning, perhaps, doing one thing fully rather than several things partially? Or does he mean that "justice" is doing only one's job—"One man, one job" (433c)?

CONCLUSION

1. To the names of Plato, John Dewey, Alfred N. Whitehead, and the authors of NCTM and other national curricular standards, we may add A. N. Applebee, *Curriculum as Conversation: Transforming Traditions of Teaching and Learning* (Chicago: University of Chicago Press, 1996); D. Barnes, *From Communication to Curriculum* (London: Penguin, 1976); C. B. Cazden, *Classroom Discourse: The Language of Teaching and Learning* (Portsmouth, N.J.: Heineman, 1988); A. H. Schoenfeld (see works cited in Chapter 7, note 20); J. T. Bruer, *Schools for Thought: A Science of Learning in the Classroom* (Cambridge: MIT Press, 1993); H. Gardner, *The Disciplined Mind: Beyond Facts and Standardized Tests—the K–12 Education That Every Child Deserves* (New York: Penguin, 2000); C. A. Chinn and R. C. Anderson, "The Structure of Discussions That Promote Reading," *Teachers College Record* 100:2 (1998): 315–368; S. Michaels, C. O'Connor, and L. B. Resnick, "Reasoned Participation: Accountable Talk in the Classroom and in Civic Life," in *Studies in Philosophy and Education* (in press); S. Michaels and C. B. Cazden, "Reading Comprehension in Class Discussion," in *Literacy Standards for the Middle Grades* (Pittsburgh: New Standards and the University of Pittsburgh Press, in press).

2. G. Hull, M. Rose, K. L. Fraser, and M. Castellano, "Remediation as Social Construct: Perspectives from an Analysis of Classroom Discourse," *College Composition and Communication* 42:3 (1991): 299–329, 319.

3. G. L. Sunderman, J. S. Kim, and G. Orfield, *NCLB Meets School Realities: Lessons From the Field* (Thousand Oaks, Calif.: Corwin/Sage, 2005).

4. K. Zumwalt, "The Misunderstood Curriculum," in *A Life in Classrooms: Philip W. Jackson and the Practice of Education,* ed. D. Hansen, R. Arcilla, and M. Driscoll (New York: Teachers College Press, 2007), 130–131.

5. Whereas Sunderman, Kim, and Orfield, *NCLB Meets School Realities,* offer a recent negative assessment, D. Meier, *Will Standards Save Public Education?* (Boston: Beacon, 2000), offers an earlier critique that identifies serious limitations in the basic assumptions of the standards and testing movement.

6. See Chapter 1, note 65.

7. W. E. B. Du Bois, "Diuturni Silenti (1924)" in *The Education of Black People* (New York: Monthly Review Press, 1973), esp. 65–73.

8. J. U. Obgu, *Minority Education and Caste: The American System in Cross-Cultural Perspective* (New York: Academic Press, 1978); C. D. Lee, *Culture, Literacy, and Learning: Taking Bloom in the Midst of the Whirlwind* (New York: Teachers College Press, 2007).

INDEX

"About What Happened to a Young Man Who Married a Very Wild and Unruly Wife." *See* "The Unruly Wife"

Adler, M., 152–53, 205*n*1

Agreed-on facts, 201*n*12

Alice in Wonderland, 6, 8, 11, 12, 16

"Allah Will Provide": agreement among students on, 53–54; changes in students' positions on, 53–54, 64; and clarification of discussants' meaning, 128, 129, 134; cluster of questions for, 104–9; discussion-leading practices for, 120, 123, 125, 128, 129, 133–36; discussion of, at Central School, 49–56, 63–64, 67, 72, 85, 104–5, 107–8, 123, 125, 128, 129, 133–36, 160–61, 181, 203*n*1; discussion of, at Sheridan School, 123, 125, 128, 129, 160–61, 182; evaluation of proposed resolutions using textual evidence on, 108–9; evaluative questions on, 63, 125, 203*n*1; identification of similarities and differences between different speakers on, 128, 134–36; interpretive questions on, 104–9, 123; and leaders' directing participants to find specific lines or passages, 131; leaders' interpretation of, 105–6; participation rate and number

of comments on, by discussants, 160–61, 181–82; personal experience in discussion on, 51–54; and repetition of discussant comments by leaders, 128, 134; shared point of doubt in discussion on, 133–36; shift from evaluation to interpretation of, 49–55, 120; and spontaneous use of text by discussants, 131; synopsis of, 49; testing theory in discussion on, 52–55; textual evidence in discussion of, 51, 52, 55, 63, 67, 107–9, 120

Ambiguity: Bakhtin on, 196*n*42; and cluster of questions, 91–92; and deepest point of doubt (DPD), 8; definition of, 7; and discussable text, 166–68; Empson on, 7; in *The Giving Tree,* 92; in "Jean Labadie's Big Black Dog," 111–12; in "Kaddo's Wall," 102; and second reading of text, 202*n*3; Strier on, 207*n*17; types of, 7, 195–96*n*41; in "The Unruly Wife," 115. *See also* Deepest point of doubt (DPD); Shared point of doubt

Anderson, R. C., 207*n*14, 208*n*1

Andriessen, J., 198*n*70

Applebee, A. N., 208*n*1

Argument development, 198*n*70

This sequel to Sophie Haroutunian-Gordon's acclaimed *Turning the Soul: Teaching Through Conversation in the High School* once again bridges the gap between education theory and classroom experience by taking the model of education developed in that book and applying it to a case study of two teacher candidates in elementary classrooms.

"Groundbreaking and innovative. . . . This is a major contribution to teacher education and will likely be picked up by teacher education programs interested in teaching teachers more philosophically."
SHARON M. RAVITCH, University of Pennsylvania

"This is a comprehensive and useful guide to interpretive discussion in the classroom—appropriate for classes at every level and in every discipline."
NEL NODDINGS, author of *Critical Lessons: What Our Schools Should Teach*

"Sophie Haroutunian-Gordon provides a subtle, perceptive account of the art of leading discussions in teaching, illuminating the central role that asking questions plays in that process, and arguing for making it a central part of teacher education."
NICHOLAS C. BURBULES, University of Illinois

"Haroutunian-Gordon's focus on interpretive discussion offers an exciting new approach to learning and teaching. She shows how classrooms come alive as students share their understanding of the text with each other and the teacher."
BERTRAM COHLER, University of Chicago

Sophie Haroutunian-Gordon is director, Master of Science in Education program, and professor, School of Education and Social Policy, at Northwestern University.

Yale UNIVERSITY PRESS
New Haven & London
yalebooks.com   www.yalebooks.co.uk

ISBN 978-0-300-16830-3